Suffolk

Local, characterful guides to Britain's special places

Laurence Mitchell

EDITION 1
Bradt Travel Guides Ltd, UK
The Globe Pequot Press Inc, USA

Suffolk

Suffolk is ideal for Slow exploration. Cycling, sailing and walking are all good options for enjoying the county's landscapes, discovering its varied wildlife and delving into its rich historic past. Along the way you will find plenty of characterful places for refreshment.

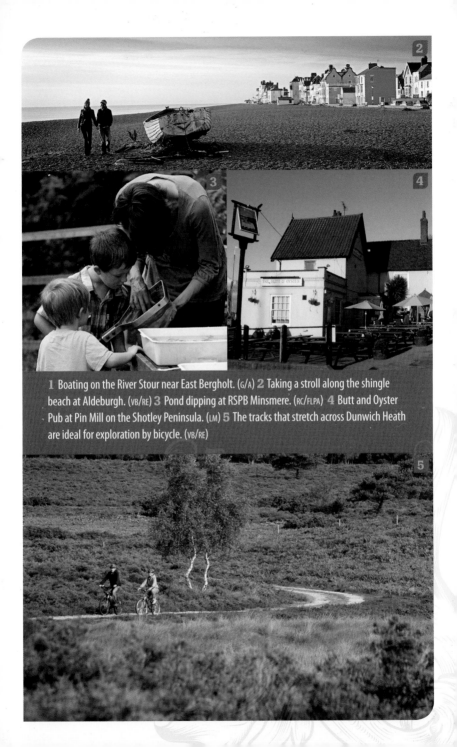

1 Boating on the River Stour near East Bergholt. (G/A) 2 Taking a stroll along the shingle beach at Aldeburgh. (VB/RE) 3 Pond dipping at RSPB Minsmere. (RC/FLPA) 4 Butt and Oyster Pub at Pin Mill on the Shotley Peninsula. (LM) 5 The tracks that stretch across Dunwich Heath are ideal for exploration by bicycle. (VB/RE)

SUFFOLK LANDSCAPES & WILDLIFE

Suffolk has a wide variety of landscapes ranging from coastal estuaries and marshes to grazing meadows and dry heaths. The county also has a considerable amount of tree cover, including small pockets of wildlife-rich, ancient deciduous woodland as well as large, dense tracts of conifers planted by the Forestry Commission in the 20th century.

5 Trimley Marsh, close to the Port of Felixstowe, is a nature reserve with pools full of wading birds. (ss) **6** The rare Dartford warbler may sometimes be seen in the gorse bushes of Dunwich Heath. (rc/flpa)

1 Rutting red deer in Thetford Forest. (ps/flpa) **2** Santon Downham in the middle of Thetford forest is a small isolated village that developed around the forestry industry. (lm) **3** Fen raft spider, the largest native spider in Britain, can be seen at Redgrave and Lopham Fen on the Suffolk–Norfolk border. (jl) **4** Freston Wood near Ipswich is an ancient wood that is carpeted with bluebells in spring. (ss) **5** Trimley Marsh, close to the Port of Felixstowe, is a nature reserve with pools full of wading birds. (ss) **6** The rare Dartford warbler may sometimes be seen in the gorse bushes of Dunwich Heath. (rc/flpa) **7** Grazing cattle in the wet meadows of the Waveney Valley near Beccles. (lm)

SUFFOLK TOWNS & VILLAGES

From picture-perfect Tudor villages with half-timbered, pink-washed cottages to market towns with a wealth of historical buildings, Suffolk's settlements are as much a draw as the attractive countryside that surrounds them.

1 The historic coastal village of Orford with its 12th-century castle and 14th-century church. (DH/FLPA) 2 The Aldeburgh Food and Drink Festival is held in the town and at Snape Maltings each September. (SC) 3 Pink thatched cottages and church at the picture-perfect south Suffolk village of Cavendish. (SS) 4 The House in the Clouds, an eccentric landmark at the coastal resort of Thorpeness. (VB/RE) 5 Kersey, with pink-washed and timber-framed cottages lining its main street, is considered by many to be the prettiest village in Suffolk. (LM) 6 Ipswich Waterfront has undergone large-scale regeneration in recent years. (IBC)

How did it all happen? George (my then husband) and I wrote the first Bradt guide – about hiking in Peru and Bolivia – on an Amazon river barge, and typed it up on a borrowed typewriter. We had no money for the next two books so George went to work for a printer and was paid in books rather than money.

Forty years on, Bradt publishes over 200 titles that sell all over the world. I still suffer from Imposter Syndrome – how did it all happen? I hadn't even worked in an office before! Well, I've been extraordinarily lucky with the people around me. George provided the belief to get us started (and the mother to run our US office). Then, in 1977, I recruited a helper, Janet Mears, who is still working for us. She and the many dedicated staff who followed have been the foundations on which the company is built. But the bricks and mortar have been our authors and readers. Without them there would be no Bradt Travel Guides. Thank you all for making it happen.

Hilary Bradt

AUTHOR

Laurence Mitchell has at various times worked as an English teacher in Sudan, surveyed farm buildings in Norfolk, pushed a pen in a local government office and taught geography in a rural secondary school. Having finally settled for the uncertain life of a freelance travel writer and photographer, he specialises in places firmly of the beaten track like the Balkans, central Asia and the Middle East when not wandering around his home patch of East Anglia. As well as writing several guides for Bradt, his work

has appeared in publications like *Geographical*, *Walk*, *Discover Britain*, *Wild Travel* and *hidden europe*. Laurence is a member of the British Guild of Travel Writers and the Outdoor Writers and Photographers Guild. His website can be found at ⌐ www.laurencemitchell.com and blog at ⌐ www.eastofelveden.wordpress.com.

AUTHOR'S STORY

I have lived in East Anglia for the best part of four decades. Admittedly my home has always been over the border in Norfolk, but Suffolk has long been a feature of my life too. As an incomer originating from the West Midlands I like to think I can view either county with equal magnanimity. I do not have any particular tribal loyalty or county allegiance to affect my judgement and so hopefully I am able to be fair-minded about what lies on either side of the River Waveney.

The Suffolk coast always was a draw, especially back in the days when I was a keen birdwatcher. The Waveney Valley with its lovely countryside became a natural magnet too. In the Waveney Valley, no-one really seemed to bother too much about which side of the county border they were on. I liked that: identifying with a region rather than an

artificial political entity – surely that is what 'sense of place' is all about? And 'sense of place' is really what *Slow Suffolk* is all about.

Since the publication of *Slow Norfolk and Suffolk*, the predecessor to this book, I have tried to seek out more of those places that make Suffolk special – towns, villages and hamlets that have a uniqueness about them, an identity forged by the people who live there and the landscape that shapes them. Researching this book, as well as revisiting old familiar haunts, I have discovered many places that hitherto had just been names on the map. Villages especially – wonderful little places that I hardly knew existed like Boulge, Middleton, Mendham and Harkest, to name just a few. I am happy in the knowledge that there are still plenty more such places waiting to be discovered.

First edition published April 2014
Bradt Travel Guides Ltd, IDC House, The Vale, Chalfont St Peter, Bucks SL9 9RZ, England
www.bradtguides.com
Print edition published in the USA by The Globe Pequot Press Inc,
PO Box 480, Guilford, Connecticut 06437-0480

Text copyright © 2014 Bradt Travel Guides Ltd
Maps copyright © 2014 Bradt Travel Guides Ltd
Photographs copyright © 2014 Individual photographers (see below)
Series Editor: Tim Locke
Project Managers: Maisie Fitzpatrick, Anna Moores & Laura Pidgley
Series design: Pepi Bluck, Perfect Picture
Cover: Pepi Bluck, Perfect Picture

ISBN: 978 1 84162 550 8 (print); e-ISBN: 978 1 84162 781 6 (e-pub);
e-ISBN: 978 1 84162 625 3 (mobi)

British Library Cataloguing in Publication Data
A catalogue record for this book is available from the British Library

Photographers
Front cover image Beach huts at Southwold (NS/A)
Back cover image View of Clare (PB/A)
Title page image Timber-framed Tudor houses, Lavenham (S/GO)
Alamy: geogphotos (g/A), nagelestock.com (NS/A), Phil Barnes (PB/A); David Falk (DF);
FLPA: David Burton (DB/FLPA), David Hosking (DH/FLPA), Paul Sawer (PS/FLPA), Robert Chittenden
(RC/FLPA); Ipswich Borough Council (IBC); James Lowen (JL); Laurence Mitchell (LM); Philip Vile (PV);
Shutterstock: Colin D. Young (S/CY), Elle1 (S/E), Gergo Orban (S/GO), Martin Fowler (S/MF),
Peter Gyure (S/PG), Mike J Roberts (S/MR), Paul Wishart (S/PW), Robert Bowden (S/RB);
SuperStock (SS); www.thebridgemarketing.co.uk (TBM); www.thesuffolkcoast.co.uk (SC);
Visit Britain: Britain on View (VB/BOV), Rod Edwards (VB/RE)

Maps Pepi Bluck, Perfect Picture & David McCutcheon FBCart.S

Typeset from the author's disc by Chris Lane, Artinfusion
Production managed by Jellyfish Print Solutions; printed in the UK
Digital conversion by the Firsty Group

ACKNOWLEDGMENTS

I would like to thank all the team at Bradt, in particular Donald Greig, Adrian Phillips, Rachel Fielding, Anna Moores, Maisie Fitzpatrick, Janet Mears and Laura Pidgley. Many thanks also go to Tim Locke for his patient, professional editing. My gratitude goes to those who contributed boxes – Anne Locke, Hilary Bradt and Janice Booth – and thanks go too to Wendy Ellis of Boydell & Brewer for permission to quote from John Seymour's *Companion Guide to East Anglia*, and to Helen Sibley for her information on Thornham Walks. As always, I must also pay tribute to the unstinting support of my wife Jackie, a Norfolk native who admits to quite liking Suffolk too.

FEEDBACK REQUEST

Suffolk is full of people who have specialist knowledge on their particular part of the region, and although we've tried our very best to check our facts there are bound to be errors as well as the inevitable omissions of really special places. You can post your comments and recommendations, and read the latest feedback and updates from other readers, online at ∽ www.bradtupdates.com/suffolk.

Suggested places to base yourself

These bases make ideal starting points for exploring localities the Slow way.

Swaffham

Norfolk

HALESWORTH page 129
In northeast Suffolk, with a station on the coastal train line, this quiet but charming market town is perfectly placed for exploring both the Waveney Valley and the north Suffolk coast.

BURY ST EDMUNDS page 197
Swathed in history, this mysterious, ancient town is the perfect urban base for exploring the west of Suffolk.

THETFORD

Little Ouse

A1066

A134

A1065

A11

A143

A1088

CHAPTER 6

LAVENHAM page 159
A picture-perfect Tudor wool town in south Suffolk, Lavenham has a wide choice of atmospheric and quite luxurious accommodation as well as easy access to the Stour Valley and central Suffolk.

A134

A1101

BURY ST EDMUNDS

A14

Newmarket

CAMBRIDGE

A14

Cambridgeshire

Stowmarket

CHAPTER 5

CLARE page 179
One of the most attractive yet little-visited of the former wool towns in this region, and a convenient base for the Stour Valley, Bury St Edmunds and the far west of the county.

A143

A134

Lavenham
A1141

Clare

A1092

Stour

Sudbury

A1071

A1307

A134

Stoke-by-Nayland

STOKE-BY-NAYLAND page 171
One of the slightly less well-known of the Stour Valley villages, attractive Suffolk-pink Stoke-by-Nayland makes a good central base for exploring the Constable Country of the Suffolk-Essex border.

A1131

Essex

COLCHESTER

BECCLES page 76
One of the larger market towns in north Suffolk, Beccles has everything that you might expect of a historic riverside town and makes the perfect base for exploring the Waveney Valley.

NORWICH

GREAT YARMOUTH

Norfolk

LOWESTOFT

CHAPTER 2

Bungay

Beccles

Diss

Waveney

Halesworth

Southwold

NORTH SEA

N

0   5 miles
0   10 km

SOUTHWOLD page 22
A small but perfectly formed seaside town with an old-fashioned, well-heeled resort feel to it, Southwold seems still to belong to the 1950s.

CHAPTER 4

Dunwich

Framlingham

CHAPTER 1

ALDEBURGH page 45
A smart, slightly upmarket seaside resort that gives Southwold a run for its money, Aldeburgh is also a convenient base on the Suffolk coast for visiting Thorpeness and Snape Maltings.

Aldeburgh

CHAPTER 3

Orford

Woodbridge

Orford Ness

IPSWICH

ORFORD page 55
Far enough away from other settlements on the Suffolk coast to feel rather isolated, this picturesque seaside village has good places to eat and stay and provides convenient access to Orford Ness.

FELIXSTOWE

HARWICH

WOODBRIDGE page 110
Close to Suffolk's county town, stylish Woodbridge has a wealth of excellent independent shops and places to eat as well as good transport connections to Ipswich and the coast.

CONTENTS

FOLLOW BRADT

For the latest news, special offers and competitions, follow Bradt on:

 www.facebook.com/BradtTravelGuides   @bradtguides

 @BradtGuides   www.pinterest.com/bradtguides

GOING SLOW IN
SUFFOLK

Slow Suffolk? What does that mean exactly? Well, it is nothing to with a slur on the character of the people of that county for a start. Sometimes referred to as 'Silly Suffolk', it is easy to assume that the term is just a mild pejorative that refers to the natives of the county as being a bit slow on the uptake. It doesn't mean anything of the sort of course: 'Silly Suffolk' is simply a corruption of the expression 'Selig' Suffolk, selig meaning 'holy' or 'blessed' in Old English, on account of the vast number of churches in the county. The majority of the churches that stand today were erected at a time when Suffolk was one of the richest counties in England thanks to profits from the wool trade. It was this wool-wealth that paid for both the construction of the churches and the fine timber-framed houses that still stand proud, if sometimes a little crookedly, in Suffolk towns like Lavenham today.

"You'll find beaches, saltings, spits, estuaries, muddy tidal creeks and reedbeds, Sandling heaths, river valleys and the sandy wastes of the Brecks."

Like Norfolk, its neighbour to the north, Suffolk was largely bypassed by the Industrial Revolution. And like Norfolk, the county's heyday was not in the 19th century but much earlier, in the medieval period. Suffolk's medieval history is second to none, and the material evidence is still there to be seen – an abundance of fine Tudor buildings in many towns and villages, an enormous wealth of medieval churches and a good showing of castles too.

The county is distinguished in terms of geography too. The landscape is low-lying but rarely flat, and it is surprisingly varied. Take a transect across the county and you'll find sand and shingle beaches, saltings, spits, estuaries, muddy tidal creeks and reedbeds, Sandling heaths, river valleys and the sandy wastes of the Brecks. Among these landscapes is a countryside filled with rolling farmland, tracts of ancient woodland, stands of modern forestry, a handful of market towns and countless small villages, each with its church. More than anything, it is the villages that make the county what it is and Suffolk has villages in spades. With the exception of Ipswich, which is by far the largest urban area though not a city – there are only a few towns of any size in the county. Suffolk has no motorways either and, despite being home to a number of bomber bases during World War II – a handful still exist – there is also no airport to speak of.

The way I see it, the essence of Slow is to find the extraordinary in the commonplace. It is to identify the unique patina created by history, landscape and custom that makes a place a bit special. Everywhere has these qualities to some extent; it is just that Suffolk probably has more than its fair share.

But Slow is about slowing down too; it's taking the time to look closely and savour something, to not hurry too much, to not get too caught up with the need for instant gratification that seems to dominate the current zeitgeist. As the Welsh poet (and tramp) William Henry Davies (1871–1940) once put it:

What is this life if, full of care,
We have no time to stand and stare.
No time to stand beneath the boughs
And stare as long as sheep or cows.

There's plenty of scope for staring in Suffolk.

HOW THIS BOOK IS ARRANGED

This book divides Suffolk into six fairly distinct geographical areas starting with the Suffolk Heritage Coast and ending with the Brecks and the area around Bury St Edmunds in the west of the county. *Chapter 1* covers the Suffolk coast from Lowestoft down as far as the north bank of the River Orwell, and also includes the coastal hinterland between the sea and the A14. This includes much of the area of the Suffolk Coast and Heaths AONB (Area of Outstanding Beauty), the remainder of which is covered in *Chapter 3*. *Chapter 2* deals with the most northerly region of Suffolk along the Waveney Valley between the coast and the river's source at Redgrave Fen. This chapter also occasionally veers across the river into Norfolk as the Waveney Valley sits astride both counties. *Chapter 3* focuses on the southern part of the Suffolk coast that includes the Felixstowe and Shotley peninsulas as well as the county town of Ipswich and its immediate surroundings. *Chapter 4* moves further inland to cover the eastern and central part of Suffolk that is centred upon the market towns of Halesworth, Framlingham and Stowmarket. *Chapter 5* deals with the Stour Valley and its hinterland – the southern part of the county that lies close to the Essex border. *Chapter 6* concludes with the far west of the county, effectively two discrete regions – the Brecks of northwest Suffolk near Brandon and the region of 'high' west Suffolk that has Bury St Edmunds at its centre.

MAPS

Each chapter begins with a map with **numbered stopping points** that correspond to numbered headings in the text. The featured walks have maps accompanying them.

THE SLOW MINDSET

Hilary Bradt, Founder, Bradt Travel Guides

We shall not cease from exploration
And the end of all our exploring
Will be to arrive where we started
And know the place for the first time.

T S Eliot 'Little Gidding', *Four Quartets*

This series evolved, slowly, from a Bradt editorial meeting when we started to explore ideas for guides to our favourite country – Great Britain. We wanted to get away from the usual 'top sights' formula and encourage our authors to bring out the nuances and local differences that make up a sense of place – such things as food, history, nature, geology, or local people and what makes them tick. So without our realising it at the time, we had defined 'Slow Travel', or at least our concept of it. For the beauty of the Slow movement is that there is no fixed definition; we adapt the philosophy to fit our individual needs and aspirations. Thus Carl Honoré, author of *In Praise of Slow*, writes: 'The Slow Movement is a cultural revolution against the notion that faster is always better. It's not about doing everything at a snail's pace, it's about seeking to do everything at the right speed. Savouring the hours and minutes rather than just counting them. Doing everything as well as possible, instead of as fast as possible. It's about quality over quantity in everything from work to food to parenting.' And travel.

So take time to explore. Don't rush it, get to know an area – and the people who live there – and you'll be as delighted as the authors by what you find.

Suffolk is a fairly large county and requires a total of seven 1:50,000 Landranger OS maps to cover it fully. Another useful map for the Waveney Valley is the double-sided 1:25,000 scale OS Explorer OL40 The Broads, which shows much interesting detail and has plenty of walker- and cyclist-friendly information.

FOOD & DRINK

I've listed some of my favourite pubs, cafés, tea rooms and places to eat, favouring those places that serve local produce or are worth a visit for some other reason, such as appealing quirkiness or distinctive character. In a few cases I have listed an establishment simply because it is a convenient option in a place that offers few alternatives.

ACCOMMODATION

Accommodation has been recommended on the basis of location and because it embraces a Slow approach in its 'green' ethos or its overall feel. Hotels, B&Bs and self-catering options are indicated by the symbol ♠ after town and village headings, and campsites by ⋏, with a cross-reference to the full listing under *Accommodation*, pages 211–17.

GETTING AROUND

Cycling and walking make the ideal methods of Slow travel. I'd like to encourage people to **visit without a car** wherever possible but I appreciate that this can be difficult in some parts of Suffolk, particularly if attempting to travel up and down the coast where progress is impeded by river estuaries that need to be circumnavigated (it is the same for cars too).

Details of how best to get around are given in detail at the beginning of each chapter. Below is a brief overview with suggestions of how to reach Suffolk from other parts of the country.

A useful website for **planning journeys by bus or train**, or a combination of the two is ⋔ www.travelinesoutheast.org.uk.

TRAINS

You have several options for getting around by train within the county, with regular Greater Anglia rail services between Ipswich, Stowmarket and Norwich, Ipswich and Felixstowe, Ipswich and Lowestoft, and between

Stowmarket, Bury St Edmunds and Newmarket. Ipswich is connected to London by frequent direct trains from Liverpool Street station and to the Midlands and North by means of a change at Ely or Peterborough. Lowestoft can also be reached by direct trains from Norwich. Greater Anglia has timetables online at ⁀ www.greateranglia.co.uk.

Greater Anglia offer a range of **Anglia Plus tickets** valid throughout Suffolk, Norfolk and parts of Cambridgeshire. These include One Day Rangers and 'Three Days in Seven' Flexi Rover tickets, both allowing travel for up to four accompanied children for a little extra payment.

BUS & COACH

Ipswich and Bury St Edmunds both have long-distance coach services with National Express that connect the city with London. Ipswich also has a daily service to and from Liverpool via the Midlands, and a coach service to Stansted and Heathrow airports. Bury St Edmunds has coach connections with Cambridge and Stansted Airport. Several different bus companies provide routes within the county, most notably First in Norfolk & Suffolk, Anglian Bus, Galloway, Stephensons of Essex, Beestons and Simonds. Bus travel details for a locality are given at the beginning of each chapter. Suffolk County Council produces booklets of **bus timetables** that helpfully combine all the various routes in each locality and come in useful for planning; they are widely available in shops, pubs and tourist centres and can be downloaded from ⁀ www. suffolkonboard.com.

CYCLING

Suffolk has plenty to offer cyclists, from quiet country lanes and disused railway lines to off-road routes that follow bridleways and forest tracks. Details of suggested routes and areas with good potential for cycling are outlined at the start of each chapter, as are local outlets for cycle hire. The website ⁀ www.cycle-route.com has many good suggestions for routes in the county, as does ⁀ www.discoversuffolk.org.uk. For off-road cycling probably the best part of the county to head for is Breckland where a large number of routes criss-cross Thetford Forest.

WALKING

Suffolk abounds with walking potential, from windswept coastal strolls to circular walks through forest and open farmland. As well as walking suggestions made at the beginning of each chapter a number of personal favourites are offered throughout the book together with a sketch map and directions for the walk. Walking in Suffolk is rarely very demanding thanks to the reasonably flat topography. The going is mostly easy and so walkers just need to decide how far they are prepared to walk if attempting a route. Any obstacles, such as they are, are limited to nuisances like overgrown nettles, hungry mosquitoes, obstructing herds of cows or the occasional cropped field that bears no trace of the footpath marked on the OS map. Otherwise, it's ideal, especially when a walk takes in a country pub and/or an interesting village church to explore *en route*.

Several notable **long-distance paths** run through the county. Longest of all is the **Suffolk Way**, a 113-mile route that begins at Flatford and crosses central Suffolk to finish at Lowestoft. The best known though is probably the **Suffolk Coast Path** between Lowestoft and Landguard Fort at Felixstowe. This route connects with the **Stour and Orwell Walk** to continue around the Orwell and Stour estuaries to reach Cattawade near Manningtree. This, in turn, is the starting point of the **Stour Valley Path** that threads through the Constable Country of the Stour Valley to end at Newmarket. Another long-distance route in the coastal region that follows a route a little way inland from the coast itself is the **Sandlings Walk** between Ipswich and Southwold. Away from the coast, the **Mid Suffolk Footpath** runs for 20 miles between Hoxne and Stowmarket. In west Suffolk, the **St Edmunds Way** connects Bury St Edmunds with Manningtree in Essex via the Stour Valley. In the Waveney Valley of north Suffolk, the **Angles Way** that runs between Great Yarmouth and Thetford uses paths on both sides of the River Waveney and the Norfolk –Suffolk border.

John Harris's **Walking in Suffolk** website (www.walkinginsuffolk. co.uk) features a wealth of links to downloadable maps and walk guides.

THE SUFFOLK HERITAGE COAST

1
LOWESOFT

2
Benacre
Covehithe

Reydon

3
SOUTHWOLD

5
Blythburgh

A1095

4
Walberswick

B1125

8
Westleton
Middleton
Theberton

6
Dunwich

7
DUNWICH HEATH
& MINSMERE
RSPB RESERVE

10
SAXMUNDHAM

A12

9
Leiston

13
Snape

A1094

12
Thorpeness

11
ALDEBURGH

B1069

Iken

14
Tunstall Forest, Chillesford
& Butley

A1152

B1078

RIVER ALDE

15
Orford

16
Orford
Ness

WOODBRIDGE

B1084

17
RENDLESHAM
FOREST

B1083

RIVER DEBEN

IPSWICH

A12

18
Shingle Street

20
Ramsholt

19
Bawdsey &
Bawdsey Quay

RIVER ORWELL

A14

FELIXSTOWE

RIVER STOUR

CHAPTER 1
page 14

CHAPTER 4
page 126

CHAPTER 3
page 98

0   4 miles   N
0   5km

1
THE SUFFOLK
HERITAGE COAST

Swoul, and Dunwich, and Walderswick
All go in at one lousie creek.
Suffolk coastal rhyme

It may be tempting to think that the workaday town of Lowestoft typifies this coastline. This couldn't be further from the truth, as the port is an exception and, from Kessingland all the way down to Bawdsey, the Suffolk coast is mostly rural and peaceful, with a couple of old-fashioned resorts interspersed by tiny villages up against the shingle. It is not an undiscovered coastline – far from it – but somehow Suffolk's unhurried, gentle pace of life has managed to persist without too much intrusion from the 21st century. Some things have changed quite dramatically over the past half century, of course, particularly the economy of the region and the incomers who have come to live here, but overall its character has survived without it ever becoming too much of a museum piece.

This coast has always attracted outsiders. The Scottish Art Nouveau architect and designer Charles Rennie Mackintosh came here to paint flowers when his architectural career was in the dumps. Benjamin Britten, having taken his leave of his home town of Lowestoft, made his home at Aldeburgh and wrote an opera about a fisherman, *Peter Grimes*. Southwold and Walberswick have always been popular with BBC television producers, authors and politicians, and you might even catch a glimpse of a vacationing rock star or Hollywood royalty at Aldeburgh's better hotels and restaurants. There is no doubt about it: the Suffolk coast exudes a certain type of understated glamour – classy and comfortable, like a pair of old but expensive shoes.

Between Lowestoft and Felixstowe, various inlets and estuaries punctuate the coastline. The rivers Blyth, Dunwich, Minsmere, Alde, Ore, Deben, Orwell and Stour all flow into the North Sea along this stretch, and the larger of these once brought trade and prosperity to the wool villages of the Suffolk hinterland. These rivers were once far more important than they are today, and far more navigable too. Look at the River Ore that flows through Framlingham – a mere brook these days – and shake your head in disbelief that stone for building the town's castle was once shipped here all the way from the coast.

As well as the coast itself, this chapter also covers the immediate hinterland, roughly east of the A12 Lowestoft to Ipswich road. A good chunk of that terrain constitutes what's known as **The Sandlings**, which has light sandy soil akin to that of Breckland in the west of the region. The Sandlings has a similar history to Breckland too: early settlement by Neolithic peoples thanks to easily workable soil; medieval overgrazing by sheep; widespread gamekeeping and forestry in the first part of the 20th century; arable crops in the second half. Today, it is an area characterised by sandy heaths, forestry plantations and wide fields of grain.

"A good chunk of that terrain constitutes what's known as The Sandlings, which has light sandy soil akin to that of Breckland."

The urban centre, **Lowestoft**, by far the biggest place along this stretch of coast, gets a mention but is hardly representative of the rest. However, if you are at all interested in Southwold sailors, bedevilled Blythburgh or disappearing Dunwich, or are curious to experience the sensation of 'orfordness', then read on. I start by working down the coast north to south, detouring inland as seems appropriate. Away from the comfortable respectability of resorts like **Southwold** and **Aldeburgh** are some real oddities. **Dunwich**, now little more than a pub, a café and a car park, was one of England's great ports back in the 12th century. **Orford Ness** was a top-secret military research site that was firmly off-limits until quite recently, while **Snape Maltings**, now an extensive arts and music complex, was a working maltings until not so very long ago.

GETTING AROUND

There is no coast road as such. Away from the busy A12, plenty of minor roads veer off towards the sea, although travelling between places along the coast itself, say between Aldeburgh and Orford for example, often involves circuitous journeys to get round estuaries. Southwold to Walberswick, which is really just a pleasant stroll on foot using the footbridge across the River Blyth, is a case in point and driving involves a long detour around the estuary to Blythburgh. Really, it's best to park up somewhere convenient and get your hiking boots on.

PUBLIC TRANSPORT

This is so-so: quite good in the north but progressively worse as you head south along the coast. Lowestoft is well connected to Norwich by a regular **train service** and frequent buses – the X2 operated by First in Suffolk & Norfolk runs every half-hour or so, as does the X1 that runs between Peterborough and Lowestoft via King's Lynn, Norwich and Great Yarmouth. The East Suffolk Line railway, run by Greater Anglia, connects Lowestoft with Ipswich at roughly two-hour intervals stopping at Halesworth, Darsham, Saxmundham, Wickham Market and Woodbridge along the way. You need the local **bus service** to reach the coast itself. The Anglian Bus 61 service runs between Great Yarmouth, Lowestoft and Southwold, while service 89 connects Southwold with Beccles. The Nightingales of Beccles 521 service connects Halesworth with Beccles, Saxmundham, Leiston and Aldeburgh, and First in Suffolk & Norfolk service 65 connects Aldeburgh with Snape, Woodbridge and Ipswich. With a bit of judicious timetable juggling you should be able to travel around the coast as long as you avoid Sundays. There are no regular buses to Orford, but Coastal Accessible Transport (✆ 0845 604 1802, Mon–Fri 08.15–16.00 ⌂ www.cats-paws.co.uk) provides a local service from Woodbridge that must be booked the day before travel.

CYCLING

Cycling is generally enjoyable away from the A12. Although the narrow roads to the coast can get pretty busy in the summer months, most of the traffic is tourist vehicles that are not in any great hurry and are generally respectful to those on bikes. There are some excellent bridleways to explore too. The OS Landranger 156 map covers the area.

If you are arriving by train, bicycles may be picked up at Darsham station by arrangement with Byways Bicycles (✆ 01728 668764 ⌂ www.bywaysbicycles.co.uk) or at Lowestoft at Streetlife (✆ 01502 585968). You can also transport your own bike using the Greater Anglia rail services although, as there is usually only provision for four bikes per train and it's on a first-come first-served basis, there is a slight risk you won't be able to take it aboard. Darsham is perhaps the best station to use as a base, as it has both Dunwich and Minsmere within easy pedalling distance. Saxmundham station is reasonably convenient for Snape, Aldeburgh and Thorpeness. Bear in mind that at as a cyclist you can also make use of some of the passenger ferry services outlined in *Walking* below, which could save some quite considerable detours. For those without their own bike, there is also the convenient Eastbridge Cycle Hire Company (✆ 01728 830154 ⌂ www.theeastbridgecyclehirecompany.co.uk) based at the Eel's Foot Inn in Eastbridge near Minsmere.

WALKING

This is very special country for walkers. As well as beach walks and quiet country lanes, the coastal region is criss-crossed by footpaths. Some of the most enjoyable hikes are along estuaries, such as that of the rivers Blyth and Alde, and you'll find plenty of scope for forest walks too, especially to the south in the extensive Tunstall and Rendlesham plantations. Those areas notated on the map as 'walks', such as The Walks near Leiston or Westleton Walks near Dunwich, refer to the old sheep 'walks' that ranged on the coastal hinterland but you can still walk there, even without a white woolly coat. There's a selection of downloadable circular walks on ⌂ www.eastsuffolklinewalks.co.uk.

As a walker (or a cyclist) rather than a driver, you have a distinct advantage in the Suffolk coast region in being able to make use of the **passenger ferries** across some rivers that flow to the coast. There is a rowing-boat ferry across the Blyth between Southwold and Walberswick (although walking via the pontoon bridge is not so much of a detour), another across the Butley River west of Orford and a third one across the River Deben between Bawdsey Ferry and Felixstowe Ferry.

ℹ TOURIST INFORMATION

Aldeburgh 48 High St ✆ 01728 453637
Lowestoft The East Point Pavilion, Royal Plain ✆ 01502 533600
Southwold 69 High St ✆ 01502 724729
Suffolk Coast & Heaths AONB ⌂ www.suffolkcoastandheaths.org
Suffolk Coastal ⌂ www.suffolkcoastal.gov.uk
Visit Suffolk Coast ⌂ www.visit-suffolkcoast.co.uk
Visit Sunrise Coast ⌂ www.visit-sunrisecoast.co.uk

FOOT FERRIES ON THE SUFFOLK COAST

Three foot-ferries operate along the Suffolk coast, all are seasonal and operate between Easter and October; all can take bicycles. A small charge is made for people and bicycles, dogs travel free.

Walberswick Ferry ✆01502 478712. This ferry, one of the UK's last remaining rowed ferries, between Southwold and Walberswick at the mouth of the River Blyth runs daily from late May to September between 10.00–12.30 and 14.00–17.00 in Easter holidays; weekends only in late April, early May and October.

Butley Ferry ✆07913 672499. Running between the Capel and Gedgrave banks of the River Butley, this claims to be the smallest licensed ferry in Europe. Run by volunteers, this operates between Easter Saturday and the end of September from 11.00–16.00 on weekends and bank holidays.

Bawdsey Ferry ✆07709 411511. Crossing the River Deben between Bawdsey Quay and Felixstowe Ferry, the Bawdsey Ferry operates from May to the end of September 10.00–18.00 and also at weekends 10.00–17.00 during Easter and in October.

Two long-distance walks pass through the Suffolk Coastal region. The **Suffolk Coast Path**, sometimes referred to as the Suffolk Coast and Heaths Path, is a 100-mile route between Lowestoft and Landguard Point at Felixstowe. Much of this walk follows the coast itself, with some long optional stretches of beach walking. The **Sandlings Walk** is a meandering 60-mile route between Southwold and Ipswich that, as its name implies, traverses the dry heathland of the Sandlings region just inland from the coast. Both of these routes connect with a third one, the **Stour and Orwell Walk** that follows the edge of the Stour and Orwell estuaries that are covered in *Chapter 5*.

THE SUNSHINE COAST: LOWESTOFT TO COVEHITHE

The Suffolk coast begins in the north at **Corton**, more or less a suburb of Lowestoft, which distinguishes itself by having a naturist beach. Lowestoft sprawls north and south of Britain's most easterly point, Lowestoft Ness, and extends as far as Pakefield, a village that is effectively a southern suburb of the town. The Suffolk Coast Area of Outstanding Natural Beauty (AONB) begins shortly beyond here at Kessingland, a small holiday resort. Further south along this stretch of coast lies Benacre Broad, a national nature reserve, and the tiny hamlet of Covehithe, which has a church built within the walls of an older demolished one. All of the north Suffolk coast is particularly vulnerable to severe sea erosion.

1 LOWESTOFT

Lowestoft has probably seen better days. In his book *The Rings of Saturn* W G Sebald describes being 'disheartened' by the town's deserted streets but, there again, he was always a writer whose glass was considerably less than half full. Like Great Yarmouth, just across the county boundary to the north, Lowestoft has seen service as both a fishing port and a resort and, rather like Cromer and Sheringham in Norfolk, the two towns have always been great rivals. Lowestoft's fleet of trawlers were decommissioned in 2002 and, like Yarmouth, it saw tourist numbers dwindle during the last quarter of the 20th century. William A Dutt, in his *Highways and Byways in East Anglia* published in 1900, writes of 'Clapham and Brixton primly disporting themselves on the south beach or placidly promenading the pier' back in the days when Brixton was a solidly middle-class part of London.

"Gaze out to sea here and you can satisfy yourself in knowing that, temporarily at least, you are the most easterly person in the United Kingdom."

Much has changed, and these days 'Loos-toff', as East Anglians tend to call it, is redolent of faded memories. If you are curious, you might want to check out **Lowestoft Ness**, close to the Birds Eye fish-finger factory, which is the most easterly point in the British Isles. Gaze out to sea here and you can satisfy yourself in knowing that, temporarily at least, you are the most easterly person in the United Kingdom. The giant compass-like piece of artwork known as the Euroscope that marks the spot will inform you of the bearings and distances to various points in the British Isles and Europe. Both of Britain's southern and northern extremities are evocatively distant: The Lizard, the British mainland's most southerly point, lies 352 miles away, while Dunnet Head, the most northerly, even further, some 465 miles distant. It might seem a shame that, given its longitudinal importance, the Ness occupies such an unprepossessing setting. Bear in mind, though, that both The Lizard and John O'Groats (which has unashamedly usurped the 'most northerly' claim for many years now) are little more than windswept headlands with overpriced car parks, so the lack of romance at such places is nothing unusual.

Lowestoft has several 'most easterlies' it can boast of. There's **Christ Church**, Britain's most easterly church, a modest Victorian building that served a poor fisherman's parish which suffered Zeppelin raids in World War I, aerial bombing World War II and devastating floods in 1953 – there is a sign to this effect outside. On a less spiritual note, the town also has the Green Jack Brewery, the nation's most easterly brewery, which produces some splendidly hoppy and appositely named ales, like Trawlerboys Best Bitter and Rising Sun Pale Ale. Close to the bus station stands the Catholic church of **Our Lady of The Star**, the most easterly Catholic church in the United Kingdom, decorated in tasteful Arts and Crafts style and probably the grandest Catholic church in all Suffolk, in which the Virgin Mary is represented as a guiding star for seafarers. Seafaring was always the mainstay here and, although burly fishermen in oilskins are a rare sight these days, there is a reminder of former times on the swing bridge over the harbour, where a monument of a trawlerman in full seafaring attire gazes wistfully out to sea.

If you wish to get a taste for what life aboard a fishing trawler was like you could always visit the *Mincarlo* (℡ 07500 603734 ⌂ www.lydiaeva. org.uk, open Tue–Thu 10.00–16.00) at Heritage Quay in Lowestoft harbour, the last vessel of its kind to be made in the town that now serves as a boat museum owned by the same charitable trust that owns the *Lydia Eva* just up the road in Great Yarmouth.

¶ FOOD & DRINK

Triangle Tavern St Peters St ℡ 01502 582711 ⌂ www.triangletavern.co.uk. Probably the best pub in Lowestoft and undoubtedly the best place to sample the range of Green Jack ales. No food, live music some nights.

2 BENACRE & COVEHITHE

Head a little way south of the town along the 'Sunrise Coast' (a recent marketing ploy) and you reach **Kessingland** with its holiday village and Africa-themed Suffolk Wildlife Park. Just south of Kessingland is where the Suffolk Coasts & Heaths Area of Outstanding Natural Beauty (AONB) begins – a broad swathe of deservedly acclaimed coastal landscape that, with the exception of the urban enclaves of Felixstowe and Ipswich, stretches all the way to the Essex border at Manningtree.

A little way beyond Kessingland you reach **Benacre**, which until recently was home to an isolated freshwater broad of the same name, a national nature reserve managed by Natural England. In recent years regular incursions of seawater have breached the shingle bank that separated the broad from the sea and as a result its ecosystem has changed dramatically. Dead trees killed by salt spray and saltwater inundation litter the beach here – highly photogenic but in an apocalyptic sort of way. It is only a matter of time before the last vestiges of Benacre Broad are engulfed and reclaimed by the sea.

South of Benacare, you soon encounter further evidence of a rapidly disappearing coast. **Covehithe** was a small town in the medieval period but has been whittled down by North Sea erosion to a mere village these days, with the oddity of the partly dismantled church of St Andrew having a later, smaller church built within it. The road that leads past the church to what would have once been more of the village ends abruptly at a cliff, its tarmac surface severed and recycled by the North Sea. The coastline has retreated over a quarter of a mile here in the past two centuries and offers a taste of what is to come at Dunwich, beyond Southwold, a far more dramatically reduced place.

SOUTHWOLD, DUNWICH & AROUND

3 SOUTHWOLD

🏠 **The Swan** (see page 211)

⛺ **Harbour Camping and Caravan Park** (see page 211)

It's hard to imagine anyone not being seduced by Southwold: that this most bewitching of seaside towns manages to exude such easy charm without much trace of smugness is to its great credit. George Orwell (real name Eric Blair), who lived and taught in the town in the early 1930s, may have been critical of Southwold's comforting gentility but for most, this is actually its draw. Southwold seems still to belong to the 1930s (in the nicest sense) in many ways.

A lighthouse stands right in the middle of town, and there's a pier, lines of colourful beach huts and a brewery where casks are delivered locally by horse and cart. Despite all this, the town has more than enough grit to keep it real, and deeper layers exist here beneath the shiny veneer of cream teas, overpriced real estate, gleaming 4x4s and metropolitan accents. There are retired folk licking ice-cream cornets, kids making sandcastles on the beach, wet fish for sale at fishermen's huts along the Blyth River, and even a reading room for sailors.

The town's genteel feel is partly serendipitous thanks to a devastating fire that tore many of its buildings down in 1659. This created a handful of open areas that were left as fire breaks and never rebuilt upon, and it is these **greens** that contribute towards the town's wholesome air of uncluttered space. The best known of these is above the beach at Gun Hill, where cannon commemorate the Battle of Sole Bay fought just offshore from here, a rare contretemps in which the English and French fleets combined forces to fight the Dutch.

The town's ultimate landmark is its **lighthouse**, built in 1887 to replace three lighthouses threatened by coastal erosion. Tours are possible at certain times of year or you could simply contemplate its white pepper-pot form from one of the outside tables at the Sole Bay Inn just across the road. The lighthouse was automated in 1938 but, before this, the keeper must have had the least lonely posting in the land, with the option of enjoying a pint in one of the town's hostelries whenever the fancy took him. The lighthouse's close neighbour, the **Adnams Sole Bay Brewery** was built in the same year (1890) that the lighthouse first went into operation. This replaced an earlier brewery on the same site, so the legend 'established 1660' that you see on bottles of Adnams ales is not mere hyperbole. The town is peppered with

"The lighthouse keeper must have had the least lonely posting in the land, with the option of enjoying a pint whenever the fancy took him."

splendid Adnams houses all serving up delicious, well-hopped beer, a phenomenon that in this instance at least gives the word 'monopoly' a newfound respectability. The Sole Bay Inn is perhaps the best known but the Lord Nelson, Harbour Inn and others are equally good places to sup a pint. Sometimes I do wonder why a pint of Adnams bitter costs quite a bit more here at a pub right next to the brewery than it does at my local in Norwich 35 miles away. But this is Southwold and it would be simply vulgar to ask. Besides, the sea view and the briny air come absolutely free of charge.

Southwold Pier (⊕ www.southwoldpier.co.uk) re-opened for business in 2001 but the original structure dates from 1900 and stood until 1934 when a gale virtually destroyed it. The pier is proudly claimed to be the first to be built in Britain for over 45 years, which in itself is quite something. Take a stroll along it and you will find that it is not quite as run-of-the-mill as you might first have imagined. Thanks to the wacky and inventive mind of Tim Hunkin, the pier's machine arcade has a wealth of bizarre but charming Heath Robinson-like slot machines that put a smile on the most serious of faces. Here at the **Under the Pier Show** you can enjoy playing 'Whack a Banker', help old ladies cross the road (usually unsuccessfully) in the face of murderous traffic in 'Help the Old Lady' and even get to decide the fate of a lovable lamb in a game of 'Pet or Meat'. The arcade is worth half an hour and a couple of pounds' worth of change of anyone's money. You might also wish to be present for the rather rude, half-hourly chiming of Hunkin's water clock, although it rarely seems to go off exactly when it should. As well as the arcade, you'll find a couple of gift shops and cafés. And if it is not too windy there are also some rather stylish benches to sit on and ponder the giant white golf ball of Sizewell B nuclear power station clearly visible along the coast to the south.

"You might also wish to be present for the rather rude chiming of Hunkin's water clock, although it rarely seems to go off exactly when it should."

Southwold's **North Beach** lies beneath the pier with its wooden groynes jutting out to sea. There's sunbathing in deckchairs and sandcastle making aplenty on the sand, while many more visitors are content to stroll the promenade above the beach huts. The town's beaches continue south of the town too – along **The Denes** by the inlet of the River Blyth. Heading inland along the river's northern bank, you'll find a **rowing-boat ferry** across the river that has been operated by the same family since the 1920s and a handful of wooden huts selling very fresh fish at relatively low prices. This part of town, sometimes referred to as **Blackshore**, is my favourite corner of Southwold, atypical though it might be. There's always plenty of activity along here – visitors strolling with children and dogs in tow, sailors pottering with their boats, fishermen unloading their catch. It's picturesquely nautical without a hint of gentrification – a bit more barnacle-rough than the rarefied gentility of the town centre. There's a campsite here too just before the river inlet, and a pub and a café a little further inland before you reach a footbridge across the river to the Walberswick bank.

The **Sailors' Reading Room** above the seaside promenade is a modest building that has photographs, newspaper cuttings and all manner of maritime memorabilia. Effectively, it serves as an informal museum and, sailor or not, you are free to enter, although photography is not allowed inside the building, presumably because it would interfere with the sailors' reading. The last time I visited, little reading was taking place and the sailors within were, instead, playing a spirited game of pool in the back room. A more formal museum is the **Southwold Museum and Historical Society** (✆ 01502 726097 ⌂ www.southwoldmuseum.org) in a Dutch-gabled cottage on Victoria Street. This covers the whole span of history of the town with a range of interactive displays. The museum, which has equal-access facilities, also organises Tuesday evening lectures throughout August at the Methodist hall on East Green.

Almost as well known as the lighthouse are the town's three hundred or so colourful **beach huts**. Those by the pier below Gun Hill are the most sought after. Other places along the East Anglia coast have similar huts, but none have quite the cachet that goes with owning one on Southwold beach. In truth, the huts are little more than well-appointed garden sheds but this has not prevented them from becoming highly prized *pieds-à-terre* in this neck of the woods. For about the same price as an East Midlands terraced house, you get a single wooden room next to a busy thoroughfare where local by-laws permit you to make tea, snooze in a chair and watch the sea. You are not permitted to sleep overnight in them, however. What can you expect for an asking price that might start around £45,000? Well, not running water and an electricity supply, obviously.

Away from the seafront, the town's high street heads inland past cafés, galleries and old-fashioned shops to **St Edmund's Church**, a towering 15th-century building constructed of imported Caen stone with flint dressing. Look up as you enter and you will see the forlorn-looking figure of a tied-up Edmund above the door. The church's interior is quite beautiful, with an exquisite angel-bedecked roof and intricate steeple-like font cover that is 24 feet high. There's also a figure called 'Southwold Jack', a soldier from the War of the Roses, who carries a sword and has an axe that rings a bell when the service is about to commence (there's another Southwold Jack figure on the wall of Adnams Brewery that also appears on the corporate logo). The east window, which is by Sir Ninian Comper, has scenes from St Edmund's martyrdom and is a 1954 replacement of an earlier window blown out by a German bomb landing just across the road in 1943.

A little way inland from Southwold is the larger but far more workaday village of **Reydon**, a pleasant enough but unspectacular place where house prices are no doubt considerably cheaper than those of its coastal neighbour. There is an interesting group of almshouses here, dated 1908, that have crow-step gables and an elegant gateway that bears the inscription 'The Rest for the Aged', which pretty much tells it as it is.

¶¶ FOOD & DRINK

For food in Southwold, you are fairly spoilt for choice with so many tearooms and pubs, but there are plenty of places to buy quality do-it-yourself ingredients too. The High Street has the **Black Olive delicatessen** at 80a/80b (01502 722312), which has locally smoked fish and delicious pies, while the **Sole Bay Fish Company** (Shed 22e Blackshore 01502 724241 www.solebayfishco.co.uk) has its own boats with fish for sale at its shed in the harbour and at Southwold's **Monday market**. The shed also serves a range of fish platters that can be eaten in the room next door. It is unlicensed but customers can bring their own wine or beer and bread; it gets busy at weekends so booking ahead is a good idea. The greengrocers' shops at the Market Place also have a good range of local seasonal produce. Despite the presence of several characterful tea rooms and cafés in the town, a well-known coffee chain (whose very name suggests the coast . . . in Spanish) has opened up a branch

BEER FROM THE COAST: THE ADNAMS STORY

Adnams claim that beer was brewed on the same Southwold site back in the 14th century but the family themselves did not get involved until 1872 when George and Ernest Adnams bought the Sole Bay Brewery with help from their father. George wasn't cut out for the brewery business and soon upped sticks to Africa, where he met an unfortunate fate with a crocodile, but Ernest persisted with the enterprise to establish Adnams & Co Ltd in 1890.

Jack and Pierse Loftus bought themselves a stake in the business in 1902 and the company progressed modestly though the 20th century until 1970 when there was a substantial modernisation of the brewery. The same year also saw, perhaps a little counter-intuitively, the reintroduction of dray horses for deliveries around town. The brewery's 'Beer from the Coast' marketing campaign was launched in 2002, together with a charming set of posters, postcards and coasters which featured many Southwold icons – beach huts, the lighthouse and pebble beaches – all with cleverly disguised Adnams motifs hidden in the scene.

Adnams has strong ties with its Southwold home, most notably through its charitable trust that was set up to provide assistance to organisations within a 25-mile radius in the town in recent years much to the chagrin of some residents. The last time I visited it was actually doing brisk business in defiance of the notices that had been posted outside some of the other cafés encouraging visitors to boycott the big city interloper and visit their establishment instead.

If it's afternoon tea you're after, Southwold has more tea rooms and cafés than you can shake a buttered scone at. If you're looking for something more substantial and/or a beer then simply choose from any one of a number of Adnams houses in the town. Two other very well-liked pubs in addition to those below are the **Harbour Inn** right by the boats on Blackshore and the friendly **Lord Nelson**, centrally placed in East Street.

Buckenham Coffee House 81 High St, Southwold ✆ 01502 723273. In a basement beneath an art gallery, this place does good coffee – it blends its own – cakes, soups and light lunches.

The Crown 90 High St, Southwold ✆ 01502 7222275 🖱 www.adnams.co.uk. Of all the splendid Adnams establishments in the town, this hotel bar-restaurant is the most sought after and pre-booking is a very good idea, if not essential. The elegantly beamed interior oozes metropolitan sophistication, while the wood-panelled snug to the rear might appeal more to alehouse traditionalists. There's a good range of gutsy world-travelled dishes on offer and an excellent wine list in addition to Adnams ales.

Harbour Inn Blackshore, Southwold ✆ 01502 722381 🖱 www.harbourinnsouthwold.co.uk.

of the town. Adnams was awarded the Queen's Award for Enterprise: Sustainable Development in 2005 and in the following year constructed a new, ultra eco-friendly distribution centre. It was in this same year that the last of the brewery's dray horses were retired, as the road between the brewery and the new distribution centre was too busy and too far for the horses to travel. This was a sad day for Southwold, as the drays had become a familiar sight around town and had played a part in perpetuating the resort's old-fashioned image.

Ever keen to forge ahead on its sustainability route, Adnams went on to reduce the weight of its 500-millilitre bottle by almost half and set about constructing a new, energy-efficient brew house. This opened in 2007 to produce East Green, a new brew that would become the UK's first 'carbon neutral' beer, a feat achieved by using local high-yielding barley, aphid-resistant hops and lightweight beer bottles and by offsetting the tiny amount of CO_2 left over. It really amounts to something when you can claim that by supping beer you're doing your bit for the environment. The bonus is, East Green tastes good too. It's light, golden, hoppy and bitter – all the familiar characteristics of a traditional Adnams ale.

At the side of the River Blyth close to the bailey bridge across to Walberswick, this has excellent credentials as a seafarers' pub and serves up a range of mains dishes that feature mostly locally caught fish, although there are a few meat and vegetarian options too. There is the full range of Adnams ales and a good wine list too. The outside wall has a plaque showing the water level of the 1953 flood and, inside, the bars are full of old photos and seafaring memorabilia.

Randolph Hotel 41 Wangford Rd, Reydon IP18 6PZ ✆ 01502 723603 🖰 www.therandolph.co.uk. In a neighbouring village, just inland from Southwold, this late Victorian pub-hotel has a summer garden and modern good looks. There's Adnams beer, and local fish and game.

Sole Bay Inn East Green, Southwold ✆ 01502 723736 🖰 www.solebayinn.co.uk. With the lighthouse rising behind it like a minaret, this is another Adnams favourite and about as close as you can get to the brewery. Do they have a direct beer pipe? Good solid unpretentious food and predictably excellent draught beer.

4 WALBERSWICK

🏠 The Balancing Barn (see page 212)

Just across the water from Southwold, Walberswick is a former fishing village where the pace of life can make its neighbour seem almost frenetic in comparison. Long adopted by artists, Walberswick has slowly morphed over the years from bohemian to shabby chic. There's still a modicum of fishing taking place but most of the boats sloped in the estuary mud are of the hobby variety these days, and more than half of the properties in the village are holiday homes. Historically, Walberswick took over where Dunwich left off as a trading port. When Dunwich harbour became irretrievably silted in the late 13th century, Walberswick exploited its position at the mouth of the River Blyth to become its replacement.

Like Dunwich, it declined slowly over the years but managed to survive as a working port until the early years of the 20th century. What remains is the mere shadow of what was once a much larger place. The village has been associated with artists since the late Victorian period: in the 1890s and 1900s, the circle of English Impressionists associated with Philip Wilson Steer came here to paint, and Charles Rennie Mackintosh made it his home in 1914 when, disillusioned with architecture, he came here to paint watercolours (it didn't all go smoothly for him though: he was arrested as a possible spy in 1915). The village remains inordinately popular with media types, with a number of actors and other celebrities

A stroll from Walberswick

✳ OS Landranger 156 or Explorer map 231; start: the car park at the Flats, grid reference TM501746.

A fine circular walk can be made by following the west bank of the creek past the campsite as far as the derelict windmill, then heading away from the sea towards the trees at East Hill and following the path along the edge of the wood to reach a minor road.

Turn left along the road for a short distance then turn right through a gate with a bridleway sign to head diagonally across a meadow towards a wood – Sallow Walk Covert.

Follow the edge of the wood and continue along the bridleway, which follows the route of the Sandlings Way, beyond the end of the wood. Walberswick church will now be visible ahead to the right, as will the buildings of Southwold beyond.

Approaching the B1387 that lies a little way ahead, take the waymarked footpath to the right across a field towards a farmhouse. Turn right at the road and then left immediately after the farmhouse through a gate that has a **Walberswick National Nature Reserve** sign. Follow the track straight ahead across the common in the direction of Southwold's water tower ahead in the distance. Ignore the path on the right that leads to Walberswick's church and continue across the common to reach a tarmac track alongside a large reedbed. To the left, on the other side of the river, is a capped windmill.

Continue to reach the Bailey bridge that crosses the **River Blyth**. Turn right to return to the village along the river's southern bank. If you are feeling particularly energetic, you could then cross over to Southwold by way of the ferry or the Bailey bridge a mile inland.

The bridge is all that remains of the old **Southwold to Halesworth Light Railway** that ran its last train in 1929 after 50 years of service and was locally famous because its carriages had originally been intended for the Emperor of China. Reportedly, the forms of Chinese imperial dragons could just about be detected beneath the paintwork. Parts of the old railway route are still walkable, particularly between Blythburgh and Southwold.

maintaining homes here; there's a handful of famous Freuds too. As John Seymour dryly remarked when writing of the village in 1968: 'It is indeed, the haunt of ex-theatrical folk and lady watercolourists, but it is very attractive nevertheless.'

As well as an artistic retreat, Walberswick is popular with walkers, birders and young families who come here to go crabbing. A very popular spot for this activity is the small bridge that crosses the channel by the main car park at the area known as The Flats. My mother once saw former England striker Gary Lineker dangling a line here. The Suffolk Coast Path passes right through the village and it's a lovely walk to Dunwich. It is even possible to walk all the way to Dunwich along the beach, although not really advisable as it is shingle the whole distance and really hard-going. Plenty of shorter, circular walks that take in the marshes and bird-filled reedbeds are other options.

¶ FOOD & DRINK

The Anchor Main St ✆ 01502 722112 ⌂ www.anchoratwalberswick.com. This Adnams house serves dishes to match the beer and uses produce from local butchers and organic vegetable growers. There's a sun terrace overlooking allotments and beach huts, and occasional summer barbecues out on the lawn.

Parish Lantern Tea Room The Green ✆ 01502 723178. Set in a sheltered walled garden, this is a good, if pricey choice for lunch or tea and cakes.

5 BLYTHBURGH

A few miles inland from Southwold at the head of the Blyth estuary, the village of Blythburgh clusters around the busy A12. The estuary itself is quite a sight, especially when the tide is in and its wading birds are squeezed in closer to view, but the major attraction here is undoubtedly the village's remarkable church. Just south of the village, at the junction of the B1387, is the Toby Walk's picnic site, named after the ghost of a dragoon drummer reputed to haunt the area.

Holy Trinity Church

Like Cley in north Norfolk, Blythburgh's parish church is a reminder of prosperous times when the village served as an important wool port. The church, towering above reedbeds close to the river, and sometimes referred to locally as 'the Cathedral of the Marshes', is a beacon for miles around and unsurpassed in the area for both its scale and beauty. Like the River Glaven at Cley, the Blyth eventually silted up and Blythburgh's importance waned. The church too fell into decay, but the most devastating occurrence took place in 1577 when lightning struck the tower and it fell into the nave, killing two of the congregation. This, at least, is one explanation. A more fanciful one is that the legendary hellhound Black Shuck ran riot in the church before leaving scorch marks in the north door and scurrying off to Bungay's St Mary's Church to create similar havoc there (see page 81). Despite spiteful mid 17th-century defacing by the arch-puritan William 'Smasher' Dowsing (see page 144), the church is still a remarkable building, with carved angels flying across its roof space. In his *England's Thousand Best Churches*, Simon Jenkins calls it the 'queen of the Suffolk coast' (although he gives one more star to Southwold's St Edmund's) and it is by far the most evocative of the various settings used for summer concerts in the annual Aldeburgh Festival. Beneath the gaze of the benign angels overhead are poppyhead-carved pews that portray the Seven Deadly Sins. The church also has a wooden bell-striking figure, a brother to 'Southwold Jack' at St Edmund's, Southwold. As well as the angels in the roof of the church there is another to be seen outside on the green. The Blythburgh village sign, renewed as a local Millennium project, features as a remarkable wooden angel with spread wings clutching a shield.

Henham Park

Henham Park, Beccles NR34 8AN ✆ 07900 553426 🖰 www.henhampark.com. Limited open days for walks.

Just up the road from Blythburgh in the cleft of the A145 and A12 is Henham Park, a glorious estate set in lush parkland landscaped by Sir Humphry Repton in 1791, with ancient oaks, redwoods and even rare service trees and black poplars. Indeed the oaks seem so old and wide in girth here that you cannot help but wonder how they didn't end up as ships' timbers during the Napoleonic Wars at the start of the 19th century. The estate is currently in the ownership of Keith Rous, the sixth Earl of Stradbroke, known as 'The Aussie Earl' because of his work as a sheep farmer in Australia prior to his inheriting the property. You can walk in the estate at certain times of year but most people turn up for the **Latitude Music Festival** at the end of July, a family-friendly rock music festival that also features theatre, comedy, poetry, literature and cabaret.

The estate is also used as the location for summer food festivals, steam rallies and game and country fairs. In case you thought that Adnams had a complete monopoly in these parts, the estate is also home to Hektor's Brewery.

¶¶ FOOD & DRINK

White Hart Inn London Rd ☎ 01502 478217 🖰 www.blythburgh-whitehart.co.uk. A 17th-century Dutch-gabled coaching inn that once served as the local courthouse and jail but is now an Adnams house with standard gastropub fare. Stirring views of the Blythburgh estuary may be had from the outside tables in the pub garden.

6 DUNWICH

🏠 **The Ship** (see page 211)

A visit to Dunwich is not so much about what there is to see now – a pub, car park, café, a few ruins – but what has disappeared from view. As W A Dutt reports in *Highways and Byways of East Anglia*: 'the story of Dunwich seizes upon the imagination; though when one sees how little remains of what may once have been the chief city of East Anglia it is difficult to believe that Dunwich, too, was not a phantom city of a land of dreams'. That was in 1900 and almost nothing has changed – if anything the remaining village is even smaller today. Hard to believe, perhaps, but Dunwich was once the capital of East Anglia: a thriving port and shipbuilding centre with several churches, priories and even the seat of the East Anglia bishopric. With the confluence of the Blyth and Dunwich rivers forming a natural harbour, the town grew prosperous as a result of the wool trade in the early medieval period but, as has been the case elsewhere on this coastline, natural harbours are rarely permanent features. Today, the place is reduced to the status of a small village with a large beach car park. It's a popular place for day trippers to take the air, eat fish and chips and stroll along the shingle – all pleasant enough, but the real thrill is to come here and contemplate what existed before.

"The town grew prosperous as a result of the wool trade in the early medieval period."

Given that most of old Dunwich lies buried beneath the waves, it is perhaps inevitable that there's plenty of hyperbole describing the place as some lost Atlantis or Saxon Camelot. Old tales speak of 52 churches that used to exist here, and of tolling church bells heard out to sea during storms. However, Rowland Parker, author of the splendid *Men of Dunwich*, scoffs at such notions, saying that there were never more than six churches standing at any one time in the town, and that he has never heard any local talk of bells tolling out at sea. If you wish to learn more of the history of Dunwich and medieval Suffolk, Parker's book is highly recommended: although it contains a staggering amount of historical detail, it is as gripping as a good detective story.

Dunwich's early history has some grey areas, but what is certain is that, although the place was known to the Romans, it was Saxons who first developed it as a port. The Christian missionary St Felix of Burgundy founded the East Anglia bishopric here in the mid 7th century when the place was known as Dommoc. The bishopric moved to North Elmham

THE DUNWICH DYNAMO

For a bicycle ride with a difference, you might want to consider participating in the annual Dunwich Dynamo.

You'll need legs of steel, and night vision would be a distinct advantage too. The ride takes place each year on the Saturday night closest to the full moon in July. The 'Dynamo' leaves Hackney in London on the Saturday night and arrives in Dunwich the following morning – a gruelling 120-mile overnight ride, part of the way marked by decidedly low-tech tea lights in jam jars, and ending up with breakfast on the beach.

This punishing event started back in 1993 when a group of London cycle messengers decided to go on a fun run to the coast. Since then, the route, planned by the London School of Cycling, has been organised on a turn up and go basis, with an increasing number of competitors taking part but less competition between them (if that makes sense). There were 700 participants on the 2006 run, or 'DD' as it is commonly known,

while the 2007 event had 450 participants of whom only 400 finished because of problems caused by bad weather. The largest turnout yet was in 2009 when an estimated 1,000 riders started from Hackney, one of whom was riding a penny-farthing bicycle. Even more foolhardy, perhaps, was some brave soul who managed to complete the route on a hired Boris bike in 2011.

A turn-out of around a thousand participants is now pretty much standard and no doubt in future years participants will continue to find increasingly more challenging ways of completing what is already a demanding overnight ride. This is no race – there's no official start time and no prize for arriving first to the coast. There's no safety car either, so participation is not to be taken lightly. It is certainly no picnic. It is 120 miles ... at night ... all the way through East London, Essex and Suffolk.

For further information see ⌁ www. southwarkcyclists.org.uk.

in 870 before later transferral to Thetford and finally Norwich. Dunewic, a Saxonised version of its original name, is recorded as being a small town in 1060 with a single church. The Norman Conquest brought expansion to the port and within 20 years of the conquest, Dunwich had a population of around 3,000, a considerable number for those days. By the mid 13th century, it had become a vitally important seaport. A conjectural map of the town and harbour of circa 1280 in Parker's book gives an idea of what might have been found here at that time: five churches, two priories, a guildhall, a market place, shipyards, a quay, town gates, a hospital, a leper hospital and even a bit of topography – Cock Hill and Hen Hill.

Dunwich's demise started in the same century. In 1286, a ferocious sea surge swept many of the town's buildings out to sea and the Dunwich River became partly silted up. The next century was no kinder. A storm in 1328 finished off Dunwich's harbour and this was the cue for Walberswick, just to the north, to take over the port trade. This resulted in such hostility between the two towns for the following century or so that confrontations often erupted into violence. That which remained was lost to the sea over the next few hundred years thanks to further coastal erosion.

All that can be seen today are the ruins of Greyfriars, the Franciscan priory, and fragments of the leper hospital (for a leper hospital in fine condition you might want to check out Lazar House along Sprowston Road in Norwich). The church that stands today, St James, is relatively recent, and dates from 1832. Marine archaeologist Stuart Bacon, who has been working here since 1971, has located the remains of two of the town's former churches, All Saints' and St Peter's, out to sea, and recent evidence of the town's shipbuilding industry has also been discovered. All Saints' was the last of Dunwich's medieval churches to be lost. It reached the cliff edge in 1904, although its tower did not collapse until 1922. Old postcards show the ruins of this church, a buttress of which was salvaged for incorporation into the structure of St James's Church. You can also see a brass taken from All Saints' inside the modern church.

Dunwich Museum on St James Street, open from April until September, has some fascinating displays outlining Dunwich's 1,500-year-old history. Even better, it's free to enter although a small donation is welcomed.

7 DUNWICH HEATH & MINSMERE

North of Dunwich is the dense coniferous plantation of Dunwich Forest and a large marshy area – Dingle Marshes and Westwood Marshes – an uninterrupted squelch as far as Walberswick. A couple of footpaths lead across the marshes – consult the OS map – or alternatively you could trudge north along the shingle beach, but that would be hard work all the way to Walberswick. A more rewarding area for walkers is that to the south of the village – Dunwich Heath, Westleton Walks and the Minsmere RSPB nature reserve.

Dunwich Heath is National Trust-owned and above the cliffs a convenient car park looks down over the Minsmere reserve and on to the giant golf ball of the Sizewell B nuclear power station. The attractive white coastguard cottages next to the car park hold the National Trust visitor centre and a tea room. Dunwich Heath itself is a rare example of typical, unimproved Sandlings habitat, with rare Dartford warblers lurking in the gorse bushes and nightjars at dusk during summer.

Sizewell B nuclear power station

This structure resembling a giant golf ball perched atop a massive concrete block can be seen from much of the Suffolk coast, certainly from as far away as Southwold and Orford Ness.

Contaminated water leaked from Sizewell A in January 2007 as the earlier power station was being decommissioned. Notwithstanding this, most locals are pretty blasé about its presence and some people even prefer to swim on the beach near the water extraction pipes because 'the water's a bit warmer there'. The power station management team has cultivated good relations with the nearby RSPB reserve over the years and has also provided welcome employment for the residents of Leiston. It may be unpalatable to eco-warriors but the reality seems to be that nuclear power stations are becoming generally less controversial than wind farms.

The beach here is a favourite place for local dog walkers and the shingle shelters lots of typical heathland plants like harebell, centaury and lady's mantle. The concrete buildings themselves also, surprisingly perhaps, provide a home for wildlife; in this case, birds – black redstart and kittiwakes. The beach also has a café next to the car park that is open more or less year-round.

A heath, marsh & shingle walk around Minsmere

✳ OS Landranger map 156 or Explorer maps 212 and 231; start: Dunwich Heath National Trust car park, grid reference TM477678.

This excellent walk provides the full Suffolk coast experience, with sea, shingle, reedbeds, grazing marshes, woodland and heath all putting in an appearance along the way. Although this does not actually enter the RSPB reserve it overlooks parts of it and catching sight of interesting birdlife is pretty well guaranteed. An alternative starting point would be to park at the Eel's Foot Inn in Eastbridge and do the walk after eating lunch there.

Start at the National Trust car park and descend the steps down to the shore. Follow the path along the shingle, passing a couple of entrances into the reserve and concrete World War II anti-tank blocks along the way. At Minsmere Sluice turn right away from the sea and follow the waymarked path inland past a fragment of what was once Minsmere Abbey (see page 42). This passes grazing marshes and reedbeds, eventually reaching a minor road. Turn right and follow the road past the Eel's Foot Inn and over a bridge at a stream to arrive at an area of dense coppiced woodland to the right. Follow the road to the right that leads to the RSPB visitor centre and veer left when it forks to leave the wooded area.

Continue through an open area with views of the coast and Sizewell B and continue across a crossroads of tracks through an avenue of oaks to reaching a footpath to the right that is waymarked Sandlings Walk. Follow this through more woodland to emerge at a gate and a sign announcing 'NT Dunwich Heath', at the point where it emerges at open heath, a wide expanse of brilliant purple in August. Continue in the same direction across the heath aiming for the white coastguard cottages and the National Trust car park ahead.

Minsmere RSPB Nature Reserve

Minsmere, Westleton IP17 3BY ☎ 01728 648281. Open daily 09.00–dusk; RSPB.

Minsmere is well known, a flagship reserve established in 1948 with year-round interest in its pools and reedbeds. The reserve is a popular place with both twitchers and beginner birders and there's a wealth of information about the place in the visitor centre. Two circular trails around the reserve take you through a variety of habitats, and some of the seven hides are accessible to wheelchairs. Typical reedbed species such as bittern, marsh harrier and bearded tit are all present and it's pretty hard to miss the elegant black-and-white avocets that grace the ponds here. You are far more likely to hear a bittern – a deep 'boom' reminiscent of a distant foghorn – than see one. You might hear nightingales, too, in early summer in the woods close to the visitor centre. The visitor centre has a shop and a tea room and there are guided walks available as well as plenty of activities for children.

¶¶ FOOD & DRINK

Eel's Foot Inn Eastbridge ✆ 01728 830154 🕾 www.theeelsfootinn.co.uk. A village pub, close to the Minsmere RSPB reserve, that has good Adnams beer and regular folk music nights. Full meals and lighter options, all locally sourced, but no pre-booking of tables. The inn also offers rooms and a cycle-hire service

Flora Tea Rooms Beach Car Park, Dunwich ✆ 01728 648433. Famous for their fish and chips as well as for location (you are at the mouth of what was once Dunwich's great harbour), this is a plain no-frills place serving good fish and chips, pots of tea and ice-cream sundaes. Outside are trestle tables for dining on fine sunny days, while there's also plenty of seating inside for less inclement weather.

The Ship St James St, Dunwich ✆ 01728 648219 🕾 www.shipatdunwich.co.uk. This popular former smugglers' inn, virtually on the beach and well placed for walkers and birdwatchers, has excellent fish and chips and Adnams in the bar, as well as a modern dining room where generous portions of comforting traditional food are served. There's also a conservatory and a large back garden. See also *Accommodation*, page 211.

8 WESTLETON, MIDDLETON & THEBERTON

These three villages sit between Dunwich and Yoxford on the A12. Westleton lies on the direct road to Dunwich and Minsmere RSPB reserve, while Middleton is just off it on another minor road. Theberton, lies just south of Middleton. All three are inviting, with scattered old houses that seem to determine the route of the road that curves around them rather than the other way round.

Westleton is the largest and most visited of the three, a fairly large attractive village with a green and St Peter's Church, a thatched 14th-century church that was built by monks from Sibton Abbey, close to Peasenhall just across the A12. Legend has it that no grass can grow over the 'witch's stone' near the priest door of the church, and if you put your handkerchief in the grating of the wall and make an anti-clockwise circumambulation of the church you will hear the sound of the Devil clanking his chains beneath the grating. You may notice that this large church is lacking in one department – it has no tower or spire. The original tower collapsed in high winds in 1776. It was rebuilt but its replacement also collapsed during World War II, this time the result of a German bomb. The church stages occasional orchestral concerts as well as hosting Westleton's annual **Wild Flower Festival**.

The village also has two pubs, unusual for a village of this size, and a nicely idiosyncratic secondhand bookshop with an emphasis on rare collectables, **Chapel Books** (℅ 01728 648616 ⌂ www.chapelbooks.com), homed in a former Methodist chapel opposite the post office and village shop. Nearby, tucked away behind the Crown pub, is the village duck pond where an inscribed bench proclaims: 'Eighteen Lime Trees for Eighteen Men 1914–1918'. The commemorative lime trees line the path behind.

"Middleton, straddling a road that goes nowhere in particular, has the distinction of being the only village in Suffolk that has its own moor."

Close to the village on the road to Darsham just east of the A12, you'll find the **Emmerdale Farm Shop** (℅ 01728 668648 ⌂ www.emmerdalefarmshop.co.uk), which stocks well-matured beef from a local herd of Suffolk Red Poll that are reared in the old-fashioned way, grazing on marshes in spring and summer, as well as locally grown vegetables like potatoes and asparagus and products from other local suppliers; it also has a coffee shop. There's another farm shop just south of the village at **Reckford Farm** (℅ 01728 648253) by the Middleton turn-off, which sells its own fruit and vegetables in addition to produce from other local enterprises

Middleton, straddling a road that goes nowhere in particular, has the distinction of being the only village in Suffolk that has its own moor, actually just a big field a mile from the village centre. After following a narrow lane for about a mile from the turn-off, the village comes as surprise when you get there. Middleton is a self-contained little place and its isolation from the main road might help explain its timeless atmosphere. Its church dominates, towering above the village on a rise. Below is a tiny green that has benches, a telephone kiosk and a metal sculpture on a plinth at its centre. The faded village sign featuring a cockerel looks more like it belongs outside a pub. But the village pub, a cosy thatched building next to an optimistically large car park, is actually called The Bell and already has its own sign. A path leads up from the green to the churchyard, its gate flanked by tidy cottages with impressive floral display in pots and hanging baskets – all very attractive but not the slightest bit twee. The village church, Holy Trinity, is welcoming, or at least it seemed that way when I last visited around Harvest Festival time. There were apples in the porch and sweetcorn plants growing in pots in the chancel as well as vases filled with slightly faded bunches of flowers gathered from village gardens. With the pervading scent of ripe apples, sunshine

MOLLY DANCING IN EAST ANGLIA

Molly dancing is the East Anglian version of Morris dancing, a more earthy tradition that is altogether scarier and might even be described as 'Morris dancing with menace'. Molly involves a type of dance traditionally performed by ploughboys in midwinter. It mostly existed in the Midlands and East Anglia and, before the recent revival, the tradition was last witnessed in Cambridgeshire in the 1930s.

Molly dancing is usually associated with Plough Monday, the first Monday after Epiphany ('Twelfth Night'), a day on which ploughboys would tour their village and offer to dance for money for local landowners, meting out 'trick or treat'-style mischief to those who refused to pay. The commonest penalty would be to plough a furrow across the lawn or garden of the offending party. Anonymity was vital, as it would be these same landowners who would provide employment once the farming season got under way. Consequently, faces would be blackened with soot, Sunday-best clothes modified with coloured scarves and one of the team would cross-dress as a woman.

The revived tradition incorporates all of these elements with a modern twist. East Anglia has several Molly 'teams': Old Glory, who also perform the Cutty Wren Hunt at Middleton (see page 40), Ouse Washes Molly Dancers and Gog Magog Molly.

As well as Plough Monday and the Cutty Wren Hunt, Old Glory Molly can also sometimes be seen dancing at Southwold and Walberswick on Christmas Eve. Whatever the occasion, the proceedings usually have a solemn, dark edge. Old Glory don't smile or talk when they perform, and they don't perform outside winter. They do tend to scare small children though. It's a serious business that seems both primordial and quintessentially English. In fact, one witness is reported to have said that the Molly experience was 'so English, it brought tears to my eyes'.

streaming through the stained glass and the sound of children's laughter drifting in from the primary school playground next door it all seemed delightfully idyllic.

There's an old tradition in the village called the **Cutty Wren Hunt** that is based on an ancient tradition in which a wren is captured on the evening of St Stephen's (Boxing Day) for purposes of divination. The custom finally died out at the beginning of the 20th century, but a modified version of it was resurrected in 1994. Originally, a wren would be captured and killed, and then fastened to a holly and ivy-bedecked broomstick to be taken around the village by boys who would demand gifts from the householders.

These days, real live wrens are spared and the ritual consists of a lantern-lit procession bearing a wooden wren that goes from the village hall to the Bell Inn where the Old Glory Molly Dancers perform. The ritual may have prehistoric origins but is a curious one, as it is generally considered unlucky to kill them. There may be a connection here with the midwinter tradition of topsy-turvydom in which the usual rules of behaviour are turned upside down, and the wren's perceived association with the underworld is symbolically challenged. Although similar traditions exist in Ireland and Britain's Celtic fringe, the one at Middleton appears to be unique for England. All this bird abuse so close to Minsmere!

Theberton is another village with a thatched church, St Peter's; in this case, a much smaller one than at Westleton but at least complete with tower, a fine round tower no less, topped with an octagonal belfry. A trio of fearsome gargoyles glare down on anyone entering the porch, the Gothic horror effect only marginally diluted by the lengths of modern piping that protrude from their mouths A Zeppelin airship was shot down here during World War I and 16 German airmen perished in the crash. There is a memorial in the cemetery across the road from the church, and a piece of the airship itself mounted in a glass case in the porch. The story of the crash in English and German, together with black and white photographs from newspaper cuttings, can also be found in the porch, as can a selection of secondhand paperbacks. Fragments of the Zeppelin were recycled into all sorts of new uses such as keepsake brooches made from bits of recycled airship brass, and it's thought various bits and pieces, handed down through the generations, survive in the area today.

🍴 FOOD & DRINK

Bell Inn Middleton ☎ 01728 648286. A cosy thatched Adnams pub with a small dining area and a relaxed bar with sofas; limited choice of food but a welcoming atmosphere.

Westleton Crown The Street, Westleton ☎ 01728 648777 🖥 www.westletoncrown.co.uk. This former coaching inn claims to have provided 800 years of continuous service to travellers. There's an open fire to warm wind-chilled walkers and a huge map of the locality on the wall. The extensive menu is mostly sourced from local butchers or Lowestoft fishing boats. The food may be pricey but the quality is consistently high. Very popular with dog owners.

White Horse Inn Darsham Rd, Westleton ☎ 01728 648222 🖥 www.westleton-whitehorse.co.uk. This has much more of a village local feel to it than the Westleton Crown, with an excellent range of Adnams beers and decent pub meals for sustenance.

9 LEISTON & LEISTON ABBEY

Leiston used to be a mere village but expanded rapidly in the late 19th century when it became a centre for cast-metal goods and munitions at the factory of Richard Garrett & Sons, better known simply as the 'Leiston Works'. Once a hive of industry, the town is fairly humdrum these days and not as well-to-do in comparison with other towns along this coastal strip like Aldeburgh and Southwold. The close proximity of Sizewell B does not exactly endear Leiston to visitors either, although some townsfolk are grateful for the employment that the nuclear plant provides. Leiston is the home of Summerhill School, founded by A S Neill, the first so-called 'free school' that is based in the former mansion of Richard Garrett, owner of the Leiston Works. In all honesty though, there's precious little to see in the town itself other than the **Long Shop Museum** (☎ 01728 832189 🖥 www.longshopmuseum. co.uk) at the former Leiston Works, which is definitely worth a detour if you have an interest in steam engines or want to get a taste of what Victorian industrial life was like. Otherwise, it's probably best to make straight for Leiston Abbey, a mile or so north of the town on the Westleton Road.

Leiston Abbey

Free entrance; English Heritage

Set just off the main road, this is a highly impressive set of monastic ruins, the largest of its kind in the county. Most of what you see dates from the 14th century when the abbey, which followed the Premonstratensian rule, was moved here from a less healthy, flood-prone location on swampy ground nearer the coast close to present-day Minsmere (where a fragment of St Mary's Chapel, part of the original abbey, can still be seen close to Minsmere Sluice). Although Leiston Abbey's buildings date from the second half of the 14th century, the materials used are largely recycled parts of the earlier abbey and 12th-century Norman in style. The new monastery was considerably larger than its predecessor, and several new chapels were added during the extensive rebuild.

What is most impressive, besides the delicate tracery around the windows and lofty perpendicular arches up to 45 feet high, is that so much material was successfully reused from the earlier abbey, a remarkable feat of architectural salvage considering how difficult it must have been to transport large chunks of wall and archway even the short distance from Minsmere.

The large house that abuts the nave and north transept is a later addition, built after the Dissolution when the church and other buildings saw use as farm buildings. The house was extended in the Georgian period and currently it is in the ownership of the Pro Corda music school. Concerts are sometimes staged in the adjoining barn and the site, in the guardianship of English Heritage, is also occasionally leased as a venue for weddings and corporate events. The Lady Chapel, the only other complete structure, was restored and furnished in 1918, although when I visited there was a rather unfriendly 'Keep Out' notice posted on its door.

The ruins ooze atmosphere and make an ideal place to wander around in at twilight or when there's a mist over the land. There is a vantage point of the whole complex in the centre of the ruins where steps lead up to a viewpoint over the refectory. There's a good chance that you may well have the place to yourself, although the site is also popular with Leiston dog-walkers as there is a direct footpath from the town.

10 SAXMUNDHAM

⋏ **Mill Hill Farm Caravan and Campsite** (see page 213)

This small market town lies a few miles west of Leiston at the end of a road that passes through some of the less inspiring countryside this coastal strip has to offer – a slightly dreary flat expanse of prairie-type arable fields with few hedgerows, not really typical of the area. This is the exception rather than the rule, and things get much better just a little way south, or indeed north, of here. Saxmundham is not really that close to the coast at all but since it lies just east of the A12, and on the road to Sizewell, Leiston and Aldeburgh, it might be best to include it here. In some ways, the town is a bit like Framlingham but without the castle, the successful independent shops and the gentle buzz. What Saxmundham does have is a functioning station on the East Suffolk coastal railway line, a handy link to Lowestoft and Ipswich. Mostly though, 'Sax' is a quiet, old-fashioned place with ironmongers, bakery and barbers' shops clustered cosily alongside each other in the centre – the classic small market town, although you sense

"'Sax' is a quiet, old-fashioned place with ironmongers, bakery and barbers' shops clustered cosily alongside each other."

that the high street has seen better days and is slowly dying. It tends to come a little more alive on Wednesday market days but otherwise most of the excitement seems to emanate from the car park of Waitrose down near the church. Sad to say, the opening of a massive branch of Tesco immediately opposite appears to be more of a magnet for local shoppers, and to provide more Sax-appeal, than any number of quality bookshops or organic farm shops. To its credit, Saxmundham does still have a representative of the former, notably Old Print Works Gallery & Bookshop (☎ 01728 602026) at 27 High Street but the farm shop, Peakhill Farm Organics, that once also stood on the High Street has been forced to close although you can still buy direct from the farm at nearby Theberton (see page 40). Like it or not, the supermarkets are what draw most local people to the town these days, and despite a rather blatant sign outside Tesco saying 'High Street This Way, Shop Local' many visitors to the town do not bother to venture as far as this.

St John the Baptist Church, just up the hill from the Waitrose car park, which has a lovely bright sign at its entrance welcoming visitors, has an intriguing font with a pair of **woodwoses** on opposite sides. The woodwose – a hairy, wild-looking man with a club – is sometimes referred to as 'The Old Man of Suffolk', but for my money, it is really just another expression of what many would call 'the Green Man'. Of the pair here, one has his club raised, the other lowered. The church literature puts it politely: 'clubs raised by the unregenerate, lowered by the regenerate' without venturing red-faced into any explanation as to what the symbolism of the club might actually be. I'll leave you to draw your own conclusions, although its seems a little topsy-turvy to me; as Freud observed, 'sometimes a cigar is just a cigar'. If you are more interested in medieval carpentry than prurient symbolism, look upwards to the fine hammerbeam roof. The graveyard has a highly unusual headstone, that of one John Noller, which takes the form of a sundial.

The **High Street**, despite being ignored by many supermarket shoppers, has a number of handsome buildings along its length. There's a cluster of pubs – Queen's Head, White Hart and Bell Hotel – with an attractive white market hall next to the last, a former coaching inn that was closed for business at the time of writing, as was the White Hart. Market Place is a little further along, just off to the left, where there is a 16th-century timber-framed building that was once an inn, and an iron hand pump, cast by Garretts of Leiston just down the road.

Returning to the High Street and continuing towards the railway bridge you should be able to spot a crinkle-crankle wall, a Suffolk speciality, fronting one of the gardens. The **town museum**, which has displays on local history in a well-preserved 1940s railway booking office, is a little further on, close to the railway bridge at number 49. The museum also has a cinema room where you can see an archive film about East Anglian railways. It is open Monday to Saturday, mornings only.

Not far from the town, a little way to the east, **Peakhill Farm** (✆ 01728 602248 🖰 www.peakhillfarm.co.uk) is a long-established organic establishment based at Theberton near Leiston. The farm run by Rob and Karen White has a herd of South Devon cattle, some sows and a field of vegetables and salads, all of which are cultivated organically.

¶¶ FOOD & DRINK

There are few choices in the town unless you are fond of supermarket cafeterias. If it's an atmospheric real ale pub with good food you are after then there are several a few miles drive in any direction – see individual listings elsewhere in this chapter. In the town itself, both the places listed below are worth a visit.

Bistro at the Deli 26a High St ✆ 01728 605607 🖰 www.bistroatthedeli.co.uk. A deli selling continental and local produce, and home-baked pies and quiches made from local, seasonal ingredients. It also doubles as a café, with daily specials, good sandwiches, cakes and coffee.

Trinity's at No. 14, 14 Market Pl ✆ 01728 604664. Formerly the Corner House Café, this is a convenient stop on the way to and from the railway station.

ALDEBURGH, ORFORD & BRITTEN COUNTRY

South of Leiston and Sizewell, the Suffolk coast curves gently south-southwest as the River Alde meanders slowly seawards dividing the mainland of Suffolk from the elongated spit of Orford Ness, the nearest thing to an offshore island in these parts.

11 ALDEBURGH

⌂ Aldeburgh Cottage, Martello Tower and **Arch House** (see page 212)

Aldeburgh is the Suffolk coast's other main contender for the role of favourite seaside resort: a former shipbuilding and fishing town that went into decline when fishing boats became too large to drag up the beach and other, more suitable ports were favoured for the construction of ships. Before this happened though, ships as illustrious as Sir Francis Drake's *Pelican* (famously later renamed as *Golden Hind*) were built here. There's still some fishing done from Aldeburgh's shingle beach and one of the town's great pleasures is to buy ultra-fresh fish from one of the huts on the beach and go off and cook it. Of course, you could have fish from the very same catch cooked for you instead – more on this later.

This town these days is a place of wealth and refinement, with barely a rough edge apart from the workaday fishing huts and 'punts' on the beach. As you might expect, there is a considerable number of incomers and those that live here year-round tend to know that they are on to a good thing, which gives the place just the slightest hint of self-satisfaction. Aldeburgh's connections with the composer **Benjamin Britten** (actually a Lowestoft man) and the annual Aldeburgh Arts Festival bring such kudos to the town that you wonder what a real-life Peter Grimes might make of it – a little hifalutin perhaps?

Despite the widespread fame of its fish and chip shops, it is immediately obvious that Aldeburgh is as much about pan-fried sea bass on a big square plate as it is about fish and chips in paper. It is undeniably lovely though, with bracing sea-scented air, a Blue Flag shingle beach, some interesting buildings and, of course, fantastic fresh fish.

The most striking building is the **Moot Hall**, a Tudor timber-framed building that looks a little odd sitting right next to the beach, and holds a museum of the town's history (✆ 01728 454666 ⌂ www.aldeburghmuseum.org.uk). Its current location is thanks to longshore drift rather than eccentric town planning as it used to sit smack dab in the town centre. As elsewhere on this coastline, the relentless North Sea has shaved great chunks off what was once the original medieval town.

A better-known landmark these days is *The Scallop*, a large stainless-steel sculpture in the shape of a shell that stands on the northern beach close to the car park. The sculpture, the work of Suffolk artist Maggi Hambling, was unveiled in 2003 to much controversy. It is dedicated to Benjamin Britten and the upright shell bears the words: 'I hear those voices that will not be drowned', taken from Britten's *Peter Grimes*. Some clearly consider *The Scallop* to be an eyesore and a despoilment of a beautiful natural setting. As a result, the work has received a lot of flak since it was first erected, with graffiti, paint splattering and petitions all brought to bear in the case against. It is hard to see why the sculpture has been quite so vilified in some quarters; it is, after all, a natural, seaside form – a shell.

Such protest may be nothing new. The poet George Crabbe who was born in the town and in 1810 wrote *The Borough*, the lengthy poem in which the solitary character of Peter Grimes first surfaced, notes a certain philistinism in the local character:

... a wild, amphibious race,
With sullen woe displayed in every face;
Who far from civil arts and social fly,
And scowl at strangers with suspicious eye.

Thankfully, there's not really that much scowling going on these days, nor a lot of flying away from civil arts. It's not always that highbrow either: most who come to see *The Scallop* seem to prefer to have their photographs taken sitting on it rather than contemplating its words.

Aldeburgh's 14th-century flint church of **St Peter and St Paul** on a low hill above the town has further local artistic interest. Here, there's a memorial bust of George Crabbe and a gorgeous stained-glass window by John Piper that depicts three Britten parables of the Curlew River. Benjamin Britten and his partner Peter Pears are both buried in the churchyard. For those wishing to uncover more about Britten's time in Aldeburgh there's a **Britten Trail** (⌂ www.brittenpears.org) to follow, which as well as the church takes in the **Red House**, where the composer lived with Peter Pears and now the home of the Britten–Pears Foundation, the **Crag House**, where Britten lived for ten years shortly

ALDEBURGH'S ULTIMATE CHIPPIE

Walk one minute inland from the seafront to the High Street and if it's lunchtime or early evening you will almost inevitably come across a lengthy queue. The chances are that this is a hungry crocodile patiently waiting for service at the **Aldeburgh Fish and Chip Shop** at number 226.

The Fish and Chip Shop – yes, that's its name – has been listed as one of the country's top ten by *The Observer* and eulogised by chefs like Rick Stein and Nigel Slater. The secret, according to the owner Margaret Thompson, is that no flour is added to the batter and that vegetable oil, not beef dripping, is used for frying. It has been a family business since 1967. Some even claim it to be the best in the country. A place that can prosaically call itself The Fish and Chip Shop rather than 'The Codfather', 'This is the Plaice' or something similar just has to be good. There's another branch further along the High Street that is run by the same concern but this one is the original. By the time you get your fish supper you'll undoubtedly be very hungry. Walk back to the sea wall to enjoy your food by the sea but beware of local gulls that have become very adept at aerial fish theft.

after World War II, and **Aldeburgh Jubilee Hall**, an important music venue in the early years of the Aldeburgh Arts Festival (see below).

Just south of the town past **Slaughden**, once an important centre for boatbuilding, now a yachting marina, you reach a narrow spit with a **Martello tower**. This is the most northerly of a string of 103 squat defensive towers that stretch from here south as far as Seaford, East Sussex. Twenty-nine of these were built in Suffolk and Essex between 1808 and 1812 as defences against possible invasion by Napoleon, and as well as being the most northerly the one at Slaughden is also the largest, effectively four towers combined into one in a quatrefoil form. The spit pushes south with the River Alde on one side and the sea on the other to become Orford Ness – a very long trudge along the shingle and best visited on the National Trust ferry from Orford Quay (see page 58) as this route is theoretically closed to the public anyway. The **Aldeburgh Arts Festival** (www.aldeburgh.co.uk), an annual June festival of mainly classical music founded by Benjamin Britten in 1948, has become famous over the years. Most of the action takes place along the estuary at the purpose-built concert hall at Snape Maltings but some events use other venues like Blythburgh church. The town has become the home of more annual festivals in recent years: the **Aldeburgh Poetry Festival** (www.aldeburghpoetryfestival.org) in November;

the **Aldeburgh Literary Festival**, run by the owners of Aldeburgh Book Shop (⊕ www.aldeburghbookshop.co.uk) in March; and the **Aldeburgh Food & Drink Festival** (⊕ www.aldeburghfoodanddrink.co.uk) in September. The last, in part sponsored by Adnams Brewery and Suffolk County Council, has been running since 2006 and takes place both in the town and at Snape Maltings. The festival's purpose is to celebrate the abundance of local produce and to help people reconnect with the local countryside and the food it produces – all very consistent with the Slow philosophy. There's a different slant to proceedings each year: recent themes have included food security for the nation and for Suffolk, and helping children and their parents reconnect with food, where it comes from and how it is produced.

ᵞᵞ FOOD & DRINK

For fresh produce to cook yourself, as well the very obvious fish huts on the beach, there's **Hall Farm Shop & Tea Room** on the Saxmundham road (✆ 01728 453666), which has Aldeburgh saltmarsh beef and lamb and other local foods. The high street has a couple of good delicatessens like **Lawsons Deli** (✆ 01728 454052 ⊕ www.lawsonsdelicatessen. co.uk) at number 138, and a **farmers' market** is held on the morning of the third Saturday of each month at Aldeburgh Church Hall.

Aldeburgh Fish & Chip Shop 226 High St and **The Galleon** 137 High St; both under the same ownership (✆ 01728 454685 ⊕ www.aldeburghfishandchips.co.uk). Of these two highly rated fish and chip shops, the former is considered to just about have the edge – witness the queues – and considered by some to be the best fish and chip shop in Suffolk, some say the world (see box, page 47).

Cragg Sisters Tearoom 110 High St ✆ 07813 552181 ⊕ www.craggsisters.co.uk. Established in 1949, this traditional tea room offers a wide range of loose-leaf teas and excellent homemade cakes and scones. Local seasonal produce is used wherever possible.

Cross Keys Crabbe St ✆ 01728 452637 ⊕ www.aldeburgh-crosskeys.co.uk. Right next to the offshore lifeboat station on the seafront, here you can sup a pint of Adnams and eat briny fresh seafood caught by local fishermen. You can drink and dine outside in the garden and courtyard or take refuge inside by a log fire in cold weather. You can even take your drink over the road and sit on the sea wall.

Lighthouse 77 High St ✆ 01728 453377 ⊕ www.lighthouserestaurant.co.uk. With a good wine list and helpful staff, this popular restaurant specialises – surprise, surprise – in fish dishes, making full use of fresh local produce.

Regatta 171–3 High St ✆ 01728 452011 ⊕ www.regattaaldeburgh.com. Another high street restaurant where fish is king, although non-fishy dishes are also available. From April to September the emphasis is on fresh fish landed on Aldeburgh beach with daily specials according to what is available. Vegetarian, meat and poultry dishes are available all year round that make use of quality seasonal ingredients from other local producers.

12 THORPENESS
⌂ The Dune House (see page 212)

Heading north from Aldeburgh along the coast, you soon reach the village of Thorpeness, an odd place created from scratch by a Scottish barrister, Glencairn Stuart Ogilvie, in the Edwardian period. A hamlet had existed before but it was Ogilvie who decided to build a private holiday village here as a place where his friends and family could spend their summers. Work commenced in 1910, with a country club, a golf course and holiday homes in Tudor and Jacobean styles all appearing over the next decade or so. The village remained largely in the ownership of the Ogilvie family until 1972 when much of it was sold off to pay death duties.

The village's iconic landmark – it appears on Suffolk guidebooks as readily as Cley-next-the Sea's windmill does to represent Norfolk – is the **House in the Clouds**, a wooden house on a high, five-storey plinth. The plinth was originally a disguised water tower but once mains water had been installed in the village, it was converted into further living accommodation and a games room. You can rent it – very expensively. The views must be quite something. Thorpeness's other main sight is its artificial boating lake called **The Meare** that was inspired by *Peter Pan*, whose author J M Barrie was an Ogilvie family friend. A regatta takes place here each August in the week after Aldeburgh Carnival.

Whether you like Thorpeness or not tends to depend on your taste for mock Tudor. In some ways, the village has something of Portmeirion in Wales, albeit without the Italianate architecture and the cult appeal of the Portmeirion-set television series *The Prisoner*. Like that place, it feels rather like a film set, although Thorpeness is still waiting for the definitive film.

13 SNAPE, SNAPE MALTINGS & THE ALDE ESTUARY

Snape is a small village a few miles inland from Aldeburgh, close to the Alde estuary, although most people tend to think immediately of Snape Maltings at the head of the estuary itself. Snape village tends to get overlooked in favour of the retail and cultural opportunities on offer just down the road but it's certainly worth a mention in its own right. Surprisingly for a village of just a few hundred, Snape manages to support two dining pubs – The Crown and the Golden Key – although its proximity to the Maltings is a clearly a factor.

The four-panelled **village sign** depicting an Anglo-Saxon ship, a monk, a curlew and a bridge neatly summarises Snape's history. The ship is a reference to the site of an Anglo-Saxon ship burial discovered nearby, while the bridge depicts the old brick bridge that stood here over the River Alde until it was demolished in the 1960s. The praying monk is a reference to the Benedictine order that once had a priory here, and the curlew, a common-enough bird in these parts, is a nod to *Curlew River*, a work by Benjamin Britten, who drew much inspiration from the area.

ST BOTOLPH'S CHURCH, IKEN

East of Snape Maltings, just north of the tiny village of Iken on the southern shore of the estuary stands **St Botolph's Church**, marked on the OS map as 'The Anchorage'. St Botolph's has an exquisite situation, isolated on a bluff above the water, suggesting that arrival by boat would make far more sense than coming by road. This ancient church, founded AD654, stands on a former site of an island and was likely built on the same site as St Botolph's 7th-century abbey. Inside this small flint, thatched church you can see a large stone Saxon cross, discovered in the wall of the church tower and carved with symbols associated with St Botolph. This dates from the 9th century and probably commemorates the destruction of the original monastery by marauding Vikings around AD870. An awful lot of marauding went on along this coast in the past and Vikings always seemed to go about their duties with great gusto. Naturally enough, given the church's history as an early flag-bearer for Christianity in the region, this is a place of pilgrimage. Isolated geography has its part to play too and St Botolph's has pilgrimage written all over it (quite literally – even the church sign spells out 'St Botolphs Church Iken Welcomes Pilgrims').

Even without any interest in church architecture or history this is an undeniably magical spot – mysterious and charged by its sense of isolation at the edge of the world ... or at least Suffolk. With the snaking channel of the River Alde threading through the glistening mudflats of the estuary below and the piping of redshanks and plaintive cry of curlews on the wind, it is a highly atmospheric setting. The gentle and comically hirsute Highland cattle that munch the grass in the field next door might seem a little incongruous elsewhere in Suffolk; here they just add to the tangible sense of other-worldliness.

Snape Maltings

🏠 Admiral Cottage, Blaxhall (see page 212)

The Maltings (📞 01728 688303 🌐 www.snapemaltings.co.uk) are an impressive collection of shops and galleries converted from an assortment of Victorian riverside buildings. Malt production finally ceased here in 1965 and since then a slow restoration and conversion of the buildings has been taking place. A bespoke concert hall was built in 1967 and the slow process of conversion of the existing buildings has been taking place ever since. Currently, its businesses include craft shops, home and garden stores, restaurants, art galleries, jewellery and fashion and even old-fashioned children's toys. Some buildings have been restored and converted for holiday or residential use. The concert hall, which serves as the centrepiece for the Aldeburgh Arts Festival, finds use all year round as a concert venue. It is a lovely venue, although as something of a cathedral in wood it can be uncomfortable if you are sitting for any length of time. It is probably best to do as Snape regulars do and bring your own cushion. The Maltings are also used as the venue for the annual Aldeburgh Food and Drink Festival. A **farmers' market** is held in the main car park here on the first and third Saturday of each month.

The Maltings sit in a superb natural environment that is virtually surrounded by reedbeds. The RSPB, who have an office here in the small Virginia-creeper-clad building by the quay, provide guided walks every Thursday and also put on a range of activities for children and families. For a brief glimpse of the river and estuary, the 92-seater boat *Enchantress* makes 45-minute **river trips** in summer; these can be booked at the craft shop (📞 01728 688303) by the quay. Alternatively, you might prefer to strike out along a **riverside footpath**. One of these leads to the village of **Iken** and its isolated church on the south bank (the boat trip sails past here too), while another that links up with the Suffolk coast and Heath Path at Snape village leads north of the estuary along the **Sailors' Path** to Aldeburgh and the coast. **Canoeing** is a possibility too: there is a canoe and kayak hire place, Iken Canoe (📞 01728 688267 🌐 www.ikencanoe.co.uk; open Apr–Oct), at Iken Cliff close to the car park and picnic site. Walk right from the bottom of the car park and follow the river path to reach a green boatshed.

A couple of miles west of The Maltings lies the village of **Blaxhall**, where writer George Ewart Evans, author of *Ask the Fellows who Cut*

Two Alde estuary walks

✳ OS Landranger map 156 or Explorer map 212; start: Snape Maltings car park, grid reference TM393574.

Snape Maltings to St Botolph's Church, Iken

The riverside walk to the church at Iken is about 4½ miles there and back and will take about two hours if you do not stop much. Obviously it is much better to take your time, enjoy the scenery and make enough allowance for a look around the church when you get there. Leave the Maltings' car park at the exit beyond the music-school building. Follow the footpath across Farmland and then along a short piece of boardwalk through a reedbed. Continue through an area of saltmarsh that might possibly be flooded during very high tides (if this is the case – unlikely – you will have to wait a short while for the water to subside) then through a little more farmland to reach the Iken picnic site and car park where there's a wooden replica of the stone Saxon cross that you will soon be seeing in St Botolph's Church. Carry on along the riverside path, which might be muddy after wet weather, until you reach a minor road. Turn left and then, soon after, left again to follow the lane to its end at the church. Return the same way.

the Hay, used to live; and where he did just that – ask the fellows – in the pursuit of oral history. The **Ship Inn** (☎ 01728 688316 🖱 www. blaxhallshipinn.co.uk; see advert, page 67) here has always been an important place for local folk song and this tradition is continued to this day, with regular 'sing, say or pay' events and even the odd competition. John Seymour reported that here (in the 1960s) you could hear men sing folk songs like 'The Dark Eyed Sailor' and 'The Larks They Sang

The Sailors' Path

This is a long walk – six miles one-way, 12 miles there and back – although you can always use the First in Suffolk & Norfolk 65 bus service for the return leg to return back to Snape or Snape Maltings – it runs pretty well hourly throughout the day. The Sailors' Path is supposedly a historic commuting route between coastal Aldeburgh and Snape village. It was apparently also, as so many of these sort of things are claimed to be, a route once used by smugglers. Whatever the historical truth, the path is a lovely bracing walk through a variety of landscapes and in places provides excellent views over the marshes and estuary.

On the way you pass three sculptural installations by local artist Jonathan. These were installed in 2008 and have been left *in situ* to deteriorate naturally – the striking terracotta totem in Black Heath Wood that combines the pottery style of the Neolithic, Bronze Age, Iron Age, Roman and Saxon periods actually gets more beautiful with time and will probably last the longest. There are also listening posts installed along the way that give oral accounts of the history of the area.

Leave Snape Maltings by the main entrance and turn right to walk over the bridge. Turn right immediately after the bridge to follow the signed path. The path follows the edge of the estuary next to reedbeds for a while before turning sharp left away from the water past **Snape Warren**, an expanse of heathland, to the right. This soon reaches a road corner on the edge of Snape village where you turn right and follow the track past cottages and asparagus fields to reach **Black Heath Wood**, an area of mature woodland with oak, Scots pine and birch trees. Leaving the wood behind continue over the boardwalk through a marshy area next to **Hazelwood Common** to reach another area of woodland with a derelict house and a gate and follow the waymarked path gently uphill past another isolated house to eventually reach a car park by a main road. Follow the footpath to the right of the road past Aldeburgh Golf Club on the left to arrive in Aldeburgh.

Melodious'. You still can, although nowadays you are just as likely to hear a local singer-songwriter airing their compositions.

¶| FOOD & DRINK

The Maltings complex has a couple of decent cafés like the **Granary Tea Room** for snacks, cakes and coffee, and **Café 1885** (✆ 01728 687175) for lunch and all-day brunch as well as the **Plough & Sail** pub (✆ 01728 688413), while the nearby village of Snape has two dining pubs both with good food (listed below). There's also a food hall at The Maltings selling local produce and luxury food items. Blaxhall, a little west of Snape Maltings has the **Ship Inn** (see page 52 and advert, page 67), which as well as regular live music also has real ales and a restaurant serving good food made using fresh local ingredients.

Crown Inn Bridge Rd, Snape ✆ 01728 688324 ⌂ www.snape-crown.co.uk. This 15th-century Adnams inn is also a smallholding that raises all of its own livestock, so has menus that take advantage of very local meat as well as locally landed fish. There are Adnams ales and wines to choose from, and families and dog-walkers are most welcome.

Golden Key Priory Rd, Snape ✆ 01728 688510 ⌂ www.goldenkeysnape.co.uk. A 16th-century cottage-style pub in Snape village close to The Maltings that has daily menus featuring an abundance of locally sourced produce including meat from Bramfield Meats and Revett's of Wickham Market and smoked fish and meat from Richardson's Smokehouse in Orford.

14 TUNSTALL FOREST, CHILLESFORD & BUTLEY

Tunstall Forest lies immediately south of Snape Maltings, a large expanse of mostly conifers planted in the 1920s on what previously would have been Sandlings heath. Like the better-known Rendlesham Forest to the south, it was badly damaged by the Great Storm of 1987 but this at least provided an opportunity to replant with a wider variety of tree species than before. Woodlarks and nightjars can be found here by dedicated keen-eyed birdwatchers although scarce birds such as these are unlikely just to pop up on a branch in front of you. The forest rides are good for walks, although it is easy to get lost as with so many dense stands of conifers it all tends to look a bit the same. The forest is a popular haunt for mountain bikers too.

The village of **Chillesford** sits near the headwaters of the Butley River, a pleasant sleepy place with a church and a pub-restaurant The Froize (see opposite) on a rare-for-these-parts bus route. The village lies on a meandering inland section of the Suffolk Coast Path and is also very close to the Sandlings Way route between Ipswich and Southwold so there are plenty of walking possibilities in its immediate vicinity. **St Peter's**, the village church, is distinguished by being only one of two churches in the country built from coralline crag, a fossilised shell-rich sandstone quarried in the area that glows a warm apricot in the late afternoon

"The church also has some delightful modern stained-glass work by Suffolk artist Surinder Warboys."

sun. The church also has some delightful modern stained-glass work by Suffolk artist Surinder Warboys. The other coralline crag church is just up the road at St John the Baptist's in the parish of **Wantisden**; this isolated building stands right next to the perimeter fence of the disused airfield at USAF Bentwaters, once home to a huge stockpile of nuclear warheads and one of the busiest military airbases in the world, a strange juxtaposition indeed. The church was enclosed by the military area until the 1950s when a new military fence put it outside the base. The cracks in the wall are evidence of a tank-school accident in the 1940s.

Just south of here and a little way west of Chillesford is the small village of **Butley**, which was once home to an Augustinian priory founded in 1171. All that remains of it today is a highly impressive 14th-century gatehouse, which now provides the romantic setting for a wedding and events venue and an unusual and stylish holiday let. The village is also home to Butley Mill, now self-catering holiday apartments, and some converted 19th-century farm buildings that have now found use as artists' studios and workshops. The village pub, the Oyster Inn, was closed at the time of writing.

Just west of the village is **Staverton Park**, a hunting park dating from the 13th century that contains a large area of ancient woodland that has more than 4,000 magnificent pollarded oaks and extremely tall holly trees, some of the largest in the country, in a densely wooded area appropriately known as **The Thicks**. Staverton Park is privately owned but there is a footpath leading into The Thicks from the Butley to Woodbridge road.

¶¶ FOOD & DRINK

The Froize The Street, Chillesford ☎ 01394 450282 ⌂ www.froize.co.uk. *En route* to Orford, this remote village restaurant set in converted 18th-century keepers' cottages specialises in local game and retro rustic cooking served from an extensive buffet station. Adnams beer and Aspall's cider are on tap for drinkers and there are excellent desserts too.
High House Fruit Farm Sudbourne IP12 2BL ☎ 01394 450450 ⌂ www.high-house.co.uk. Pick your own fruit or buy ready-picked at this traditionally managed farm just north of Orford. They also make their own apple juice and preserves, and camping is available.

15 ORFORD

⌂ **The Crown and Castle** (see page 211)

Arriving at Orford's central square next to the church is a real pleasure, although there is little sense yet of being at the coast. For that, you will need to walk or drive the short distance down to the quay where all will be revealed.

Orford is very much a village of two halves: the village centre is a charming conglomeration of cottages around what was once a market square and hemmed in by the village church to the north and a 12th-century castle keep to the south. **St Bartholomew's Church** dates mostly from the 14th century, although there are traces of a Norman chancel. Of **Orford Castle**, which now belongs to English Heritage, only the keep remains but it is an impressive one and worth paying the entry fee just to climb up the spiral staircase for the view alone. Built by Henry II in 1165, at a time when they tended not to do things by halves, the keep has ten-foot-thick walls and is 90 feet high – a citadel that would be hard to breach with modern weaponry let alone longbows and maces. This, of course, is only a fraction of the fortifications that once stood here, which does raise the question as to what happened to all the stone that was shipped in to construct the original building.

Market Hill, around which much of the village clusters, is not much of a hill and no longer has a market but it's here you'll find a few shops, the town hall and the post office. There's a trio of narrow alleyways leading off Market Hill that connect with Broad Street and along the one next to Butley Orford Oysterage (see *Food and drink*) you'll find the **Butley Orford Oysterage Shop** (✆ 01394 459183 🖰 www.pinneysoforford.co.uk) where they have all manner of fresh and smoked fish and naturally, ultra-fresh oysters. The oysterage itself has a sign depicting a merman, which relates to the tale of a wild man-like creature that turned up in someone's fishing nets in the 12th century. In good medieval fashion, the poor creature was tortured but did not, or could not, talk and eventually managed to escape back to sea.

A five-minute stroll along Quay Street brings you to a large car park opposite the **Jolly Sailor** pub and then the **Quay**. Suddenly it becomes maritime, with sailing dinghies bobbing around on the river. The village, like many others on this seaboard, was once a thriving port but the growth of **Orford Ness**, the huge sand spit opposite, eventually denied Orford its ready access to the sea. However, judging by the number of yachts and pleasure boats here, the river seems a perfectly acceptable substitute for most modern-day sailors. There's not much else: a small

An Orford stroll

✳ OS Landranger map 169 or Explorer map 212; start: Orford Quay, grid reference TM425495.

The village offers numerous walking opportunities. A good, short circular walk is to head south of the quay along the bank of the River Ore. Where the river wall turns sharp left, turn right off the bank, cross a wooden bridge and stile then turn left through a wooden gate to reach a footpath by a ditch. Follow this through Chantry Marshes, bearing left at the sewage station, then right along a wider track. Arriving at a tarmac road turn right and then left along a footpath after passing the entrance to Green House Lane. Continue past Chantry Cottage and turn right to reach Orford Castle and the village centre a little way beyond.

National Trust shed selling tickets for the ferry across to the Ness, Brinkley's shed selling wet fish and, next door, a tea room. There's no electricity so Mrs Brinkley keeps her fish on ice – she has cod, skate and sea bass, or at least that was what she had on the day when I visited. 'There's just two boats that fish from here these days – us and another boat,' she told me. 'My husband catches the fish and I clean and sell it, so we do allright together.'

ⵙ FOOD & DRINK

Orford is very much on the Suffolk gastronomic map these days, having several places where a memorable meal might be had, particularly if seafood is involved.

Butley Orford Oysterage Market Hill ☎ 01394 450277 ⵙ www.butleyorfordoysterage. co.uk. This long-popular seafood restaurant serves Orford-caught fish landed by its own small fishing fleet and oysters grown at nearby Butley Creek. The restaurant interior is nothing fancy, plain even, but the delicious, unpretentious, uncomplicated fish dishes are superb.

Crown and Castle Hotel ⵙ www.crownandcastle.co.uk. This stylish hotel in the shadow of Orford Castle serves well-cooked locally sourced dishes from an imaginative à la carte menu of in its Trinity Restaurant. See also *Accommodation*, page 211.

Jolly Sailor Inn Quay St ☎ 01394 450243 ⵙ www.jollysailororford.co.uk. Just before

Orford Quay, opposite the town car park, this traditional 17th-century Adnams inn has two cosy, if slightly cramped, nautical-themed bars, good honest home-cooked food (the 'best cod and chips in Suffolk' according to the Ramblers, or so it says on the sign outside the pub and a beer garden.

Riverside Tearoom Orford Quay ✆ 07794 551530 ✆ www.riversidetearoom.co.uk. This is a good place for tea and scones while waiting for the ferry to Orford Ness. There's an outside sun terrace overlooking the River Ore.

16 ORFORD NESS

Quay Office, Orford Quay, Orford IP12 2NU ✆ 01728 648024. Open Jul–Sep daily 10.00–17.00, Apr–Jun & Oct Sat only 10.00–17.00; National Trust.

If you are not at Orford Quay for the sailing, your eyes will no doubt be drawn across the water to Orford Ness, which exudes an air of mystery typical of places associated with forbidden territory. From 1913 to the mid-1980s, the spit was firmly closed to the public, a top secret, no-go area dedicated to military testing and radar research. The links with its secret past are part of its appeal; otherwise, it's undeniable that Orford Ness is quite a remarkable bit of topography.

Though hardly pretty, this long shingle spit is undoubtedly evocative. Signs warn about unexploded ordnance, and everywhere you'll see tangles of tortured metal and wire netting among the teasels in the shingle. Overall, it's a rather melancholy landscape and you might begin to wonder if Orford Ness should actually be 'orfordness', a state of mind, rather than the name of a wayward landform. Of course, I am not the first to note the singularity of the place, nor will I be the last – in 2012, writer Robert MacFarlane was commissioned to write a libretto for a work titled *Untrue Island*, a performance piece combining sculpture, narration, music and real-time sounds that was performed on location at Orford Ness in July of that year. The Ness also appeared on the television series *Coast* around that time too and so the 'little known' cliché does not apply quite as much as it once did. Nevertheless, the place retains its magic and still keeps its secrets close to its chest.

To get to Orford Ness, you must take the National Trust boat. The *Octavia* runs across to Orford Ness roughly every half an hour between 11.00 and 14.00, with the last boat back around 17.00. 'Please don't miss the last boat back,' the NT boatman will inevitably warn you. 'It gets pretty nippy out there at night and there's only one loo for the whole of the spit.'

Seen from Orford Quay, Orford Ness has the appearance of being an island – it is often referred to as 'The Island' by locals. The ferry trip across the River Ore simply adds to this impression, but it's not an island – it's actually a long sand spit that begins just south of Aldeburgh and gradually widens as it follows the coast south. It is the largest vegetated shingle spit in Europe (nearly ten miles long) and it is only when you disembark at the jetty that you can really appreciate the scale of the place. The National Trust has a number of recommended waymarked routes to follow but the reality is that you won't see much unless you are prepared to walk some distance. Concrete roads lead around the spit and you have to trudge along these some way before you get to see anything of much interest. Bicycles are not permitted.

The Red Trail leads along the road and across a central dyke to the Bomb Ballistic Building, where you can climb to the roof terrace and survey the surroundings. A track leads across from here to a lighthouse on the shoreline, where there are also some ruined, boarded-up buildings. From the lighthouse, you can walk along the shingle as far as the Police Tower, where another track leads to Lab 1, the first of the military 'pagodas' that are clearly visible from the mainland.

If post-apocalyptic landscapes are not your thing then you'd be better off choosing the Green Trail and concentrating on the **wildlife**. You might be lucky enough to see porpoises out to sea from the beach by the lighthouse (someone had done so the day before my visit) but you are more likely to spot gulls and terns, and nervous rabbits and hares flitting across the shingle. As well as birds galore there are several plant species adapted to this harsh environment that you should look out for like yellow-horned poppy and sea pea, both

"As well as birds galore there are several plant species adapted to this harsh environment that you should look out for like yellow-horned poppy and sea pea."

shingle specialists. The hares here tend to be larger and chubbier than those on the mainland, although perhaps this may just be a trick of perspective in such an open environment – they really do look big. There are Chinese water deer too, and predatory birds like peregrine and marsh harrier. The Green Trail follows a circuit around King's Marshes on the landward side of the spit, where you should find plenty of waders feeding in the pools and lagoons. You could just about do both Red and Green trails if you came across on an early boat but you would have to get a move on, as that would constitute a total walk of around ten miles.

For me, the appeal of Orford Ness is to experience its other-worldly isolation and imagine (incorrectly) that I have the place to myself, alone at the edge of the world. More gregarious visitors might want to avail themselves of the various **tours** that take place on certain summer weekends – the 'Bombs and Beasties' guided tour is a good one that is quite self-explanatory. You can take a photography guided tour too – Orford Ness is enormously photogenic. All of these tours should be booked in advance; precise dates are given on the website or you can phone for bookings (☎ 01394 450900). The 'Island' is also an important place for bird migration and if so inclined you can observe migrants close up on designated 'Bird Ringing Mornings' in autumn.

Havergate Island, an RSPB reserve, lies a little further south between Orford Ness and the mainland. It's well known for its breeding avocets and there are occasional boats from Orford Quay that leave at 10.00 and return in the afternoon. Other birds regularly seen here include terns, owls, ducks and a broad range of waders. Seals are also sometimes seen in the River Ore here.

SOUTH OF ORFORD

To reach Shingle Street, the next settlement south along the Suffolk coast, requires a diversion inland from Orford around the River Butley via Chilesford and Butley. A minor road skirts Rendlesham Forest to reach Hollesley, with its HM Young Offenders Institution, before the road peters out completely at Shingle Street. Walkers can take a more direct route by way of **Butley Ferry** (☎ 07913 672499), where a boat will ferry you across the Butley River from where you can follow the Suffolk Coast Path south along the bank of the River Ore. The ferry is reached by following a minor road southwest of Orford past Gedgrave Hall and then following the waymarks to the river. Butley Ferry, which claims to be the smallest licensed ferry in Europe, operates between Easter Saturday and the end of September, 11.00–16.00, at weekends and on bank holidays.

17 RENDLESHAM FOREST

Rendlesham Forest is a vast coniferous expanse with a smattering of picnic places and forest walks. Gnarled old Scots pines scratch at the sky but plenty of plantations are relatively new, planted to replace the losses brought about by the October 1987 storm that wreaked havoc across southern England. I visited the area just after the event and I remember being shocked by the extent of the damage: huge shattered trunks, branches split like matchwood – the aftermath of the sort of extreme weather event that we are not supposed to experience in mild, moderate Britain.

The forest has experienced even stranger events than this if you can believe all that you hear. The so-called **Rendlesham Forest Incident** occurred over three successive nights during Christmas 1980, and was probably the most publicised example of a UFO incident ever to have occurred in the UK. It involved a series of unexplained sightings of lights and even the alleged landing of an alien spacecraft in the forest. There were two airbases in the area at the time, RAF Bentwaters and RAF Woodbridge, both of which were being used by the US Air Force. Although witnesses of the event were encouraged to believe that the pulsating lights they witnessed were simply those of Orford Lighthouse, there were those who insisted that they had seen a conical metallic object landing in a forest clearing. As with all events of this sort, the incident provided fertile ground for conspiracy theorists and the Ministry of Defence was accused of engineering a news cover-up after the event. The incident did not make national news until three years later when the *News of the World* published the story beneath the headline: 'UFO lands in Suffolk – and that's official'. For those intrigued by these extra-terrestrial claims, the Forestry Commission (⊕ www.forestry.gov.uk) has helpfully marked a three-mile 'UFO Trail' for walkers that begins at the **Rendlesham Forest Centre** and includes the main locations of the incident (two bicycle trails are marked from here too). Inevitably there's more on the internet: see ⊕ www.rendlesham-incident.co.uk.

Back to earth, Rendlesham Forest provides important habitat for woodlarks and nightjars – 20% of the national breeding population of the former and 10% of the latter, in fact – and three types of deer, as well as badgers and adders lurking in the woods.

18 SHINGLE STREET

This really does feel like the end of the road. On a blustery winter's night, it probably seems like the end of the world. There's really not much to Shingle Street: a row of coastguard cottages and holiday lets, a phone box, a car park and an awful lot of shingle. It does have a certain rather desolate charm; the beach is more or less empty, with wonderful views north towards Orford Ness and the mouth of the River Ore. At the southern end of this short strip of beachside houses stands a Martello tower, and you can see three more of them looking south from here framed by the distant silhouettes of Scots pines. There's virtually nothing else along this coast until you reach the Deben River estuary with Felixstowe sitting on its opposite bank. Standing on the shingle here with the coast curving south to vanishing point it seems hard to believe that Ipswich is only a dozen miles away.

Shingle Street was once a little livelier than it is today: a small fishing village and coastguard station that was home to River Ore river pilots. Unlikely as it may seem, there used to be a pub here too, the Lifeboat Inn, but this met an ignominious end during World War II when it was used for target practice for a newly developed bomb from Porton Down. At least the authorities were decent enough to evacuate the village first. Shingle Street was in fact emptied of its entire population in 1940 and this lasted for the duration of the war. Its fishing boats were destroyed at the same time and the village never recovered as a viable fishing centre, even after its people were allowed back at the end of the war. Many did not bother to return. Various conspiracies were hatched during the wartime period (perhaps this should be renamed the Conspiracy Coast given how far-fetched tales bordering on the supernatural seem to inhabit the landscape between the Alde and Deben estuaries?). There were lurid accounts of an abortive German landing and of a beach littered with burning bodies, rumours of the testing of experimental chemical bombs and of the sea being set ablaze to repel invaders. Such rumours, most of them anyway, were later proved to be false but stories like these may well have been encouraged during the war years for purposes of propaganda. The destruction of the pub is certainly true, as is the fact that the bodies of four German airmen were washed up on the beach sometime during World War II.

Leaving Shingle Street, if you want to keep going as far as the River Deben, you'll need to retrace your steps back to Hollesley (pronounced 'Hosely') then head south through Alderton to Bawdsey and then

> *"Shingle Street was once a little livelier than it is today: a small fishing village and coastguard station that was home to River Ore river pilots."*

Bawdsey Manor, where there's a passenger ferry across the estuary mouth to Felixstowe. The **Suffolk Coast and Heaths Path** goes this way too, clomping along the shore south from Shingle Street, across the Deben by way of the ferry then past another two Martello towers before reaching the outskirts of the town that is home to Britain's largest container port, **Felixstowe**, which is covered in *Chapter 3*.

Nearby **Hollesley** is home to a Category D prison and a Young Offenders Institution. The prison once had the largest prison farm in Britain and was also home to the oldest established stud of Suffolk Punch horses, which were put on display periodically at various county and national shows. The stud has since been sold to the **Suffolk Punch Trust**, a delightful charity institution that welcomes visitors.

The Suffolk Punch Trust

The Suffolk Punch Trust, Woodbridge Walk, Hollesley IP12 3JR ✆ 01394 411327 ⌂ www.suffolkpunchtrust.org. Open late May–end of Sep Wed–Mon, Oct Fri–Mon.

Although this is a working stud farm, you can visit the stables here and meet the horses as well as get a look at rare breeds of farm animals like black pigs, Red Poll cattle, Suffolk sheep and Ixworth chickens. There's a heritage museum too, where you can find out about the history of the Suffolk Punch breed, and a barn full of various horse-drawn vehicles and cultivating equipment. Three waymarked circular walks around the farm enable you to see the horses and livestock in their 'natural' environment, while a range of hands-on stuff for children includes stable demonstrations, milking a Jersey cow and various horse-related art and craft activities. The licensed café, which serves snacks and light lunches made using Suffolk ingredients wherever possible, has an outdoor terrace and picnic area and makes for a good lunch stop in a corner of Suffolk that offers few alternative refreshment possibilities.

19 BAWDSEY & BAWDSEY QUAY

The village of **Bawdsey**, a few miles south of Shingle Street and Hollesley, has little to offer other than easy access to the coast – there is a conveniently situated car park immediately east of the village close to a Martello tower. The car park, located next to a World War II gun emplacement and four rectangular ponds filled with wildfowl, is a good setting-off point for walks along the coast, either north to Shingle Street or south to Bawdsey Quay. Looking north, Martello towers dot the coast at regular intervals, the third that you can see marking the location of Shingle Street, just a low line of cottages peering through the haze. This makes for a fine two-mile walk along a raised bank between sea and marshes, with the added interest of the Martello towers as you pass them by.

Walking south in the direction of Bawdsey Quay, it is first necessary to head inland for a dog-leg around Bawdsey as the original coast path has eroded away in this section. You can reach the coast path again by turning left in Bawdsey along the main road and then taking the track across the fields once past Bawdsey Hall south of the village (follow the Suffolk Coast Path waymark signs). Heading south along the foreshore, it can be quite tough-going crunching through pebbles on a shingle beach punctuated with wooden groynes. It is worth the effort though, if only for the peace and isolation in a minimalist landscape of sea, shingle and sky. You are unlikely to see many people here even in high summer. The fact that the country's largest container port lies a just a few miles south seems highly improbable until you catch a glimpse of a container ship out to sea Felixstowe-bound.

A little way short of Bawdsey Quay is **Bawdsey Manor** (☎ 01394 412396 ⌥ www.bawdseymanor.co.uk), a strikingly odd Victorian Gothic building with Tudor-style chimney pots and a dragon weathervane. The eccentricity of the manor's architecture reflects the taste of its first owner, Sir William Cuthbert Quilter MP, a landowner, stockbroker, art collector and member for Sudbury in the late 19th century. Quilter was also a real ale aficionado it would seem, owning several breweries, and he once spoke on the subject of beer purity in Parliament, one of only two occasions on which he stood up to speak during his entire political career.

The manor came into the ownership of the Ministry of Defence just before World War II when it soon saw new life as a top secret radar research centre, the first of its kind in the world. The manor came into private ownership once more in 1994 when it was purchased by its present owners. Although the manor is closed to the public, apart from those attending educational courses, wedding functions and corporate events, occasional guided tours are organised under the Invitation to View scheme (⌥ www.invitationtoview.co.uk). The Transmitter Block of the former radar station, a concrete bunker tucked away secretively behind Bawdsey Manor, now serves as a museum managed by **Bawdsey**

Radar (📞 07821 162879 🖥 www.bawdseyradar.org.uk). The museum has a number of open days throughout the spring and summer when its Magic Ear exhibition may be seen, a comprehensive account of the history of radar development and the part it played in the Allied victory of World War II.

Just beyond Bawdsey Hall, on the north bank of the River Deben where it flows into the sea at Woodbridge Haven, **Bawdsey Quay** really is the end of the road, a long meandering road at that. If you are on foot or bicycle you can cross the river here over to **Felixstowe Ferry**. The ferry (📞 07709 411511), which operates from Easter to October, is now just a boat and you'll need to attract the attention of the skipper if he is on the opposite bank. This was once a much busier place and in the early 20th century a steam-drawn chain ferry used to operate here, the brainchild of Sir William Cuthbert Quilter from Bawdsey Manor who wanted a reliable connection with Felixstowe. The chain ferry was replaced by a launch in 1931 but the service was closed to the public during World War II when Bawdsey Manor served as a radar research centre. The ferry was contracted to RAF Bawdsey from the end of the war until 1974 since when it has become a privately operated summer-only service.

🍴 FOOD & DRINK

Boathouse Café The Quay, Bawdsey 📞 07900 811826 🖥 www.boathousecafe.co.uk. Right by the quay, with a veranda overlooking the River Deben, this is ideally situated for a drink or snack before or after taking the ferry. This has soups and sandwiches, cakes and scones baked on the premises, locally caught crabs and smoked prawns from the smokehouse just across the river. Open every day from May–Oct; Fri–Sun in Nov.

20 RAMSHOLT

On the east shore of the River Deben, halfway between Woodbridge and Bawdsey Quay lies Ramsholt, less a village and more a thin scattering of isolated farmhouses and barns. Other than some gorgeous coastal scenery, there are just two attractions here: an isolated, highly unusual church and an idyllically situated riverside pub. The only way to get here, other than by boat, is by way of the road from Shottisham, a village midway between Woodbridge and Bawdsey. The narrow road makes several 90-degree shifts of direction as it zigzags around the field boundaries on its way to the river. Eventually an even narrower road signposted 'church' leads off to the right. This road – grass growing in the middle, sand spilling over it in places – leads up to All Saints' Church. You can either take this and park by the church or continue a little further and take the next right turn to reach the pub and car park from where you can follow a bridleway from the river across marshes to the church, a distance of about three-quarters of a mile. There again, you could just grab an outside table at the Ramsholt Arms and watch the boats bob up and down on the Deben as you sip your beer. You could, but you'd be missing something.

All Saints' Church is one of 38 round-tower churches in Suffolk – you'll find a lot more in Norfolk – but the thing is it does not really look round-towered on first inspection. This is because the tower has buttresses to shore it up giving it more the oval profile of an old-fashioned medicine bottle. The church is mostly Norman but the base of the tower is probably older and of Saxon origin. The base of the oatmeal-coloured tower is of unusual material too, constructed of septaria, a brown mudstone obtained from the foreshore – one of the materials used to construct Orford Castle further up the coast.

The churchyard offers a splendid viewpoint over the tops of pines to the River Deben with its hundreds of boats below, and across the peninsula to the clustered cranes of Felixstowe Port scratching the sky in the distance. Perhaps it is the presence of these giant tools of modern-day commerce that makes this spot so special – the juxtaposition of a distant view of industry and a tangible sense of the ancient where you stand. Ramsholt was probably a sizeable settlement in medieval times but now, with the exception of the pub and a few cottages and farm buildings, the church is all that remains. The silence here has its role to play too: this is rural tranquility writ large. Enjoy it while you can as things might not be quite so peaceful down at the shore; it rather depends on how many groups of yachty types have descended on the Ramsholt Arms seeking an outside table and dinners all round.

⊤⊤ FOOD & DRINK

Ramsholt Arms Dock Rd, Ramsholt ✆ 01394 411209 ⌂ www.theramsholtarms.com. The only south-facing pub on the river, the terrace here is understandably popular in summer especially with the sailing set. Offering plenty of locally sourced seafood mains, Sunday roasts and share platters for two, this has what might best be described as posh pub grub.

67

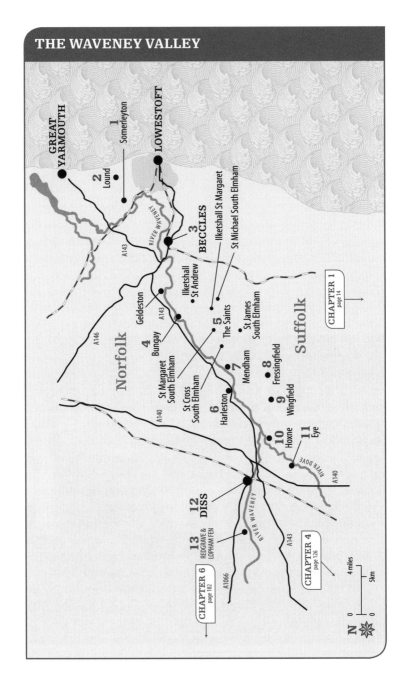

GREAT YARMOUTH

Somerleyton **1**

LOWESTOFT

2 Lound

RIVER WAVENEY

A143

BECCLES **3**

Ilketshall St Margaret

St Michael South Elmham

Ilketshall St Andrew

Geldeston

A143

St James South Elmham

The Saints **5**

A146

Norfolk

Bungay **4**

St Margaret South Elmham

Mendham **7**

Fressingfield **8**

St Cross South Elmham

Harleston **6**

Wingfield **9**

A140

Hoxne **10**

11 Eye

Suffolk

RIVER DOVE

A140

12 DISS

RIVER WAVENEY

13 REDGRAVE & LOPHAM FEN

A1066

A143

CHAPTER 1
page 14

CHAPTER 6
page 182

CHAPTER 4
page 126

N

0   4 miles
0   5km

2

THE WAVENEY VALLEY

Two rivers separate Suffolk from Norfolk, its northern neighbour. In the west, the Little Ouse River forms a natural boundary between the two counties, while in the centre and east the River Waveney defines the border. The Waveney's source lies between the villages of Redgrave in Suffolk and South Lopham in Norfolk, close to where the Little Ouse also rises. From its humble origins in Redgrave Fen, the river flows east through the small towns of Diss (Norfolk), Bungay and Beccles (Suffolk) before looping north around Lowestoft to join the River Yare at Breydon Water and eventually go to sea at Great Yarmouth. East of Bungay, the river lies within the boundary of the Broads Authority and the river is connected to Oulton Broad just west of Lowestoft by a manmade channel, Oulton Dyke. The only deviation that the county boundary makes from the river is between Great Yarmouth and Lowestoft, just north of Somerleyton where, instead of continuing north to reach Breydon Water, it veers east through Fritton Lake to reach the North Sea at Hopton-on–Sea. The reason for this anomalous diversion from the natural river boundary is administrative. It is also a relatively recent departure from topographic common sense – more on this later (see box, *The Island of Lothingland*, page 75).

Not that the Waveney forms an impenetrable barrier: the river is more of a conduit than anything, with plenty of bridges spanning it, especially in its western reaches. The Waveney Valley may not be much of a valley in physical terms but it does have a personality all of its own that is distinct from the rest of the county. I've crossed the county boundary here and there in this chapter, and so both Diss and Harleston are included despite belonging to Norfolk.

A sense of cosy isolation characterises the Waveney Valley, as south Norfolk eases into the clay country of north Suffolk. Here there are fewer big estates, and more commons, ancient hedgerows and moated farmhouses; more meandering tracks that seem to follow every field boundary before ending up nowhere in particular. There has probably been less change over the past 50 years in this region than anywhere else in southern England. Unlike other parts of Suffolk, the area is not a place that tends to lure incomers, downsizers or weekenders. The Waveney Valley has a different kind of draw. Those that have settled here have generally become more integrated into the existing community. It has long attracted artists, writers and craftsmen and there was a noticeable, if small-scale, invasion of folk escaping the city for something simpler and more wholesome back in the 1970s – they are mostly still here.

A surprising number of artists work from the towns and villages of the valley. Constable and Gainsborough may have immortalised the Stour Valley further south on the Essex border but that just happened to be where they lived. It might just as easily have been the Waveney Valley. To quote author and pioneer of sustainable living John Seymour: 'If John Constable had been born at Harleston, instead of at East Bergholt, we would have processions of motor coaches along the Waveney instead of along the Stour.' As for present-day local artists, perhaps the recently deceased Mary Newcomb (1922–2008) is the most representative for her innocent, yet evocative, vignettes of country life – not exclusively featuring the Waveney Valley but certainly evoking its spirit.

Several well-known writers are or have been based here too. Roger Deakin, who used to live in the village of Mellis just south of Diss, chronicled the changes of the season in *Notes from Walnut Tree Farm* and to a lesser extent in *Wildwood*, while nature writer Richard Mabey has more recently moved to the area and his Waveney Valley home features prominently in his book *Nature Cure*. Louis '*Captain Corelli's Mandolin*' de Bernières has settled near Bungay, and W G Sebald in *The Rings of Saturn*, his meandering introspective walk through a rather sombre Suffolk, spent enough time in the Waveney Valley to be quite spectacularly rude about a small hotel in Harleston just over the Norfolk border.

It's easy to get carried away of course. Like everywhere else, there's an element of reactionary Nimbyism here on occasion – the greatest fears seemingly being the provision of caravan sites for travellers and windfarms – but overall, it's pretty welcoming and lacking the self-satisfaction sometimes found in more high-profile parts of the county. The key words here are probably 'self-contained' and 'authentic': real places with real shops serving real people. This chapter begins close to the mouth of the River Waveney at Somerleyton and slowly works its way upstream to end at Diss, just across the border in Norfolk and the urban centre for the west of the valley.

GETTING AROUND

Making your way along the Waveney Valley is easy enough. The main towns and villages are linked by the A143 that runs from Bury St Edmunds to Great Yarmouth. From its Suffolk beginning, the road crosses the county boundary at Diss and continues along the Norfolk side of the river as it heads towards the coast, apart from a brief detour into Bungay on the Suffolk bank. For motorists, it's a convenient way of speeding east or west but the minor roads that thread through the valley are infinitely more enjoyable. Thankfully – and sensibly – the buses that run along the valley avoid the A143 for the most part, preferring to detour through the villages where most of their passengers live.

PUBLIC TRANSPORT

This could be better; there again, it could be worse. Diss has a regular **train** service to Norwich, as it lies on the main Norwich–London line. Regular trains also run between Norwich and Lowestoft, from where the East Suffolk Line (⌂ www.eastsuffolkline.com) to Ipswich passes through Oulton Broad and Beccles. **Bus** transport is somewhat restricted but reasonable enough in daylight hours, with buses running along most of the length of the valley. The Anglian Bus (✆ 01502 711109 ⌂ www.anglianbus.co.uk) 580 service runs hourly between Beccles and Diss via Bungay and Harleston during working hours, Monday to Saturday (excluding bank holidays), as does the 581 between Beccles and Lowestoft. Anglian Bus 62 runs between Beccles, Halesworth and Kessingland. Surprisingly perhaps, the Waveney Valley has much better connections to Norwich than it has to Ipswich, the latter always requiring at least one change and usually a considerable detour via Diss or Lowestoft. The Norwich to Lowestoft First in Suffolk & Norfolk service X2 connects Norwich to Beccles with half-hourly buses through the day Monday to Saturday and hourly on Sundays. The Norwich to Halesworth Anglian Bus service 588 connects Norwich to Bungay with hourly buses during working hours, Monday to Saturday, and with a two-hourly service on Sundays and bank holidays. Simonds bus service 114 connects Diss with Eye and Ipswich at approximately hourly intervals during working hours Monday to Saturday.

CYCLING

If you want to make use of muscle power alone, there is plenty of potential for cycling in the Waveney Valley, although you will want to avoid the A143 wherever possible. Otherwise, there are lots of quiet country roads and tracks to explore. You can **hire** a bike at Bungay at Outney Meadow Caravan Park (✆ 01986 892388 ⌂ www.outneymeadow.co.uk) and at Martha's Cottage Cycle Hire, The Green, Barnby, Beccles (✆ 01502 476789). **Maps** of some good circular routes, like a 19-mile Beccles loop and a 16-mile tour of 'The Saints', can be downloaded from the Visit Waveney Valley website (⌂ www.visitwaveneyvalley.co.uk). **Sustrans Regional Route 30**, which begins at Ten Mile Bank in the Fens, runs along the river to Lowestoft by way of Diss, Bungay and Beccles.

BY WATER

Transport by **boat** is an option east of Geldeston, which is the limit of navigation for motorboats a little way upstream from Beccles. Day boats are for hire at Beccles and Oulton Broad and there is scope for **canoeing** too, although the river is noticeably tidal east of Beccles. A stretch for canoeing recommended by the Upper Waveney Valley Project is the 20-mile section of the river between Brockdish, west of Harleston, and Ellingham Weir, east of Bungay. Canoe hire is possible at Bungay at Outney Meadow Caravan Park (✆ 01986 892338 ⌂ www.outneymeadow.co.uk), in Geldeston at Rowan Craft (✆ 01508 518208 ⌂ www.rowancraft.com) and at the Waveney Valley Centre (✆ 01502 677343 ⌂ www.waveneyrivercentre.co.uk) on the Norfolk bank of the river at Burgh St Peter. Contact the Waveney Valley Canoe Club (⌂ www.waveneyvalleycanoeclub.co.uk) for further advice. For a less energetic way of viewing the river, short daily tours of the River Waveney aboard the *Waveney Princess* are available in season with Waveney River Tours (✆ 01502 574903 ⌂ www.waveneyrivertours.com) at Oulton Broad.

WALKING

The Waveney Valley is a fine place for walking and there's a wide choice of lovely walks to be had, particularly alongside the river itself. Most

i TOURIST INFORMATION

Beccles The Quay, Fen Lane ✆ 01502 713196
Diss Mere's Mouth, Mere St ✆ 01379 650523
Harleston Tourist information Point, 8 Exchange St ✆ 01379 851917
Broads website ⟨🖰 www.broads-authority.gov.uk
Waveney Valley ⟨🖰 www.visitwaveneyvalley.co.uk

villages lie close enough to one another for decent circular walks to be possible and with such quiet back roads even road walking is a pleasure. The **Angles Way** long-distance route threads its way along the valley between Breckland and Lowestoft; eastwards from Beccles it follows the riverbank – the best option is to walk the nine miles from there to Oulton Broad South station and get the train back to Beccles.

LOTHINGLAND: SOMERLEYTON & AROUND

The River Waveney has its confluence with River Yare at the estuary of Breydon Water at Burgh Castle in Norfolk from where it flows into the North Sea at Great Yarmouth. This upstream section now belongs to Norfolk but south of St Olaves it is the river that defines the boundary between Norfolk and Suffolk. Somerleyton is a little further south.

1 SOMERLEYTON

🏠 **Fritton Lake Woodland Cottages** (see page 213)

Somerleyton lies on the Suffolk side of the river in the far north of the county. The village is home to **Somerleyton Hall** and although relatively remote is blessed with a very convenient stop on the Norwich to Lowestoft Wherry Line railway. Somerleyton is very much an attractive model village with estate houses, railway station, primary school and combined shop and post office all built in the mid 19th century in the same retro-Tudor style by the millionaire eccentric Samuel Morton Peto, the man responsible for rebuilding Somerleyton Hall. It was Peto who brought the railway to the village, a fortunate survivor of the Beeching cuts of the 1960s, and it was he who also rebuilt the village's then derelict church of St Mary's although you would hardly know it from the outside as he was fairly faithful to its original 15th-century style.

The hall and gardens are the obvious draw here but there are good walks to be had too – the Angles Way passes close to the hall and park and through the village on its way south.

Fritton Lake Outdoor Activity Park (✆ 01493 488288 ⏱ www. frittonlake.info) along with Fritton Lake with its lush wooded shoreline and rowing boats for hire, open to the public at Easter and between July and early September, lies just to the north of the estate straddling the county border.

Somerleyton Hall & Gardens

Somerleyton Hall, Lovingland NR32 5QQ ✆ 01502 734901 ⏱ www.somerleyton.co.uk. Open late Mar–late Sept Tue and Thu, also Wed and Sun mid-July–mid-Sept; 'garden only' tickets available on any open day.

Owned by the Crossley family who have lived here since the 1860s, this magnificent remodelled Tudor–Jacobean stately home has much to admire – an entrance hall clad in carved oak with marble panels, a ballroom decorated in crimson damask, a large elegant library and a dining room hung with oil paintings. The extensive gardens are equally impressive, and contain a walled garden with an ornate iron and glass greenhouse designed by Joseph Paxton, the architect of the Crystal Palace, and a yew-hedge maze planted in 1846.

¶¶ FOOD & DRINK

Duke's Head Slug's Lane, Somerleyton ✆ 01502 730281 ⏱ www.dukesheadsomerleyton. co.uk. Popular with boating folk, this red-brick pub five minutes' walk from the river has Suffolk real ales and a menu featuring seasonal fresh ingredients sourced from Somerleyton Estate's own farm and other farms in the locality. The beer garden here overlooks the Waveney River.

2 LOUND

East of Somerleyton is **Lound**, a small village with a duck pond, a church and the Mardle Café, an ideal place to stop if walking in the area. Lound has the interesting Anglo-Catholic **round tower church** of St John the Baptist. There seems to be a concentration of round tower churches in this neck of the woods. Others may be found nearby at Blundeston (fictional birthplace of Charles Dickens's *David Copperfield*), Herringfleet, Belton, Burgh Castle and Fritton, the last three now in Norfolk but formerly in Suffolk (see box, *The Island of Lothingland*).

THE ISLAND OF LOTHINGLAND

The Lothingland region north of Lowestoft is an island in the sense of being surrounded by water on four sides: the North Sea to the east, the River Waveney to the west, Breydon Water to the north and Oulton Broad and Lowestoft's Lake Lothing at its southern limit. Historically, Lothingland was a Half Hundred of the Suffolk Archdeaconry that was incorporated with the neighbouring Mutford division to the south to become the Mutford and Lothingland Hundred in 1763. All of this 'island' used to be part of the county of Suffolk, which extended north as far as Breydon Water; however, a redrawing of the county boundary in 1974 resulted in the most northerly settlements of the peninsula – Belton, Burgh Castle, Fritton and Hopton – being transferred from Suffolk to Norfolk. The logic behind this boundary change was to streamline administration in the wake of the Local Government Act of 1972 which aimed to allow all of Great Yarmouth's suburbs and outlying villages to be taken into Norfolk control.

Best of all for location and atmosphere is the isolated thatched **church of St Mary's** at the hamlet of Ashby a little way east of Lound, which stands alone among fields on the route of the Angles Way. Close to the gate of the churchyard is a memorial stone to the crew of a bomber that crashed near here in 1944. The sundial on the church tower sports the legend 'Aim Higher than the Mark', the meaning of which you can contemplate while taking a breather on one of the churchyard's conveniently placed benches.

ᵞᛁ FOOD & DRINK

The Mardle Café and Bakery 51 The Street ☎ 01502 730820 ⌂ www.themardlecafe. co.uk. On Lound's main street, this popular café has a real community feel to it. There's a good range of coffees, teas and snacks on offer, as well as breakfasts and excellent home-baked bread and bakery goods.

BECCLES & THE LOWER WAVENEY VALLEY

Heading upstream along the Waveney, the river changes direction near Lowestoft to lead west through a largely uninhabited marshy area to reach Beccles. These days the river is wide enough for navigation as far as Geldeston Locks, a little way beyond the town but in the not too distant past boats would have been able to travel as far as Bungay considerably further upstream. This, of course, has considerable effect on the river's character, which morphs from busy thoroughfare to a relatively sleepy backwater within a matter of miles.

3 BECCLES

Waveney House Hotel (see page 213)

The largest town in the valley, **Beccles** is a place that most tend to pass through rather than stay in but there is plenty to see here and it is certainly worth lingering here a while to soak up the town's easy-going, unhurried atmosphere. As with any market town, market day is a good time to visit if you can manage it – here it's on Friday. The town is solidly Georgian as, like elsewhere, its timbered Tudor core was destroyed by a succession of ravaging fires. The river used to have far more significance to town life than it does now, and Beccles was once a flourishing port with many wherries passing by. Herrings from the coast used to be an important commodity here and, in the medieval period, Beccles annually provided tens of thousands of the fish to the monks at Bury St Edmunds.

Boats still have a part to play, as Beccles is the most southerly point on the Broads system. The river here is not quite as hectic in summer as the Bure and Thurne are in Norfolk to the north but it's busy enough. There's some good walking on the Beccles Marshes close to the town and also along the north bank of the River Waveney to Geldeston Locks where there is a pub (see *Food and drink*). There is also a regular **boat service** to Geldeston Locks, the Big Dog Ferry (07532 072761 www.bigdogferry.co.uk), which runs from Beccles Lido between Easter and October. Short **boat trips** can be made on the Edwardian-style *Liana*. You can book them at the **Broads Information Centre** at The Quay (01502 713196).

Although there are a few specific sights worth investigating, the best way to experience Beccles is to simply wander through its attractive Georgian streets and see what you come across – you are certainly not in any danger of getting lost. Stick to the 'gates' – Saltgate, Northgate, Ballygate – and you won't go far wrong. With luck, you'll find some crinkle-crankle walls and a handful of older medieval buildings scattered here and there. Sometimes you'll get more than you anticipated. On one occasion, visiting the town with my wife, we were admiring the town's octagonal town hall on The Walk when we were approached by an elderly man. 'Are you tourists here, then?' he enquired in a friendly tone. 'Well, sort of, we live in Norwich.' 'In that case you want to take a look at that', he responded, pointing across the road. 'See that chimney pot up there, what do you think that is next to it?' It looked like a small gravestone and this is what we said. 'Yes, that's exactly what it is, although most people round here don't pay much attention to it. It's where a young boy got stuck up a chimney and died in the Victorian time. They say that he were up there for years before they found him.' This last bit didn't quite ring true but we didn't say anything as he went on tell us that there were more rooftop graves like this one in the town. After a full 15 minutes of hearing his life story, an interesting one peppered with remote Scottish and Cornish connections – his wife's family were tin miners – we made our excuses and bade him goodbye. We didn't see any more chimney-pot gravestones though, despite scouring the town's rooftops.

For the best view in town you should climb the hundred or so steps that lead up from Puddingmoor to **St Michael's Church**. Horatio Nelson's parents, Edmund Nelson and Catherine Suckling, were married here in 1749. The churchyard looks out west across the river to the marshes that lie beyond on the Norfolk bank. There are some benches here but they may well be already occupied by Beccles folk eating their sandwiches or snatching a bit of quiet time. This close to the church you cannot fail to notice that its bell tower is detached from the body of the church. It is also at the wrong end of the church, to the east rather than the west. There's a simple answer to this conundrum as if the tower had been erected where it ought to be it would be virtually on the edge of a cliff so its incorrect location makes good architectural sense. Why the bell tower only has a clock face on three of its sides is a matter of speculation. Local lore suggests that there is no clock on the western side because Beccles townsfolk do not wish to give the time of day to their Norfolk neighbours.

Close to St Michael's Church, just off Puddingmoor down by the river, is **Beccles Lido** (✆ 01502 714911 🖰 www.beccleslido.com). The Lido represents a real local success story in terms of community action. This outdoor pool was purchased by a community-run charity from the local council and since reopening in 2010 has been comprehensively refurbished, with leaks repaired and a solar power system installed to heat the water. Clean, warm, good value and fun for families, the Lido is open late May to September and gets very busy in hot weather and

A walk to Geldeston Locks & back

✳ OS Landranger map 134 or Explorer map 231; start: tourist information centre, grid reference TM422912.

The beauty of this walk is that there are several permutations. You can walk to Geldeston along the Norfolk bank of the Waveney, cross the footbridge and return along the Angles Way to Beccles, or alternatively you could return the same way – nothing wrong with that. Another possibility is to take the Big Dog Ferry to the pub from Beccles Lido and return to Beccles on foot using either bank . . . or vice versa of course. I'll just deal with the first option here. The full walk is around seven miles in all but it is good sense to break it midway with a picnic or a meal at either of Geldeston's pubs.

From Beccles Tourist Information Centre, go along Fen Street to reach Bridge Street then turn right to cross the bridge. Turn left immediately after the bridge and follow the riverside footpath for a mile and a half before the path turns inland towards a house set among trees. Turn right at the junction and go uphill along the footpath to reach a road. Follow this quiet lane through Geldeston village and just after passing the Wherry Inn turn left at the T-junction down Station Road. After crossing the course of the old railway line take the track to the left signposted Locks Inn. Continue to the inn and go over two footbridges to cross the River Waveney then head across a marshy field towards a wooden bridge. Carry on to reach a gate and stile (warning – there may be inquisitive cattle here). Go through the gate and follow the footpath left through more gates and over more stiles along the signed route of the Angles Way. This eventually reaches the main Beccles to Bungay road near Roos Hall. Turn left and walk on the grass verge until reaching Puddingmoor Lane, where you turn left and follow it back into town.

during school holidays. With good views and nice places to sit around the pool area, it's a popular picnic spot; refreshments are available at the cafeteria.

🍴 FOOD & DRINK

As well as Beccles itself, which has several decent pubs and cafés, the nearby village of Geldeston just to the west of the town on the Norfolk bank of the river has a couple of good pubs. Beccles Farmers' Market at Beccles Heliport (✆ 01502 476240 ⌂ www.becclesfarmersmarket.co.uk) has around 30 stalls on the first and third Saturday of the month.

Garden Tea Rooms 4 The Walk ✆ 01502 712631. Go through a discount shop to arrive at a bright pink dining room and a garden beyond. This small café has the usual cakes, scones, snacks and breakfasts.

Geldeston Locks Inn Locks Lane, Geldeston ✆ 01508 518414 ⌂ www.geldestonlocks. co.uk. An isolated, traditional pub with a sunny garden on the Norfolk bank of the River Waveney three miles west of Beccles. Locally sourced food, Green Jack ales from Lowestoft, regular musical events and a beer festival in September.

Waveney House Hotel Puddingmoor ✆ 01502 712270 ⌂ www.waveneyhousehotel. co.uk. With a pleasant terrace right next to the river, the Riverside Bar offers a good menu for lunch and dinner as well as afternoon tea (15.00–17.30). See also *Accommodation*, page 213.

Wherry Inn 7 The Street, Geldeston ✆ 01508 518371. Geldeston's other place to eat – a traditional pub with a good range of real ales and seasonal menu.

BUNGAY & THE CENTRAL WAVENEY VALLEY

It's just a few miles from Beccles to Bungay along the B1062, although it is considerably further by river as the Waveney meanders lazily through the Geldeston and Barsham Marshes. Following the road, you'll pass the hamlet of Shipmeadow with its large former workhouse now converted for domestic use. If you look at the village sign you'll see that the 'ship' in Shipmeadow actually refers to sheep rather than boats. Next comes Barsham, where there's yet another round tower church. Back in the 1970s the paddock next to the church used to be the location for the Barsham Faire, one of several Albion Fairs in the region at that time of which I have fond, if somewhat foggy, memories. The last was held in 1976 and I recall an event that successfully if haphazardly blended the carefree atmosphere of a medieval fair with that of a mini Glastonbury festival.

4 BUNGAY

⅄ Outney Meadow Touring and Camping Park (see page 213)

Were I in my castle
Upon the River Waveney I wouldne give a button For the King
of Cockney.

Hugh 'the Bold' Bigod, 1173

The ideal defensive site for a fortified town is either at the top of a hill or in the meander of a river. The second of these conditions is provided for perfectly at **Bungay** where the River Waveney coils like a flexing eel. The town has a hill of sorts too, and this is the site Hugh Bigod, the first Earl of Norfolk, chose for his castle in 1173, on high ground overlooking a meander. Hugh 'the Bold' Bigod was a fierce rival of Henry II (who had made his castle at Orford; see page 56) but was forced to surrender his Bungay fortress to the king as a penalty for aligning himself with an insurrection led by Henry's rebellious sons. If it had succeeded he would have gained custody of Norwich Castle; the words quoted above record his regrets.

Bungay is a self-contained, likeable place that, with a castle, an independent theatre and a distinctive eccentric character, seems to punch well above its weight for somewhere so small. Over the years, it's been a centre for leatherworking, boatbuilding and more recently printing but it has always also been an important market town for the region.

As with most small towns in East Anglia, Bungay's heart is its market place. Central to this is the octagonal **Butter Cross** that has a lead figure of Justice with her scales on top of its cupola. Like many other settlements where medieval wood and thatch predominated, a serious fire spread through the old town in the late 17th century and Bungay's plentiful Georgian buildings reflect a post-1688 rebuild. There's a pleasing mix of architecture spread throughout the centre but **Bridge Street**, with its colourfully painted houses sloping steeply down towards the river, is particularly attractive. This is a street that seems to happily harbour some of Bungay's undeniable eccentricities too: take a look at the anarchic bric-a-brac shop with its backyard chicken coops opposite The Chequers pub for a taste of what indifference to convention can do.

Most of what you see now of **Bungay Castle** was actually constructed by Hugh's ancestor Roger Bigod at the end of the 13th century. Today, there are two crumbling towers of the original gatehouse and some outer walls that you can visit and with a bit of luck they will have removed the scaffolding by the time you get here. There's a visitor centre at the entrance, which has a café and tourist information in season. To get a good view across to Earsham on the other side of the Waveney Valley you can climb up **Castle Hills** from the visitor centre. In celebration of its founder, the **Bigod Way** is a ten-mile loop around the town that starts and ends at the castle. It's a lengthy walk that takes four or five hours but there's plenty of historical and wildlife interest along the way.

Although there were said to be five churches in the town in the 11th century, just two survive today: **Holy Trinity** with its Saxon round tower, the oldest complete building in town, and **St Mary's**. St Mary's, now deconsecrated, is famous in these parts for its role in the **Black Shuck legend**, when the legendary black dog with fiery eyes ran amuck in the church and killed two worshippers having already caused untold damage at far-off Blythburgh church that same morning of 4 August 1577. This fanciful tale has long passed into local folklore, although versions of it differ quite widely. According to one account, a woman who went to school in Bungay in the late 19th century remembers Black Shuck as being a cat and recalls children singing the song:

Scratch cat of Bungay
Hanging on the door
Take a stick and knock it down
And it won't come anymore.

Whatever his form, puss or pooch, Black Shuck did not leave any evidence of his visit at St Mary's (there are at least putative 'scorch marks' at Blythburgh), although he does put in an appearance on the town's coat of arms. There's also an attractive tapestry of Bungay's history hanging in the church with a panel detailing the rampaging dog with the legend, '1577: Black Dog entered during a fearful storm and two men died.'

Bungay is not all about castles and churches. With the River Waveney just a shadow of what it used to be, it is easy to overlook the importance that the river once held for the town. Once the lock at Geldeston was established in the late 17th century, and the river canalised, wherries were able to ship goods up here from the coast. Upper Olland Street in the town centre probably gets its name from a derivation of 'oak lands' and locally plentiful oak would have been used to build wherries in

THE CHICKEN OF THE EAST

What came first, the chickens or the roundabout? The chickens did, in fact. It is thought that the colony of chickens that used to live in the middle of a roundabout on the A143 just outside Bungay were originally allotment escapees that managed to survive on grain from the nearby maltings. The chickens survived the building of a bypass in 1983 thanks to this grain, but when the maltings went up in flames in 1999 their free food supply vanished. Thankfully, this was when a local character known as the 'chicken man' appeared on the scene and began to make a two-mile round trip with his wheelbarrow most days just to feed them.

There was always considerable pressure to remove them as these very free-range chickens had been branded a potential danger to traffic by local authorities. Bungay citizens strongly resisted their removal however, and signed petitions and even dressed up in chicken costumes to promote their cause.

It seemed that the chickens were safe until a sharp decline in their numbers was reported in 2009 and, following incidents of animal abuse, the remaining few birds were removed by animal welfare groups.

The chickens may now have gone but they still seem to have a place in the hearts of most local people. A campaign was launched to install a commemorative statue to their memory in the middle of the roundabout. As one campaigner stated, 'They have the Angel of the North, why can't we have the Chicken of the East?'

Predictably perhaps, spoilsport planners have deemed such a monument a 'safety hazard' to motorists but it seems likely that even without such a memorial the chickens will live on in local folklore for many years to come. The chicken man, Gordon Knowles, who fed the birds daily for nearly 20 years, is commemorated with a plaque on Bungay's Falcon Bridge close to the roundabout.

the Staithe area of the town. Indeed, William Brighton, builder of the *Albion*, one of the few wherries that survive today, used to work here, while the boat itself used to ply its trade between Bungay Staithe and the coast at Lowestoft. These days, Geldeston is as far as navigation goes for anything larger than a canoe.

All this serious talk of history and tradition is well and good but if you ask a local for an instant word association with Bungay you'll probably end up with 'chicken roundabout'. Although now just a memory, Bungay's so-called **Chicken Roundabout** was the sort of small town silliness that local newspapers and regional television networks delight in.

The roundabout in question is just across the river where the roads to Norwich, Ditchingham and Beccles spin off and, yes, it really did once have chickens living on it. Sadly, this is no longer the case as the chickens were finally removed by animal welfare groups after becoming the target for persistent animal abuse.

For cycling, the **Godric Way** is a 24-mile route around Bungay that starts and ends at Butter Cross and passes through Ellingham, Broome, Ditchingham, Earsham, Denton, Alburgh, Homersfield, Mettingham and The Saints – all places in which a slow cycle through is worth a dozen drive-bys.

¶¶ FOOD & DRINK

Several cafés and tea rooms are dotted around the town centre in addition to a handful of pubs.

Buttercross Tea Rooms 6 Cross St ✆ 01986 893002. Just down from the Buttercross, this is an unfussy but perfectly pleasant place for a snack, coffee or all-day breakfast.

Castle Inn 35 Earsham St ✆ 01986 892283 ⌂ www.thecastleinn.net. With an imaginative menu that does its level best to utilise locally sourced food, this is probably Bungay's nicest place to eat. There's also an elegant but cosy bar that serves local cider and ales and a good selection of wines.

Earsham Street Café 11–13 Earsham St ✆ 01986 893103 ⌂ www.humblecake.co.uk. Located in an attractive 17th-century building, this is a little more upmarket than the Buttercross Tea Rooms and has a courtyard garden where a cock fighting pit once stood. Good for cakes and light meals.

Old Bank Tea Room 8 Market Pl ✆ 01986 894050. An old-fashioned, 1920s-themed tea room with a good choice of coffees, loose teas, cakes and sandwiches.

Queen's Head Station Rd, Earsham ✆ 01986 892623. Just west of Bungay in the Norfolk village of Earsham, this pub has its own real ale brewery, the Waveney Brewing Company, attached.

5 THE SAINTS

🏠 **Buckland House** Ilketshall St Lawrence (see page 213)

South of Bungay on the Suffolk side of the river is a handful of small villages known locally as 'The Saints'. They are St Mary South Elmham, St Cross South Elmham, St Margaret South Elmham, St Nicholas South Elmham, St James South Elmham, St Michael South Elmham, St Peter South Elmham, All Saints South Elmham, Ilketshall St Margaret, Ilketshall St John, Ilketshall St Andrew, Ilketshall St Lawrence and All Saints Mettingham. I suppose you might also call them 'The South Elmhams and Ilketshalls', but that does not quite have the same ring to it.

These are medieval parishes that never coalesced to form a city as they did in Norwich. It has been remarked that if one of these villages had been a port, a defensive fortress or important market place, then the history of the area might have been quite different and, instead of a clump of tiny villages, we might find a city. But it can seem as if the medieval period has not yet completely passed by in this corner of Suffolk where even Harleston and Bungay can feel a long way off.

"It's the sort of terrain where satnavs tend to have nervous breakdowns."

There are no specific sights here, apart perhaps from South Elmham Minster – the charm of 'The Saints' is, as they say, subtle – but it's an area that rewards relaxed wanderings. It is perhaps worth noting that one of the villages, St Michael South Elmham is one of only two 'thankful villages' in Suffolk (there are none at all in Norfolk). It is, in other words, a rare village in which all soldiers returned from World War I and has no need of a war memorial.

'The Saints' is definitely an area for cycling. It's the sort of terrain where satnavs tend to have nervous breakdowns. Driving around it in a car, you will inevitably get lost – cars are just too fast for this maze of narrow lanes and confusing signposts. South of the curiously named St Cross South Elmham stands **South Elmham Hall**, a 16th-century farmhouse that these days functions as a place to stay. Just south of the hall, standing alone in a field surrounded by trees, is the evocative ruin of **South Elmham Minster**. The Minster was an Episcopal chapel built for Herbert de Losinga, Bishop of Norwich, who also founded a monastery at North Elmham (in Norfolk) and a smaller one at Hoxne. It has been dated as 11th century, although a Saxon 10th-century tomb slab has been found on the same site and so some place of worship must have existed previously. It's a mysterious place and the hornbeams that surround the ruin provide a wonderful haven for birds. With luck, you may even see hawfinches here, exotic-looking birds that are about the closest thing to a parrot that you can find in Suffolk.

The land beside The Beck, the stream that runs through it, which has buttercup meadows, coppiced elm hedges (kept like this to prevent a return of Dutch elm disease) and ancient hornbeam pollards, was once a medieval deer park. Now it provides grazing for British White cattle – a rare breed – and walks for visitors. Bateman's Barn (✆ 01986 782526 🖰 www.batemansbarn.co.uk) at the hall has information about wildlife walks in the vicinity. The hall is open for guided tours on Thursdays and some Sundays and bank holidays from the beginning of April until the end of September.

Just north of St Peter South Elmham is **St Peter's Hall**, a 13th-century moated hall that was extended in the 15th century using what is euphemistically known as 'architectural salvage' from nearby Flixton Priory, hence its fine Norman stone. The hall itself is a restaurant today but St Peter's Hall is probably best known for its **St Peter's Brewery** (✆ 01986 782322 ⚲ www.stpetersbrewery.co.uk), established in 1996, that produces tasty, traditionally brewed beers in distinctive oval bottles. Local malts are used for brewing and the water used is drawn from a deep chalk aquifer beneath the ground. The rather medicinal bottle design, which dates back to 1770, helps to create the impression that what you are drinking is actually doing you good – it works for me. The visitors' shop opposite the hall is open every day.

If cider is your thing then you might wish to pay a visit to the **Cider Place** (✆ 01986 781353) at Cherry Tree Farm, Ilketshall St Lawrence, which has a wide range of ciders, country wines and meads, and has tastings most days of the week. Keeping with the apple theme, the **Metfield Stores** (✆ 01379 586204 ⚲ www.metfield.org.uk), a community shop in Metfield village, just west of St James South Elmham, specialises in local produce that includes some rare varieties like Darcy Spice. The store celebrates Apple Day (and Apple Week too) each year in October, often with a local nurseryman on hand to dispense advice. The Metfield Stores, which is, in fact, the only shop in the village, is staffed by volunteers and is very active in promoting local suppliers and produce.

ᵞ⎮ FOOD & DRINK

St Peter's Hall St Peter South Elmham ✆ 01986 782288 ⚲ www.stpetershall.co.uk. This offers fine dining in the slightly eccentric surroundings of a wood-panelled Tudor great hall, with sophisticated English cuisine that makes use of local meat and game. There's also a library bar with ales from St Peter's Brewery.

HARLESTON & AROUND

Heading west along the Waveney Valley, Harleston is the next place of any size. It lies just across the Norfolk bank of the river, the nearest market town for a sizeable chunk of north Suffolk and south Norfolk.

THE ANGLES WAY IN WINTER

I did this long-distance walk in midwinter, over eight days of the coldest weather to hit East Anglia so far this millennium. I started each stage from my home in Norwich, using public transport to reach the day's trail head. Some of the bus and train connections were tight but it was all just about feasible – on weekdays at least. The first section involved a lengthy stretch along the south bank of Breydon Water, always at its best on bright, frosty days when the water sparkles and migrant waders work the mud. The waymarked footpath left the estuary at Burgh Castle to dawdle through the dormitory village of Belton, probably the dullest stretch along the entire route. After skirting a golf course, the way led across fields to pass the Redwings Animal Sanctuary where I was delighted to see a large number of the eponymous winter thrushes congregating in the paddocks. After passing two charming churches – first, thatched and round-towered Fritton St Edmund's, then Ashby St Mary's, isolated among fields – I arrived at the slightly eccentric estate village of Somerleyton. Next day, I followed the railway line east along the marsh edge to wind up at Oulton village.

The stretch from Oulton Broad to Beccles followed the bank of the Waveney for much of the way – an elemental landscape of water and grazing marsh. Beccles to Earsham came next: hard work on my chosen day because the ground was frozen solid. I slithered my way out of the town, past Roos Hall then through fields that looked down upon the Waveney and picturesquely frozen marshes that, with only the distant thrum of traffic to remind one of the 21st century, resembled a scene from a Constable painting.

Emerging at the hamlet of Shipmeadow, I crossed the A143 to head across fields next

6 HARLESTON

Harleston is the urban magnet for this stretch of the valley, although 'urban' is probably too big a word for a pleasant little market town. As with many places of this size, medieval fires saw to it that most of the town's earlier thatch and timber frames went up in flames so what remains today is mostly solid Georgian red brick with the odd Tudor survivor. Market day, still important to the town, is on Wednesdays.

Harleston's most conspicuous landmark is the almost minaret-like **clock tower** on the market place that used to belong to St John's Chapel of Ease. The chapel was founded in the 14th century but was in a ruinous state by the 18th. A new church was built on Broad Street to replace it and the old chapel was demolished and replaced with a grocer's shop, which remains there today. As with many agricultural towns in the region, there's a conspicuous Victorian **corn exchange**: a stark white to a converted workhouse that was now a desirable residence but which must once have been a miserable place to live. Close to the ruins of Mettingham Castle, I followed a timeless green lane lined with coppiced hazel and, before I knew it, found myself gazing down on Wainford Mill just outside Bungay.

Rather than diverting into Bungay, the Angles Way crosses back into Norfolk here to follow the meander of the river. I took the track through woodland above Ditchingham Lodge and, arriving at Earsham Mill, crossed into Suffolk once more to traverse lush riverside meadows as far as the village of Mendham. After a gentle climb up the north side of the valley I arrived in Harleston. The next leg followed the south bank of the river as far as Brockdish, where the way crossed a bridge back into Norfolk and, after climbing and skirting the village churchyard, I followed another lengthy stretch of green lane and farm

tracks across beet fields to end up in Scole. Arriving at Diss Mere the following day, I found the resident ducks looked rather confused by the frozen state of things. I headed west out of town alongside Roydon Fen to reach the gorse-covered heath of Wortham Lings and eventually arrived at the source of the Waveney (and the Ouse) near Redgrave after a splendid leafy section through the woodland area of the nature reserve.

A final day's walk brought me to Knettishall Heath in Breckland where future options awaited me: the Peddars Way north to Holme-next-the Sea or the Iceni Way to Thetford and Hunstanton. I had walked around 80 miles in total – perhaps more like 90 – and had encountered virtually no-one along the way give or take the odd dog-walker. For those in search of tranquility and midwinter exercise, walks like this certainly have plenty to recommend them.

neoclassical building that was opened for commerce in 1849 but which served as a local court in later years. Since its early days, when its walls must have resounded to the bargaining cries of Norfolk farmers, the building has seen use as a skating rink, furniture market, dance hall and even a delicatessen and restaurant. At the time of writing it had just been sold after being on the market for seven years and plans were afoot to reopen it as an antique centre with a 1940s-style tea room and a museum.

The market place, which tends to be on the sleepy side apart from Wednesday mornings, has another town landmark: the J D Young Hotel, originally known as the **Magpie Inn** – the original distinctive sign can still be seen – which has served as a coaching inn for centuries. Churchill and Eisenhower are reputed to have met here during World War II, presumably not over a pint. Just across from the hotel is a large Georgian house with two enormous sequoias that look as if they will burst out of the garden like slow-growing triffids in the next century or two. The town's other coaching inn is **The Swan** in The Thoroughfare, which was built by Robert Green, a conspirator in Kett's Rebellion who may have been rewarded with this property for snitching on his colleague – hardly the noblest of ways to get a start in the pub trade.

The Old Market Place, which no longer has a market, has Harleston's oldest building at number 18, an Elizabethan hall house that originally would have been jettied. If you were wondering why there is no medieval parish church to be found in Harleston, it is because the town shares the same parish as **Redenhall**, which does have a magnificent 15th-century church.

¶¶ FOOD & DRINK

Chameleon House 3 Redenhall Rd ☎ 01379 852243 ◌ www.chameleonhouse.co.uk. A bright, colourful restaurant in the town centre that offers seasonal set lunch and dinner menus as well as morning coffee and snacks.

7 MENDHAM

Just across the Waveney from Harleston in Suffolk is the small village of Mendham. This was the birthplace of **Sir Alfred Munnings**, the East Anglian painter of horses and rural scenes and one-time president of the Royal Academy, whose father owned the mill just outside the village. If you approach the village from the south via the Witherdale road, Mendham seems remote despite its proximity to Harleston. The village is set in the river's flood valley amid lush water meadows and lines of poplars. It's a quiet, dreamy place, with a church and a single pub that is called, appropriately, the Sir Alfred Munnings. The car park opposite the pub has a noticeboard with a suggested five-mile circular walk – along Sconch Beck to St Cross South Elmham. The Angles Way passes through the village as it crosses into Norfolk and there's a footpath that leads across Mendham Marshes past the ruins of a Cluniac priory.

Alternatively, you could just saunter past the pub down to the river. This is classic Waveney Valley scenery – the sort of thing Munnings might have painted if he had not concentrated on horse fairs or attacking modernism quite so much. It's the kind of landscape that brings reverie. The iron bridge crossing the Waveney seems like a giant staple attaching Norfolk to the Suffolk mainland. Brown cows wandering the meadows contentedly graze and flick flies away, keeping their eyes on a pair of locals fishing beneath the trees and catching nothing. As poplars rustle in the breeze, the very English sound of an accordion drifts down from the Munnings pub. It could almost be the 18th century, if it wasn't for the fishermen's car parked by the road. As I am taking all this in, a man who is clearly the worse for drink ambles down the road towards the bridge. He stumbles exactly halfway across, pauses for a moment, then goes back the way he has come. It is as if he is fearful to place his feet on Norfolk soil, or there is some sort of invisible barrier. Two minutes later, a sleek Jaguar arrives from the north to pick the man up. Then it turns around and ferries him back across the bridge … into Norfolk.

"As poplars rustle in the breeze, the very English sound of an accordion drifts down from the Munnings pub."

8 FRESSINGFIELD

South of Harleston on the B1116 Framlingham road, a knot of houses cluster around a church at Fressingfield. The village has a tidy prosperous air and two thriving pubs to bear this out – unusual in a place of this size. In warmer weather, there's inevitably a handful of people enjoying a drink at an outside table of the Swan Inn, and a nearly full car park at the rather grander **Fox and Goose Inn** (just up the hill behind the church of St Peter and St Paul), built in 1509 and formerly serving as the village's guildhall. This Tudor building operates as a popular gastropub these days and even in the late 1960s it was famous for its food according to the author John Seymour, who suggested that people came from as far away as Yorkshire 'just for the eating' and recommended booking a day or two ahead. Back in those days, most pubs served just crisps and pickled eggs along with very unreal ale – or scampi and chips if you were lucky – so you have to admire the continuity of tradition here. Rumour has it that Hollywood actor Johnny Depp and party once turned up here but could not get a table because they hadn't pre-booked.

The **church of St Peter and St Paul** is a veritable cathedral to the use of unstained oak, with some marvellous 15th-century bench ends in the form of saints and a hammerbeam roof. There's a fine example of medieval graffiti here too, with the initials 'A P' incised into a bench. This is considered to be the handiwork of Alice de la Pole, granddaughter of the poet Chaucer, who was perhaps the medieval equivalent of a graffiti tagger. All that wood ripe for carving must have been just too much of a temptation and as Duchess of Norfolk she would hardly expect to be punished for her petty act of vandalism. The church is the venue for a music festival in September, the **Fressingfield Music Festival** (✆ 01379 596459 ◌ www.fressingfieldmusic.com), that attracts some big names in the world of classical music. Recent festivals have had performances by artists such as Julian Lloyd Webber, Emma Kirkby, Badinage and the Choir of Christ's College, Cambridge.

The **village sign** at the junction at the top of the hill depicts a pilgrim with a pack mule in tow. This represents the village's place on a late Saxon pilgrimage route to Bury St Edmunds. There are even older roads in the vicinity. Just east of the village there's a very obvious Roman road that links Pulham with Peasenham, following the route of the B1116 for some of the way through Weybread. There's a Saxon diversion around Fressingfield, but it re-emerges at Little Whittingham Green where it continues to Chippenhall Green, the sole survivor of the parish's common land that had been mostly enclosed by the end of the 18th century. If you take this same old Roman Road north from Fressingfield towards Harleston, you'll pass through **Weybridge** and **Weybread**, a linear sprawl of houses with a seemingly endless stretch of 30mph speed limit – imposed perhaps because of the irresistible temptation that dead-straight pieces of road like this offer to speed merchants.

Suffolk is yet to earn the reputation of Bordeaux or the Napa Valley but it does have a few vineyards where brave English wine growers do their best to conjure the spirit of Bacchus from the heavy clay soil. **Willow House Vineyard** (✆ 01379 586868 ◌ www.oak-hill.co.uk) in the centre of the village behind the church produces its own Oak Hill Wines named after an 800-year-old oak tree that overlooks the vines, the last vestige of an ancient wood. Four hundred vines of the Bacchus variety were planted here back in 1987 and the vineyard produces three types of white wine – dry, sweet and oaked.

ⵏ FOOD & DRINK

Fox and Goose Inn ✆ 01379 586247 ◌ www.foxandgoose.net. In a Tudor building that was the former guildhall, this is a highly regarded and very popular place so booking is almost essential. Most produce is sourced within a six-mile radius.

Swan Inn ✆ 01379 586280 ◌ www.fressingfieldswan.co.uk. With outdoor tables overlooking the road and the beck, this has straightforward bar food made using local produce and a decent selection of real ales.

9 WINGFIELD

Wynkefelde the Saxon held Honour and Fee

Ere William the Norman came over the sea.

West of Fressingfield is the village of Wingfield. The Wingfields were an old Saxon family who gave their name to the village. Sir John de Wingfield, chief of staff of the Black Prince, founded both Wingfield College and St Andrew's Church in the mid 14th century. Wingfield Castle, which was the seat of the Wingfields and their successors the de la Poles, Earls and Dukes of Suffolk, is now just a ruin next to a farm. **Wingfield College** was partly demolished before being remodelled in a Palladian style in the 18th century. The college's farm buildings now incorporate **Wingfield Barns** (01379 384505 www.wingfieldbarns. com), hosting arts, drama and theatrical events as well as weddings and civil ceremonies. Wingfield College itself is a private residence but the house and gardens can be visited on pre-booked guided tours (01206 769607 www.wingfieldcollege.com) at roughly monthly intervals from May to September. The collegiate church of **St Andrew** here has the stone tomb of Sir John de Wingfield alongside the wood and alabaster tombs of Michael and John de la Pole and their wives. The church also contains a curious 18th-century wooden sentry box called 'The Hud', which was used outside by priests performing funeral services in inclement weather.

¶¶ FOOD & DRINK

De la Pole Arms Church Rd 01379 384545 www.delapolearms.net. This free house has Adnams ales, hearty home-cooked British food that uses local produce. There's also a log fire in winter.

HOXNE TO DISS

10 HOXNE

Hoxne (pronounced 'hoxen') is a pretty village just south of 'The Crotch', the confluence of the Waveney and the Dove. The village has some elegant cottages and a nice pub but its real claim to fame is as the place where **St Edmund** was killed by marauding Danes. This may not be true of course – it may well have been elsewhere – but it is Hoxne that has claimed the legend and it has the monument to prove it, so there you are.

The legend dictates that St Edmund was taken prisoner here and tied to a nearby oak tree before being shot dead with arrows. A stone monument to him stands in the middle of a field at the spot where an old oak was brought down by lightning in the 19th century. When it was subsequently broken up for timber, the tree apparently revealed a Viking arrowhead. Such history may be rather tangential but it is captivating all the same. Naturally, the tree in question would have to have been at least a thousand years old.

If you walk south along the village's high street past The Swan, you'll soon come to a minor road off to the left. Turn down here and you'll see the stone **Goldbrook Bridge**, under which Edmund was supposedly discovered hiding, his glinting spurs spotted by a young, newly-wed couple who snitched to the Danes. St Edmund is said to have put a curse on all newly-weds crossing the bridge so Hoxne is probably not the ideal place for a honeymoon. The bridge makes no claims to be the original: one side bears the legend, 'KING EDMUND TAKEN PRISONER HERE – AD870' and the other, 'GOLDBROOK BRIDGE – AD1878'. Just over the bridge stands a newish village hall in brick and flint, appropriately called St Edmund's Hall and a rather impressive building as village halls go. The gable wall has a plaque beneath the window that tells of King Edmund being taken prisoner and slain, while the apex has a relief carving that shows Edmund lurking beneath the bridge with sword in hand as Danes cross above him. The car park has an information board with details of a five-mile circular walk that snakes into Norfolk to take in Billingford windmill. Thoughtfully, perhaps because this is still a pilgrimage site of sorts, there is also a picnic table for weary walkers. If you wish to see the St Edmund monument where the oak tree use to stand, then continue south a little way past some very smart thatched cottages and you'll soon see a sign pointing towards the monument in the middle of a barley field.

Further references to St Edmund can be found in Hoxne's **St Peter and St Paul Church**, as you might expect. A bench-end shows the saint's head being carried by a wolf, and an oak screen depicting events from his life is reputedly made from the tree that was destroyed by lightning where his monument stands. Hoxne's history clearly stretches back further than the Saxon time of St Edmund: in 1992, a local man looking for a lost hammer in a nearby field found an enormous hoard of over 15,000 Roman gold and silver coins, jewellery and tableware instead, probably hidden in the turbulent 5th century when Roman rule was breaking down. The Hoxne hoard, the largest ever found of its type in the United Kingdom, is now in safe keeping in the British Museum.

¶¶ FOOD & DRINK

Swan Inn Low St ☎ 01379 668275. Built in 1480 by the Bishop of Norwich as a lodge, this atmospheric listed building is all sloping floors, oak beams and open fires, with a ten-foot-wide inglenook in the main bar. It is very popular at weekends and so it's best to book ahead.

11 EYE

West of Hoxne, Eye is a quiet, self-contained little market town just south of the River Waveney. It actually lies on the west bank of the River Dove, a tributary of the Waveney, and is home to a church tower that the architectural writer Nikolaus Pevsner deemed 'one of the wonders of Suffolk'. The church in question is that of **St Peter and St Paul** and its 101-foot-high tower is remarkable for the flint flushwork on its west side. The church stands beneath a Norman **castle mound**, which is now all mound and no castle but gives quite a view of the town nevertheless. The town clings tightly to the base of this: a small maze of streets and ancient houses dominated by the brick-and-flint panel Victorian **town hall** with its ornate clock tower. The town's guildhall stands beside the church, an impressive Tudor building.

"The town of Eye is a small maze of streets and ancient houses dominated by the brick-and-flint panel Victorian Town Hall with its ornate clock tower."

The town gets its curious name from an Old English word for 'island', and when it was first settled it probably was almost entirely surrounded by water and marshland associated with the River Dove: the surrounding area still sometimes floods.

Eye Castle was constructed in the years that immediately followed the Norman Conquest and a Benedictine Priory was founded shortly after in the town in 1086–87. Hugh Bigod, the first Earl of Norfolk, attacked the castle in 1173 during the rebellion against Henry II and it never really recovered, although its prison continued in use as late as the 17th century. You can climb up to the castle mound by following the signs from the car park at Buckshorn Lane. The path takes you through a small estate of modern wedge-shaped Toblerone-like houses, across a meadow and up some steps to the top. At the top, there used to stand a building known as **Kerrison's Folly**, constructed in the mid 19th century by General Sir Edward Kerrison, reputedly as a home for the batman who had served him at the Battle of Waterloo. Part of the folly was used as a museum in the early years of the 20th century but there are just remnants of walls left now – it collapsed in the 1960s. If the story is true, then Kerrison's batman must have enjoyed waking up to a bird's-eye view of the town in his later years. You can enjoy the same perspective by climbing up the enclosed wooden staircase. The interpretive board here has a drawing of what the castle might have looked like in the 16th century when a windmill stood on the top – quite a sight in this land without hills.

Once down from the castle, the town's **Guildhall** is worth a look too: a timbered Tudor building that has the archangel Gabriel carved into one of its corner posts. There's another impressive Tudor building on the corner of Church Street and Buckshorn Lane, close to the town hall, currently a pharmacy.

¶¶ FOOD & DRINK

Queens Head 7 Cross St ℅ 01379 870153 ⌂ www.queensheadeye.co.uk. This 16th-century inn has good Mediterranean-style pub food and tapas and is the only survivor of around 15 pubs that served the town a few decades ago.

DISS & AROUND

In this upstream part of the Waveney Valley the river is little more than a stream by the time it reaches Diss in south Norfolk. A little way beyond the market town the source of the river lies in marshes close to the source of the River Little Ouse that flows westwards and delineates the Suffolk/Border in the west of the county.

12 DISS

Diss is a town of two halves. The modern part of the town, east of the centre close to the A140, is pretty undistinguished and could be almost anywhere but do not judge the town on the basis of this, as the old part of Diss is far more appealing.

Old Diss centres around a body of water, **The Mere**, a six-acre, spring-fed lake that gives the town its name, as *dice* in Anglo-Saxon means 'standing water' or words to that effect. Diss folk claim that this glacial remnant is at least 60 feet deep, with about 20 feet of water and 40 feet of mud. The common theory is that it was formed when the underlying chalk bedrock collapsed, an altogether more plausible theory than it being the mouth of an extinct volcano, as a few Diss residents still believe. The Mere was badly polluted in the 19th century, with high mercury levels brought about by local hatters and dyers making use of its water. Bizarrely, it was also around this time that The Mere was stocked with eels, which, according to some accounts, threw themselves from the water at every opportunity such was the level of pollution. Thankfully, it's clean enough to swim in these days, although this is expressly forbidden. Global warming being what it is, it is unlikely that there will ever be a repeat of the winter cricket matches and ice carnivals that were held on its frozen waters in the early 19th century.

A waterside path leads from the southern shore to what is usually referred to as the **Mere's Mouth**, where there is an information centre and the Diss Publishers Bookshop and Café, which as well as a selection of local books has café tables by the water. It's a place to feed the ducks, lick an ice cream and have a 'mardle' (local-speak for leisurely chat) on market days. These days, there's an electric fountain in the middle of The Mere that spouts like a mini Jet d'Eau on Lake Geneva.

Mere Street leads north from the Mere's Mouth up towards the **market place** past a few pubs, cafés and independent shops. There's a good showing of Tudor timber-framed buildings in addition to some fine red-brick Georgian and Victorian houses. Friday – market day – is definitely the day to be here as, unlike in much of clone-town Britain, it's still an important weekly event. As well as the weekly event, there's a **farmers' market** held here on the second Saturday of each month.

Diss Museum (✆ 01379 650618), located in a small building right at the top of the market place, is a community museum run by enthusiastic volunteers. **St Mary's Church**, just beyond, dominates the market place, a fine 13th-century building in the Decorated style. The church's most famous rector was John Skelton, who was rector here from 1504 until his death in 1529. Skelton, who had earlier served as tutor to the young Henry VIII and had been Poet Laureate of both Oxford and Cambridge universities, remains firmly in the number one place of the town's most illustrious citizens. A later Poet Laureate, John Betjeman, was another admirer of the town.

Opposite the church stands the 16th-century **Dolphin House**, a striking black and white timbered building that has seen life as a wool merchant's house and a pub in the past. These days it houses various small businesses. Further north along Mount Street from St Mary's you'll find more handsome Georgian houses lining a quiet street. If, instead, you head west along St Nicholas Street then you'll come to the **Corn Hall**, which like most such buildings in these parts is in the mid-19th-century neoclassical style. The days of cereal wheeling and dealing may be past but it is still an active place, with regular concerts and plays.

Fair Green is set apart from the rest of the old town but worth a detour. You can reach it by walking west along Park Road from the bus station and turning left at the roundabout. Once you round the corner, the contrast is extreme. Gone are the noisy lorries thundering along Park Road; you suddenly find yourself next to an idyllic village green with a café, a pub and a restaurant clustered around its eastern end. The green, which is surrounded by highly attractive 16th- and 17th-century houses, was granted a charter for a fair in 1185 and must have presented quite a sight back in the days when bear-baiting and cockfighting were regarded as quite ordinary pursuits. The Cock Inn no doubt gets its name from such activities, as do many other 'Cock' pubs in the region. The fair was finally closed by Parliament in 1872, ostensibly because of its reputation for 'disorderly behaviour'.

¶ FOOD & DRINK

If you are just looking for a coffee and a snack, there are several options along Mere Road. **Diss Publishers Bookshop and Café** (✆ 01379 644612 🖰 www.disspublishing.co.uk) at number 41 has some tables outside overlooking The Mere, as does **Mere Moments** (✆ 07790 695056) at number 44, and **Café Culture** at the Market Place further up. **The Saracens Head** (75 Mount St ✆ 01379 652853 🖰 www.saracensheaddiss.co.uk), just behind the church, has standard pub grub and steaks. The options listed below are at Fair Green, a little further away from the centre but really not that far.

Angel Café 1 Fair Green ✆ 07502 285957. Rustic, friendly and low-key, the Angel Café serves up organic meals and snacks, with plenty of vegetarian options. It's also good for espresso coffee, homemade cakes and desserts.

Cock Inn Lower Denmark St, Fair Green ✆ 01379 643633 🖰 www.cockinndiss.co.uk. With a decent selection of real ales and a great view over the green, this is a sound choice. Live music events on some nights.

BIRDWATCHING

Suffolk is one of the best counties in England for watching birds. The salt marshes of the coastal hinterland are particularly rich in wading species. The RSPB reserve at Minsmere near Leiston, with its breeding avocet population, has been established in this region since 1947.

1 Island Mere Hide, Minsmere. (DB/FLPA) **2** Avocet, an elegant black-and-white wader often seen at Minsmere. (S/MF) **3** Bearded tit, a typical species of East Anglia reed beds. (S/PG) **4** Bittern, with its deep, foghorn-like boom, is more often heard than seen. (S/MF)

RELIGIOUS & HISTORIC ARCHITECTURE

With impressive historic houses, huge wool-trade medieval churches and evocative ruined monasteries, the Suffolk countryside is replete with history at every turn.

1 A beautifully restored painted ceiling at St Mary's Church, Huntingfield, the sole work of Mildred Holland, the 19th-century vicar's wife. (LM) 2 Aldeburgh's Moot Hall once stood in the centre of town before erosion ensured that it had a seaside location. (S/MR) 3 Sundial on the flint round tower of isolated St Mary's Church at Ashby in Lothingland, Waveney Valley. (LM) 4 Inside Lavenham's Guildhall, now a National Trust museum. (SS) 5 Greyfriars Priory at Dunwich, a fragment of the extensive town that stood here in the early medieval period. (SS) 6 A church within a larger dismantled church at Covehithe on the north Suffolk coast. (LM) 7 Ickworth House near Bury St Edmunds was built in the early 19th century and now belongs to the National Trust. (VB/BOV)

SUFFOLK DEFENCES

Suffolk has its fair share of castles – the most complete examples of these can be seen at Framlingham and Orford. The coast also has the most northerly of the defensive Martello towers that were built as a chain of fortresses between Sussex and Suffolk at the time of the Napoleonic wars.

1 Framlingham Castle, where Mary Tudor proclaimed herself queen in 1553. (s/pw)
2 Martello tower near Shingle Street, one of a string of 103 defences built along the coast between Suffolk and Sussex. (lm) 3 Orford Castle was built by Henry II in 1165. (s/cy)

13 REDGRAVE & LOPHAM FEN

West of Diss, the Waveney begins as a tiny trickle at Redgrave and Lopham Fen, very close to where the Little Ouse also rises. The Fen, which covers 300 acres and is the largest surviving area of river valley fen in England, has been managed by the Suffolk Wildlife Trust for the past 50 years (although the reserve straddles both counties and the visitor centre is actually in Norfolk) and has an impressive cluster of designations as a wetland of national and international importance. It is also one of only two sites in the country that has native **fen raft spiders**, as well as being a prime habitat for dragonflies and butterflies, mammals like otters and pipistrelle bats, and a recorded 96 bird species.

Like the Norfolk Broads, the fen was traditionally used for reed and sedge cutting for thatching, as well as cattle grazing at its drier margins. Part of the Suffolk Wildlife Trust's management strategy is to use Hebridean sheep and Polish Konik ponies to control the vegetation. The black Hebridean sheep look strangely at home grazing here, as do the small grey ponies that thrive in the wet conditions. These all add to its atmosphere as quite a primeval place and the presence of the semi-aquatic raft spiders certainly fits in with this image. Arachnophobes should probably be aware that the fen raft spider is one of Britain's largest, although even here they are pretty scarce. I once spent a long time looking for them to no avail at one of the designated viewing pits but you may be luckier. There's a **visitor centre** (Low Common Rd, South Lopham ✆ 01379 688333) run by the Suffolk Wildlife Trust, and three dedicated nature trails. Be warned, the mosquitoes can be vicious here in summer, especially in the woodland areas – either lather up with 'Jungle Formula' or similar, or wear long sleeves and trousers.

"The fen was traditionally used for reed and sedge cutting for thatching, as well as cattle grazing."

If you visit here, then you might also take a look at nearby **Redgrave** village, a pleasant place that has all the essentials of village life: a pub, a green, a church and a community shop in the premises of the original post office.

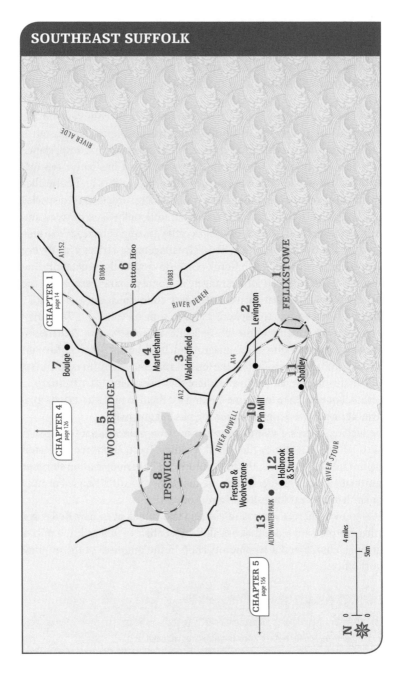

RIVER ALDE

A1152

B1084

6
Sutton Hoo

B1083

CHAPTER 1
page 14

RIVER DEBEN

FELIXSTOWE

1

2
Levington

7
Boulge

4
Martlesham

3
Waldringfield

A14

CHAPTER 4
page 126

5
WOODBRIDGE

A12

11
Shotley

8
IPSWICH

RIVER ORWELL

10
Pin Mill

9
Freston &
Woolverstone

12
Holbrook
& Stutton

RIVER STOUR

13
ALTON WATER PARK

CHAPTER 5
page 156

N

0
0

4 miles

5km

3
SOUTHEAST SUFFOLK

This chapter continues from where the first left off, dealing with the southern part of the Suffolk coast – Felixstowe and its peninsula, the county town Ipswich and its surrounding area, Woodbridge at the head of the Deben estuary and the Shotley Peninsula which extends between the ports of Felixstowe and Harwich south of Ipswich. It's a mixed bag that deals with some of the largest places in the county as well as tiny estuary villages. The various inlets and estuaries that punctuate the coastline further north continue to do so in this part of the county, although they tend to be much larger and wider. The Rivers Deben, Orwell and Stour all flow into the North Sea along this stretch and the sea trade that dwindled centuries ago in the silted-up ports of the northern part of the coast still thrives here. The Port of Felixstowe is currently the largest container port in the country, which might not suggest very much in the way of Slow credentials but the port is just one aspect of Felixstowe and the town itself has many redeeming features. Ipswich too, might seem on first inspection to be brash and traffic-blighted, but the town has far more going for it than might immediately be apparent. Woodbridge, on the other hand, has abundant Slow appeal. As for the Shotley Peninsula, if anywhere were to be awarded the clichéd epithet of 'best kept secret' then this might be a worthy contender. It's not a secret of course, just a little unsung.

GETTING AROUND

The A12 connects Ipswich with Woodbridge and Lowestoft to the north. Felixstowe is connected to Ipswich and the rest of the country by the A14, a very busy road that carries a great deal of container traffic to and from the Port of Felixstowe over the Orwell Bridge and continues west to Stowmarket, Bury St Edmunds and the Midlands. The Shotley Peninsula has just one main road running its length to reach Shotley at the end, the B1456, while the A137 runs south of Ipswich across the western end of the peninsula to reach Cattawade at the mouth of the estuary of the River Stour and the eastern extremity of the Stour Valley.

PUBLIC TRANSPORT

Ipswich, at the centre of this region, has excellent **rail connections** with London, Norwich and Stowmarket, although reaching the rest of the country directly without a connection in the capital tends to be less straightforward. There are, however, regular train services from Ipswich to Cambridge and Peterborough. Felixstowe, although somewhat out on a limb, has regular trains to Ipswich. The East Suffolk Line, run by Greater Anglia, connects Lowestoft with Ipswich at roughly two-hour intervals stopping at Halesworth, Darsham, Saxmundham, Wickham Market, Melton and Woodbridge along the way. Local **bus services** from Ipswich connect some of the smaller villages of the Felixstowe and Shotley peninsulas with the county town and, although the service is far from perfect, even the smallest villages here seems to have a bus going somewhere near them at sometime in the day. The First in Suffolk & Norfolk 75, 76, 76A, 77 and 77A services all connect Ipswich with Felixstowe and Landguard Fort via Trimley, the 64 and 65B service connects Ipswich with Woodbridge, while Ipswich Buses 98 and 202 service runs more or less hourly between Ipswich and Shotley Gate at the end of the Shotley Peninsula via Holbrook and Chelmondiston respectively. Ipswich Buses 163 runs between Ipswich and to Levington on the Felixstowe Peninsula and the same company's 172, 173 and 174 services connect Felixstowe with Woodbridge.

A couple of **ferries** are useful too. Bawdsey Ferry (℡ 07709 411511), a foot-passenger service between Bawdsey Quay and Felixstowe Ferry, operates from May to the end of September and also at weekends during Easter and in October. This is a useful lifeline for venturing north along the coast from Felixstowe Ferry to avoid a very long detour by road. The other service worth considering is the Harwich harbour Foot and Cycle Ferry (℡ 0791 9911440 🖰 www.harwichharbourferry.com) that runs between Landguard Fort and Shotley Gate calling in at Harwich in Essex along the way. This operates about five times daily between

Easter and early September, and weekends only in the last two weeks of September.

CYCLING

Away from the main trunk roads – A12, A14 and A137 – cycling is generally enjoyable in this part of the county especially on some of the quieter roads on the Felixstowe and Shotley peninsulas. The OS Landranger 169 covers most of the area in this chapter and is useful for planning quiet virtually traffic-free cycling routes and avoiding pitfalls.

WALKING

Surprising though it might seem given the number of largish towns the walking in this southeast part of the county can be extremely good. Two long-distance walking routes pass through this region: The Stour and Orwell Walk, and the Sandlings Way. Both offer great potential for day walks between points along the route or for circular walks that incorporate just part of them.

The **Stour and Orwell Walk** does pretty much exactly what its name suggests. Starting at Landguard Point in Felixstowe, where the Suffolk Coast Path terminates, it follow the southern edge of the Felixstowe Peninsula, close to the shore for much of the way, then goes in and out of Ipswich before following the entire shoreline of the Shotley Peninsula, first along the southern shore of the Orwell estuary and then along the northern shore of the River Stour. It ends at Cattawade close to the Essex border, where the Stour Valley Path begins along Dedham Vale.

The **Sandlings Way** offers an alternative route to the Suffolk Coast Path between Ipswich and Southwold, via Woodbridge, Snape and Dunwich. Rather than following the coast, the route passes through the Sandlings heaths that lie a little way inland. Really keen walkers could join all three routes together to make a continuous circuit of around 160 miles.

Far more modest undertakings are, of course, possible. **Day walks** of all the above routes are worth doing if transport connections are not a problem. For example, the first section of the Sandlings Way between Ipswich and Woodbridge, which is much better than it might seem, or the section of the Stour and Orwell Walk on the Shotley Peninsula that stretches between Pin Mill and Shotley Gate. The peaceful Shotley Peninsula is also excellent territory for short circular walks; some

TOURIST INFORMATION

Felixstowe 91 Undercliff Rd West ✆ 01394 276770 ⌂ www.visitfelixstowe.co.uk
Ipswich St Stephen's Church, St Stephen's Lane ✆ 01473 258070
Woodbridge Woodbridge Library, New St ✆ 01394 444400
Suffolk Coastal ⌂ www.suffolkcoastal.gov.uk
Suffolk Coast & Heaths AONB ⌂ www.suffolkcoastandheaths.org
Visit Suffolk Coast ⌂ www.visit-suffolkcoast.co.uk

suggestions will be indicated in the text. Fearless urban warriors might want to go for the ultimate road walk challenge and cross the Orwell Bridge south of Ipswich. There's a pavement beside the road here and it's perfectly possible to cross the bridge using this although this is probably the antitheses of a Slow experience and will not be to everyone's taste.

THE FELIXSTOWE PENINSULA

This large tract of land south of Ipswich and Woodbridge is sandwiched between two of Suffolk's principal rivers – the Deben and Orwell. At the end lies Felixstowe, a popular resort and also the location for Britain's largest container port tucked away behind Landguard Point in Harwich harbour at the mouth of the River Orwell. Away from the frantically busy A14 dual carriageway, which shuttles lorry traffic to and from the port this is mostly an area of mixed farmland like much of the rest of the county. The Deben shore is largely undeveloped, a land of marshes and muddy creeks mostly, while the east bank of the River Orwell on the western side of the peninsula is a little more populated with small villages like Nacton and Levington that have a country park and marina respectively.

1 FELIXSTOWE

🏠 **Dorincourt Guesthouse** and **Treacle Pot Cottage** (see pages 214)

Mention Felixstowe to anyone from outside Suffolk and the thing most think of is the Port of Felixstowe, hardly classic Slow territory. The port, though, is actually quite separate from the main part of the town that has long been a popular seaside resort and continues to be so despite a slight economic downturn of late. The fact that Felixstowe's role as a resort has been overshadowed in recent years is actually welcomed by many Suffolk natives, especially those of the Ipswich area, who quite like to have the place to themselves. It's all pretty much seaside-traditional and gentrification is yet to happen here, as are sky-high property prices and a deluge of well-heeled incomers. For the time being, Felixstowe does not quite have the 'Let's Move to ...' kudos celebrated in the resorts further north along this coastline. This is not such a bad thing. Certainly, the town is nowhere near as smart or refined as Southwold or Aldeburgh but it does not make any claim to be so. It's an old-fashioned seaside resort pure and simple: gastropubs, posh delis and art galleries may be a bit thin on the ground but what you do have is a pier, albeit somewhat truncated these days, a long pleasant promenade and more beach huts than you shake a stick of seaside rock at.

"It's an old-fashioned seaside resort pure and simple."

In some ways Felixstowe is actually several towns in one. There's the seaside resort that flanks the promenade and beach, there's the port of course, all swivelling cranes and multi-coloured mounds of stacked containers, and there's Old Felixstowe, an area of town that stood long before there were any notions of a holiday resort or container port. Finally, there is Felixstowe Ferry, a place apart, barely a village, where men mess about in boats, fish are landed by a handful of fishermen and not much ever happens. Most of the action takes place at the other end of the town in the vicinity of the port. It did in the past too, at nearby Landguard Fort, a redoubtable defensive structure that continues to keep watch over Harwich harbour with a steely military gaze.

Felixstowe's life as a resort began like so many similar places when the railway arrived at the end of the 19th century. A relative of Queen Victoria, Princess Augusta Victoria of Schleswig-Holstein, wife of Kaiser Wilhelm II, visited Felixstowe for an extended holiday in 1891; this put the town on the must-go-to map for London's wealthier citizens. Felixstowe water was considered to have curative properties and the town was granted 'spa' status in 1902, following which paddle steamers started to come direct from London, dropping off passengers on the pier which in those days was more than half a mile long, much longer then than it is today. Another famous visitor to the town – not quite royal in this case but very nearly – was Mrs Wallis Simpson who resided at Beach House on Undercliff Road East in the town for six weeks in 1936 in order to achieve resident status necessary to divorce her American husband and marry Edward VIII. She was clearly used to better things, though, and recorded in her diary that 'the little house in Felixstowe was dismaying. It was tiny, there was barely room for the three of us [two friends and herself], plus a cook and a maid, to squeeze into it.' The house was demolished in 1994 and so you can no longer go there yourself to check whether the wannabe queen was being a little too picky. There is a tea rooms named after her on Undercliff Road East now, which she probably would have hated too, although she obviously had some sort of interest in the catering trade as it was while staying in Felixstowe that she is said to have invented the club sandwich. Of other celebrity figures associated with the town, T E Lawrence ('of Arabia') is probably the best known. The author and World War I hero was based here incognito for two years in the 1930s while serving as an aircraftsman at RAF Felixstowe.

Felixstowe: the resort

A good way to see the best that Felixstowe has to offer is to the start at **Felixstowe Quay** north of the town. There's a car park here and a foot ferry across to Bawdsey Quay on the other side of the River Deben, where the ornate chimney pots of Bawdsey Manor can be seen to good advantage across the water. There's not that much here besides a waterfront, quay, a few huts selling fish, a café and a pub but it's a good place to watch the world go by and imbibe some briny sea air. A Martello tower stands a little way south of the quay and there's another to be seen a little further on towards the town situated a little incongruously on the edge of a golf course. There are beach huts too, the first of what must be hundreds lining the seafront on the way into town. These eventually peter out around the point where the coast bends eastwards at Cobbold's Point and a procession of groynes runs out to sea.

The sea-wall promenade begins a little further on, the cranes of the port clearly visible ahead. The promenade runs parallel to Undercliff Road East beneath a very large imposing building on top of Bath Hill that was once a hospital but has now been redeveloped into apartment units. Until recently this functioned as a convalescent care centre and before the building's construction in 1926 was the site of another Martello tower and also the Bath Hotel, burned down by suffragettes in 1914, their last major outrage before receiving the vote in 1918.

The promenade continues along Undercliff Road West past more beach huts and seafront gardens to reach the **Spa Pavilion Theatre and**

Gardens, the original building of which was also bombed and burned to the ground, this time by bombs during World War II (Felixstowe was one of the few places in the United Kingdom to be attacked by Italian planes during the blitz). The current building dates from the 1950s but at the time of writing it was closed and boarded up, a sad fate for a venue that was once a regular venue for a wide range of entertainers. Further ahead is the **pier**, a mere shadow of its former self as it was dramatically shortened during World War II as prevention against enemy landings. Constructed in 1905, it once stood over half a mile long and had its own electric tramway to bring *Belle* paddle steamer passengers from London into town. Unfortunately you can no longer walk the whole length of the pier even in its reduced state. Despite rumours at the time of writing that suggest that the pier might be demolished, other sources hint that plans are afoot for a 'new look' pier to be opened in approximately 2015.

Beyond the pier, where the cranes of the port loom ever larger as you continue south, are all the things that you might expect of a seaside resort of the old school– amusement arcades, bingo halls, ice-cream parlours and fast-food places. Continuing south you come to the third of the town's Martello towers, which now finds useful service as a coastguard lookout station. There's a caravan and campsite just beyond here and then a track across a common that leads to Landguard Fort.

Landguard Fort

Landguard Fort, View Point Rd IP11 3TW ✆ 01394 675900 🖰 www.landguard.com. Open end of Mar to early Nov; English Heritage. **Felixstowe Museum** ✆ 01394 674355 🖰 www.felixstowemuseum.org.

At the peninsula's southernmost tip is this large pentagonal fort protecting Harwich harbour. It was built in 1744 to replace an earlier structure that in turn had replaced an older building that had originally been commissioned by Henry VIII. The fort stands on the site of the last invasion of England in July 1667 when Dutch soldiers landed nearby but failed to capture it, as they were repulsed by the Admiral's Regiment, the forerunners of today's Royal Marines. The fort remained in military hands until as recently as 1971, mostly as barracks in its later years. English Heritage took the fort over in 1997 and carried out structural repair work before opening it to the public. Although the fort now lies firmly in the county of Suffolk, this territory was once considered to be part of Essex. Daniel Defoe mentions this in his account of his early 18th-century tour of East Anglia in which he observes that 'The fort is on the *Suffolk* side of the bay or entrance; but . . . our surveyors of the county affirm it to be in the county of *Essex*.' Whichever side of the county line, there's certainly plenty to see here – soldiers' quarters, magazine tunnels, ammunition chambers and so on – and the entrance fee includes a good free audio tour that describes the everyday lives of the men who were posted here. Guided tours are available too for those who prefer a live human to an anonymous voice in the ear. Tours of the outer batteries take place on Sunday afternoons, as do ghost tours.

The fort is home to **Felixstowe Museum**, housed in the neighbouring Ravelin Block, a former mine storage depot, which has various exhibits on local history as well as details of the history of the fort itself. South of the fort at the very end of Suffolk is a small nature reserve where migrating birds are kept under close observation, up-to-date details of which are usually chalked up on a blackboard outside the entrance.

The Port of Felixstowe & Old Felixstowe

You can follow the road around the back of the fort to a car park where there's an excellent view across the mouth of Harwich harbour and a very welcome caravan snack bar too. This is also the departure point for the foot ferry that crosses from here to Harwich and Shotley Gate. To the right lies the **Port of Felixstowe**, with its clattering lorries, swirling cranes and four-high stacks of containers; more than likely there'll be a massive cargo ship in dock too. If you really want a closer look at this, make for the quite surreal viewpoint, where there's a bench, directly above the dockyard a couple of miles west along the route of the Stour and Orwell Walk as it heads out of Felixstowe. A little further on, out of town but still within the acoustic shadow of all the metallic activity in the port, are **Trimley Marshes**, a nature reserve with pools full of wading birds.

Felixstowe is more than a mere appendage to a massive container port, and more than just a holiday resort too. North of the centre, **Old Felixstowe**, with its leafy streets and elegant three-storey Victorian and Edwardian houses, is well worth a wander. Fans of unusual buildings might want to check out St Andrew's Church in the town centre, which has the distinction of being England's first reinforced concrete church. Don't expect a squat bunker-like structure though – it's quite elegant, a mock perpendicular edifice rising among mock-Tudor semi-detacheds.

¶| FOOD & DRINK

The Alex 123 Undercliff Rd West ☎ 01394 282958 ⌨ www.alexcafebar.co.uk. Very convenient for the seafront, this busy café-bar with a first-floor brasserie is just across from the prom. The brasserie offers a selection of grill and seafood dishes as well as a good-value set menu while the downstairs café-bar has all-day breakfasts, snacks and light meals in addition to good cakes and coffee.

Bonnet's Café 1 Hamilton Rd ☎ 01394 282310. A long-established café and tea room with a 1930s atmosphere and specialising in teas, coffee and chocolate.

Ferry Boat Inn Felixstowe Ferry ☎ 01394 284203 ⌨ www.ferryboatinn.org.uk. Nicely situated down by the quay at Felixstowe Ferry, a great base for a seaside stroll, this has real ale, decent fish dishes as you might expect, and a good choice of gluten-free options too.

The Little Ice Cream Company 59–63 Undercliff Rd East. This is the place in Felixstowe to come for a seaside ice cream, much of which is made on the premises from local produce. There's a selection of hot food on offer too.

Regal Fish Bar Sea Rd ☎ 01394 273977. This fish bar on the front is highly rated by locals for its consistent high quality and large portions.

View Point Café View Point Rd ☎ 01394 675823. It's hardly surprising that given the name of both the road and the café, this commands fantastic views across the port and mouth of the River Orwell. This no-nonsense café is the perfect place for a mug of tea and a bacon sandwich while watching the ships come in.

The White Horse 33 Church Rd ☎ 01394 277496 ⌨ www.thewhitehorse-felixstowe.co.uk. This traditional pub in Old Felixstowe serves locally sourced home-cooked food and a good selection of real ales. There's also a beer garden for fine weather.

2 LEVINGTON

There is not a huge amount between Felixstowe and Ipswich to detain most visitors but the area around Levington on the south side of the peninsula is not without interest. The village, which these days is a peaceful little place with a thatched pub and a church overlooking the River Orwell and across to Pin Mill on the other side, was a centre for digging coprolite back in the 18th and early 19th century. Coprolite – fossilised dung from prehistoric animals – was highly regarded as a fertiliser and dug by hand from just beneath the surface in the area. The industry has long since declined and is now just a memory, but the name lives on in Ipswich where there is still a Coprolite Street, which sounds considerably better than Fossilised Dung Street (or worse).

Levington Creek just below the village has long been connected with the sea and was once a working harbour. Coal was landed by barge here up until World War I and long before this Viking boats would have made landfall here as evidenced by the discovery of remains of what was probably one of the Danish fleet that raided Ipswich in AD991. Smugglers, too, used to take advantage of the creek's inconspicuous situation and in 1817 a boat named *Daisy* was apprehended carrying 48 tubs of spirits that it shouldn't have had. Although the creek hasn't seen any barge trade since the 1920s you can still make out some of the harbour furniture, with some old mooring posts and fragments of wooden jetties still visible.

Just east of Levington Creek is the Suffolk Yacht Harbour at Levington Marina, constructed in 1967 on reclaimed land. West of the village is **Broke Hall**, surrounded by parkland landscaped by Humphry Repton in 1794. He was obliged to incorporate specific design specifications in his plan to obscure the view of neighbouring Orwell Park and also hide views of the estuary's mudflats yet keep views of the river channel itself. Repton's near 300-year-old avenue of lime trees can still be seen leading down to the hall.

3 WALDRINGFIELD

Across the peninsula on the Deben shore, Waldringfield, like Levington, was another centre for coprolite mining. Now like its counterpart on the other side of the peninsula it is a quiet village with a yacht club. Unlike Levington, there's also a river beach here, and a golf course too on what used to be Waldringfield Heath. Behind the beach is a sandy cliff of the same red crag which used to yield copious quantities of coprolite that once brought wealth to the village. Waldringfield village makes a decent enough base for walks along the marshes of the Deben River – The Maybush pub down at the water's edge is a good place to start and finish. There's also an enjoyable short walk from here up to the village's hilltop church, All Saints', with its Tudor red-brick tower.

Southwest of the village, just outside Newbourne you'll find **Newbourne Springs nature reserve**, a Site of Special Scientific Interest (SSSI) managed by the Suffolk Wildlife Trust that has an impressive array of wildlife from willow tits, siskins and orchids in its swampy woodland to butterflies and nightingales on the heath. The various springs here provided the water supply for Felixstowe until the 1980s and what was once the pumping station is now the visitor centre. There's also a disused crag pit, once a source of coprolite, across the road from the car park that now has sand martins nesting in its steep, red crag slopes.

¶¶ FOOD & DRINK

The Maybush Cliff Rd ℰ 01473 736215 ⥁ www.debeninns.co.uk/maybush. Beautifully situated on the west bank of the Deben River at Waldringfield, this former 15th-century farmhouse has excellent views of the waterfront, Adnams beer and a decent menu that features local game and fresh seafood.

4 MARTLESHAM

Martlesham sits at the head of the peninsula, west of Waldringfield, close to and more or less midway between Ipswich and Woodbridge. The village is probably best known for being the Suffolk Constabulary headquarters and also for its aviation museum in the former control tower of what used to be RAF Martlesham Heath. Hopefully you will not require the services of the former but might want to investigate the latter. **Martlesham Heath Control Tower Museum** (ℰ 01473 624510 ⥁ www.mhas.org.uk; open from Apr to end Oct Sun afternoons only; free) has interesting displays about the aerodrome's history. Both Peter Townsend and Douglas Bader once flew missions from here.

Martlesham Creek, an inlet where the River Fynn forms a confluence with the River Deben, is a little way northeast of the village. Once a centre for contraband smuggling, now a haunt for wading birds and boat enthusiasts, it is a strangely quiet place given the proximity of Woodbridge just to the north and Ipswich to the west. A riverside footpath here follows the route of the Sandlings Way along the west bank of the River Deben all the way into Woodbridge, an excellent way to approach the town.

IPSWICH & WOODBRIDGE

Suffolk's county town, its largest by far, sits on the River Orwell straddling the head of two peninsulas, Shotley and Felixstowe. Far smaller Woodbridge lies a little way northeast on the bank of the River Deben. In many ways, the two towns are like chalk and cheese: one brash, noisy and traffic-addled, the other traditional, refined and relatively peaceful. An over-simplification perhaps, but while Woodbridge seems a natural contender for honorary Slow status almost any way you look, in Ipswich it is necessary to be rather more selective.

5 WOODBRIDGE

🏠 **Church Farm, The Crown, Martello Tower** and **Teachers House** (see pages 213–14)
⛺ **Forest Camping Limited, Mill House Camping, Secret Meadows** and **Suffolk Yurt Holidays** (see pages 214)

William A Dutt in his turn-of-the-century *Highways and Byways* referred to Woodbridge as 'a delightful little town – one of the prettiest little country market towns in England'. Dutt was quite right: it is. This was not one of those cases where you lament how things have changed since imagined halcyon days. No, it's a fact: take away the cars on the streets and the town really hasn't changed that much since Dutt wrote his account. The urban blight that has despoiled parts of neighbouring Ipswich seems to have kept well clear of Woodbridge. It is a living, breathing market town, well-to-do, certainly, but it still belongs in the real world rather than just the glossy lifestyle pages of the Sunday supplements.

The town stands at the head of the River Deben estuary, where you'll find yourself if you arrive by train – and perhaps by car too, as there's a big, convenient car park down here by the railway lines. From here, there's a footbridge across the railway and a riverside path that leads south along the estuary past reedbeds and rowing clubs. If you head in the opposite direction and walk around the back of the riverside theatre you'll soon reach a quay that has one of the town's most distinctive buildings, the **Tide Mill** (☎ 01394 385295 ⬦ www.woodbridgetidemill. org.uk; open Easter–Oct). This elegant, white-planked 18th-century building operated until the 1950s and, as its name suggests, harvested the power of the incoming tide to turn a waterwheel. The mill still works, but the pond that used to store the tidal water has been replaced by a much smaller one while the original has morphed into a kidney-shaped **yacht harbour** that is closed to the general public unless you are wearing the right kind of sailor's hat. Much less fancy but, I think, more characterful, boats are moored at the quay beside the tide mill. Some of these look as if they have been here a long time and you can detect a real sense of community in the slightly battered craft with pot plants and bicycles on their decks moored in the boatyard beyond the yacht harbour. Also down on the quay near the tide mill, the

Riverside Restaurant and Theatre (✆ 01394 382174 🖰 www.the riverside.co.uk) offers tempting deals that combine a three-course dinner with a film in its retro-style cinema. Close by is the Woodbridge Art Club (🖰 www.woodbridgeartclub.co.uk), which has regular exhibitions by local artists.

Away from the riverside, central Woodbridge is delightfully traffic-free, with the pedestrianised streets of Quay Street, Church Street, New Street and The Thoroughfare combining to provide a compact shopping and strolling area. One of its glories is that there are so many small retailers and so few chain stores: the Woodbridge Town Centre Management Group has come up with the slogan, 'Choose Woodbridge for real shopping', and it kind of makes sense. The Thoroughfare, in particular, has several independent bookshops and tea rooms. In fact, the town as a whole has so many coffee houses and tea rooms you suspect that the town council may have shares in Twinings.

"One of its glories is that there are so many small retailers and so few chain stores: Woodbridge town centre has come up with the slogan 'Choose Woodbridge for real shopping'."

Woodbridge's **historic core** lies a little further uphill. Woodbridge is surprisingly hilly and slopes sharply away from the river. Melton Hill, which has St John's Church, is claimed by some to be the inspiration for the 'Grand Old Duke of York' nursery rhyme although there is no historical evidence of 10,000 soldiers marching up and down this particular hill. Other Woodbridge hills have been suggested, as has Ipswich, which has an actual Grand Old Duke of York pub. The Duke of York in question, Frederick Augustus, the second son of George III, actually had far more than 10,000 men under his command in his Napoleonic campaign, and he wasn't old either – just 31 at the time. The song more than likely came about following an unsuccessful campaign in Flanders, and that is probably where the hill in question is. Returning to terra firma in Woodbridge, Church Street and New Street merge at Market Hill where the imposing Dutch-gabled **Shire Hall** has pride of place. Built by Thomas Seckford in 1575, the ground floor of this building once served as the town's corn exchange while the upper level was used for judicial purposes. In front of the shire hall on Market Square stands an elegant stone pump built in 1876. The **Woodbridge Museum** (✆ 01394 380502), with its exhibits detailing the history of the town and its people, especially local luminaries Thomas Seckford and Edward FitzGerald, lies just opposite. You can get a great view of the rooftops of the town by climbing up the steps to the small balcony on the southern side of the Shire Hall. North of the Shire Hall, there's a pleasant shady square, a surprisingly tranquil spot to find right in the centre of town. Keep going along Theatre Street and you reach **Buttrum's Mill** (✆ 01473 264755), a nicely restored six-storey tower mill dating from 1836 and open for visitors on summer weekends and bank holidays.

◍ FOOD & DRINK

You have a wealth of cafés and pubs to choose from in Woodbridge – below is just a small selection. Among the excellent food shops are a couple of excellent delis in town. **Loaves and Fishes** (✆ 01394 384040) at 52 Thoroughfare has a great selection of cheese, smoked fish and organic produce, while **Woodbridge Fine Food Company** (✆ 01394 610000 ✆ www.woodbridgefinefoodcompany.co.uk) at 2a New Street has fresh shellfish, wines, picnic foods and their 'world famous pies'. **The Cake Shop** (✆ 01394 385515 ✆ www. cakeshopbakery.co.uk) at 19 Thoroughfare not only has beautiful cakes but also a fantastic range of artisan breads.

Cherry Tree Inn 73 Cumberland St ✆ 01394 384627 ✆ www.thecherrytreepub.co.uk. A traditional inn with home-cooked food and a good selection of cask ales and wines.

Georgian Coffeehouse 47a Thoroughfare ✆ 01394 387292 ✆ www.georgiancoffee house.co.uk. One of several traditional tea rooms serving light meals and afternoon teas.

King's Head 17 Market Hill ✆ 01394 387750 ✆ www.kingsheadwoodbridge.co.uk. An Adnams-run inn in one of the oldest buildings in town, this has good ales, a decent pub menu with meats from Five Winds Farm in nearby Melton, and a roaring fire in winter.

Waterfront Café: The Granary Tide Mill Way ✆ 01394 610333 ✆ www.the waterfrontcafe.co.uk. A stylish café and seafood restaurant in a former granary next to the Tide Mill and under the same ownership as the Woodbridge Fine Food Company. The menu offers high-quality seasonal food: lobster, crab and oysters, game like pheasant and venison in autumn. Salad leaves are locally grown and organic and there's an excellent wine list.

Whistlestop Café Station Rd ✆ 01394 384831. A conveniently situated, good-value and friendly café right next to the station.

6 SUTTON HOO

Trammer House, Sutton Hoo, near Woodbridge IP12 3DJ ✆ 01394 389700. Open Apr–Oct daily, Nov–Mar weekends only; National Trust.

Just across the Deben estuary from Woodbridge is the **Sutton Hoo Burial Site**, unearthed in 1939 to reveal a large Anglo-Saxon ship. This had been buried stuffed with treasure which included magnificent garnet-set gold jewellery, silver, drinking horns and armour: Anglo-Saxon notables tended to leave this world in great style. Ship-burials seem to have been a Suffolk speciality: there were others here, and one in nearby Snape, but treasure-hunters raided the Sutton Hoo mounds in the 16th century and only missed finding this one by a few inches. The notable in question here is most probably Raedwald, who was King of East Anglia in the early 7th century. As famous as the ship-burial is the beautiful silver and gold ceremonial helmet found at the site.

The discovery is a saga in itself: the landowner, Mrs Edith Pretty, a widowed spiritualist, commissioned a self-taught local archaeologist, Basil Brown, to excavate some grassy mounds which she somehow sensed had some significance. To his everlasting credit, rather than simply digging down for treasure, Brown recognised that the lines of metal rivets in the sandy soil represented all that was left of a ship's hull, still in position, and excavated with great skill. But once the discovery became national news, he was sadly sidelined by the 'professionals' directed by the British Museum. At least Brown gets to tell the tale: it is his voice that does the narration on the audio guide.

"Brown recognised that the lines of metal rivets in the sandy soil represented all that was left of a ship's hull."

The mounds, with their pagan associations, were later used as a place of execution: join one of the tours led by local volunteers to get the best sense of what happened here. Run by the National Trust, the site is set in a 245-acre estate with attractive woodland and estuary walks. There's an excellent view of the estuary to be had from the terrace of the café. The exhibition hall has a full-size reconstruction of the burial chamber and displays that tell the story, describing Sutton Hoo as 'page one of English History', which somewhat overlooks the Romans and Iceni tribes that came before.

7 BOULGE

You may struggle to find tiny Boulge on the map. The village – more just a collection of lanes – does have an interesting story to tell though. Across the A12 from Woodbridge and a little further north, a minor road leads west to the village of Bredfield. After less than a mile it comes to a junction with a water pump and some fancy wrought ironwork that has finger signs pointing in every direction. Take the one that says 'Boulge, Debach and Clopton' and just after Partridge Farm you should notice a crude hand-painted sign pointing along a rough track to Boulge church. Take this and you'll soon come to **St Michael's Church**, hidden away on the edge of a small wood, a delightfully peaceful spot that seems much further from the A12 than it really is. The graveyard here is the resting place of Edward FitzGerald, a slightly oddball Victorian polymath who was responsible for translating Omar Khayyám's *Rubáiyát* poems from the Persian. FitzGerald's family owned the Boulge Estate to which the church belongs – the hall was destroyed in the 1950s – and he lies buried in the graveyard here under a simple carved granite slab. Some straggly rose bushes around the grave are rather more special than they might first appear, having been planted by admirers from the Omar Khayyám Club in 1893, ten years after FitzGerald's death. The original rose was raised from seed brought from the grave of Omar Khayyám in Nishapur, Persia, and more have been planted since, although none of them appeared to be doing very well the last time I came here. Nevertheless, their oriental origin provides an exotic touch to what might seem a perfectly ordinary, half-forgotten Suffolk graveyard.

Edward FitzGerald lived a life somewhat at odds with the rest of his family, and that his grave lies separate from the large family tomb is probably indicative of the alienation he felt. FitzGerald disliked the stuffy life of the estate and spent much of his adult life at Woodbridge where he dressed in odd clothes and befriended herring fishermen at the quay. One in particular, Joseph 'Posh' Fletcher, had a long-term relationship with FitzGerald that was most probably not entirely platonic – quite scandalous at the time. Ironically, FitzGerald's Woodbridge boat was named *Scandal* too. If you think Edward FitzGerald sounds like a typical W G Sebald character, then you are right. Sebald passed this way in *The Rings of Saturn* and wrote movingly of FitzGerald's predicament.

8 IPSWICH

🏠 **Freston Tower** and **Kesgrave Hall** (see pages 213–14)

Ipswich, Suffolk's largest town by far, may not seem to readily fit with the notion of Slow. For a start, although the Suffolk county town has 'town' status, it is the size of a city, with a population comparable to that of its rival Norwich across the county border to the north. It is perhaps a little unfair to compare Ipswich to Norwich – I will confess to a personal bias here as I live in the latter – but while planning mistakes have certainly been made in the Norfolk cathedral city these are as nothing compared with the way that Ipswich has been shoddily redeveloped in places and carved up by a traffic system that does no favours for its historic core.

Ipswich has plenty of fine sights and much of historical interest; the trouble is the sights seem to sit in isolated pockets. Here you'll find half-timbered Tudor houses juxtaposed next to concrete car parks and slapdash 1960s development. There are exceptions though, most notably the pedestrianised zone in the town centre. The newly regenerated waterfront area shows plenty of promise too, although it is still a work in progress. The problem is, at present these two areas are not very well linked together, especially for walkers.

The town centre

Quite a few specific things are worth seeking out in the town centre, parts of which still retain a medieval character. For pargeting aficionados, the town has what is perhaps the very best example in the county at the 17th-century **Ancient House** on the corner of St Stephen's Lane and Buttermarket. This was once a merchant's house but is now a branch of the kitchen utility chain, Lakeland. Here, four pargeted panels represent the continents of Europe, Asia, Africa and America as seen through Tudor eyes (Antarctica and Australasia are both missing, unknown at the time). Some of the imagery, as you might expect, reflects the perceived stereotypes of the period, with Africa represented by a naked man with a spear. Just around the corner from here, an interesting story concerns the bells at **St Lawrence's Church** on Dial Lane, currently used as a café and community centre. In 2009, the church's five bells were returned to their place in the tower after a 25-year absence. Cast in the mid 15th century, they are the oldest circle of bells in the world. They were removed in 1985, but have now been overhauled and reinstalled. Their sound is reckoned to be unique and beautifully mellow by those able to judge these things. Whatever the quality of this genuinely medieval sound, it is humbling to think that when these bells first chimed in the streets of Ipswich, Columbus had not yet discovered America. Although you are unlikely to hear its ancient bells peal during your visit, it is worth stopping for a drink and a look at the church's cavernous, heavily Victorianised interior. As you sip your mug of tea you can admire the wooden pulpit and the stained glass above the kitchen area, and heed the instructions of the frieze that circuits the wall: 'Blessed are the pure in heart for they shall see God . . . Blessed are the . . .' and so on. St Lawrence's is just one of many, mostly disused, medieval churches in Ipswich, enough indeed to give even famously church-rich Norwich a run for its money. South of Buttermarket on St Stephen's Street the town's tourist information centre also makes use of a redundant church, **St Stephen's**, which ceased to be used as a church in 1975.

Central to the whole of this pedestrian zone at Cornhill is **Ipswich Town Hall**, an impressive Victorian edifice that looks as if it should belong in a middle-sized city rather than a county town. There is a market in front of the town hall four days a week and just around the corner on Queen Street you'll find a bronze statue of Grandma, the character created by *Daily Express* cartoonist Giles who used to work in the offices opposite. For more timber-framed buildings you should head to St Nicholas Street and Northgate Street, where Oak House dates from the 15th century as does nearby Pykeham Gatehouse. A little way west of Cattle Market bus station on Silent Street is a modern **statue of Cardinal Wolsey** with a cat at his side, opposite his childhood home. The cardinal, Henry VIII's chancellor, wanted to build a college in the town that would act as a feeder school for Cardinal (now Christ Church) College, Oxford, which he had also founded. But thanks to the Reformation and Wolsey's fall from power the college was closed and demolished within a year of opening. All that remains now is Wolsey's Gate on College Street and the nearby church of **St Peter's by the Waterfront**, which was commandeered by Wolsey to become the college chapel. The church, probably on the site of Ipswich's very first church, is now a heritage centre and music venue. It is just south of the town centre close to the waterfront as you might expect from its name, but the river probably once ran even closer to the church than it does today (to reach the waterfront proper from here, turn right down Foundry Lane then left along the quayside to arrive at the new Neptune Marina development). St Peter's is home to the **Ipswich Charter Hangings** – eight tapestries commissioned to celebrate the millennium and depict the 800 years since the town received its charter from King John. The tapestries, which took over three years for a team of 30 to complete, have the River Orwell as a constant theme on each of them along with a collage of buildings, coats of arms, ships, town life and prominent figures in Ipswich history from the Viking period through to the present day.

PARGETING

Pargeting is the traditional art of decorative plastering on the walls of houses. The technique involves moulding wet lime plaster to create a form of bas-relief. Pargeting is most commonly seen in Suffolk although there are examples in other parts of East Anglia like Norfolk, Cambridgeshire and Essex. There would have been plenty of pargeting on show in London too before the Great Fire of 1666 destroyed it all. It is most commonly seen on buildings that date from the 16th or 17th century when the art reached its zenith although there was also a revival of interest during the Arts and Crafts Movement of the late 19th century. There are also a few contemporary examples. The art probably began in the time of Henry VIII but no pre-Elizabethan examples survive. The best examples in the county are The Ancient House in Ipswich (see page 115) and on the County Museum (also known as 'The Ancient House' in Clare (see page 179).

Ipswich Waterfront

The Waterfront is Ipswich's current big project – a large-scale regeneration begun in 1999 that has entailed the building of a large number of new apartments, a hotel, several restaurants, university buildings and a marina. At the centre of all this is the **Old Customs House** (✆ 01473 231000) a Victorian neoclassical building that now serves as the offices of the Ipswich Port Authority. Nearby is the Waterfront union building of the University of Suffolk, which has its campus near here. Across the water on the other side, just west of the customs house, stands the Jerwood Dancehouse, the permanent home of Dance East, built on the site of a former mill. Given time, the Waterfront will, no doubt, become a highly enjoyable place to visit; a place to drink, eat, stroll and watch the boats come and go. For the time being though it all seems a bit unfinished as if all this squeaky-new development needs a little more time to bed in. Part of the problem is a sense of disconnection from the town centre, as the area between this and the waterfront still has an air of run-down abandonment about it. But the same could be said of the Waterfront itself a few years back and it's undoubtedly a huge improvement on what was here before.

This being the Waterfront, naturally enough there are boats here aplenty. One permanently moored here sees service as Mariners, a smart floating restaurant (see box, page 118), while another, *Orwell Lady*, moored at Orwell Quay, runs regular **cruises** along the River Orwell in the summer months (✆ 01473 258070 ⌂ www.orwellrivercruises.com), from a short 50-minute trip passing underneath the Orwell Bridge to various theme-night trips and what it calls 'English Afternoon Tea Cruises', which involve either a 2½ hour trip to Pin Mill and back or a 3½ hour exploration of Harwich harbour. A wind-powered trip can be had on the old Thames sailing barge *Victor* (⌂ www.sbvictor.co.uk), which sails from the Old Customs House on a variety of cream tea, supper and do-it-yourself picnic cruises in summer.

Christchurch Park

Ipswich has several pleasant parks but Christchurch Park, formerly the grounds of an Augustinian priory, is by far the most special. Sloping down to the town centre from the north, this large leafy space is a great place to come for leisurely walks and picnics, and on sunny Sundays that is exactly what many Ipswich folk do – it's deservedly popular with locals. There's plenty for children here too, with duck ponds, ice-cream kiosks and a dedicated play area. The park also has two arboretums to investigate and free tennis courts. At its centre stands a red granite **monument** to the nine Ipswich martyrs executed during the reign of (Bloody) Queen Mary.

The **Christchurch Mansion** (✆ 01473 433554), a handsome Tudor building at the bottom end of the park, was presented to the town by Felix Thornley Cobbold, a philanthropic brewer, in 1892 and now serves as a museum. The mansion has a collection of Victorian toys and games and an interesting Tudor kitchen as well as an art gallery that includes works by notable Suffolk artists like Alfred Munnings and a good collection of paintings by John Constable and Thomas Gainsborough. At the rear of the building you'll find a tea room.

A BOAT OF MANY FLAGS

The boat that currently serves as Mariners floating restaurant at Neptune Quay down at Ipswich's Waterfront began life as the SS *Argus* in Bruges in 1889. Requisitioned for the Belgian Navy and sunk by the Germans in 1940, it was raised and repaired by them before becoming a Dutch Red Cross hospital ship renamed *Florence Nightingale* in the 1950s. Following this, it became a party boat for a while before being brought to Ipswich to be opened as an Italian restaurant in 1990. Nowadays, it is a French brasserie – truly an international vessel.

¶¶ FOOD & DRINK

Ipswich has a wide choice of cafés, restaurants and pubs – a small selection is given below. Probably the most atmospheric place to eat and drink, certainly the most up-and-coming, is at one of the restaurants that line the quay at the newly developed Waterfront area.

For food shopping there are a couple of places for quality Suffolk produce close to the town. Just south of Ipswich, close to the west side of the Orwell Bridge, is the **Suffolk Food Hall** (℅ 01473 786610 ⌂ www.suffolkfoodhall.co.uk), probably the largest and best-known farm shop in the county. This is open seven days a week and stocks a huge array of local produce – bread, cheese, meat and fish – as well a bistro restaurant, café, a cookery school and activities for children. Nearby at Wherstead is **Jimmy's Farm** (Pannington Hall Lane, Wherstead IP9 2AR ℅ 01473 604206 ⌂ www.jimmysfarm.com; see page 120), a rare-breed farm open every day except Christmas Day, with shop, restaurant, woodland trail, events and courses, a butterfly house, a vegetable garden, petting farm, and special activities for children.

Dove Street Inn 76 St Helens St ℅ 01473 211270 ⌂ www.dovestreetbrewery.co.uk. With an excellent range of real ales and other drinks, including beers from their own brewery next door, this friendly pub is well located close to the city centre and university campus. Good homemade pub grub and a choice of different rooms to sit in as well as an outdoor beer garden.

Fat Cat 288 Spring Rd ℅ 01473 728524 ⌂ www.fatcatipswich.co.uk. Sister pub to Norwich's famous Fat Cat, itself something of a legend in the real ale movement, this lies east of the city centre between the university campus and hospital. Like its sister, this has an enormous choice of real ales – more than a dozen on tap. Inexpensive snacks are available too like pasties, pork pies and Scotch eggs, and there's all the (lack of) amenities you'd expect in a traditional pub – no fruit machines, no jukebox or TV.

Mariners Neptune Quay ℅ 01473 289748 ⌂ www.marinersipswich.co.uk. Down at the Waterfront, this floating brasserie is located in a 1899 Belgian gunboat. This is one of the smartest places to eat in Ipswich and so quite formal and expensive, although the set meals are reasonably priced. Although the food might be described as French with a modern twist almost all ingredients are locally sourced.

Museum Street Café Westgate House, Museum St ℅ 01473 232393. A rare vegetarian café with tasty, imaginative food.

St Lawrence Centre Café Dial Lane ℅ 0844 7369710. Decent, inexpensive food and snacks in the lovely stained-glass setting of a disused church right in the heart of town. This is a social enterprise business which provides work for adults with disabilities.

Waterfront Bar Bistro 15 Regatta Quay ℅ 01473 226082 ⌂ www. waterfrontbistroipswich.co.uk. A French-influenced place on the waterfront with an outside terrace.

BACK FROM THE BRINK: JIMMY'S FARM SAVES THE ESSEX PIG

Jimmy Doherty's farm is one of the best known in the country thanks to a BBC2 television series that documented the trials of raising rare-breed pigs. Jimmy's business goes under the name of the Essex Pig Company and you might be fooled into thinking that the farm stands on the wrong side of the River Stour. It doesn't – it's in Suffolk, just south of the A14 near a village called Wherstead. The pigs, however, have an impeccable Essex pedigree.

The Essex Pig is a direct descendant of the breed that once foraged East Anglia's wildwood. Modernisation brought about a dramatic decline in their numbers following World War II, and by 1967 the breed was considered extinct. Luckily, one farmer, John Crowshaw, managed to keep his pedigree Essex bloodline pure. Although the Essex Pig remains officially extinct, Jimmy Doherty is currently hard at work building up the numbers of this rare animal. Jimmy's Essex porkers are in suitably aristocratic company, having both Saddlebacks and hefty Gloucestershire Old Spots as farmyard neighbours.

THE SHOTLEY PENINSULA

South of Ipswich, a finger of land extends southeast, delineated by the River Orwell to the north and the River Stour to the south. At the tip of the finger is Shotley Gate, once a naval training base, isolated from the rest of Suffolk by land yet close to both Felixstowe and Harwich in Essex by sea, both of which lie just a mile or two away across the water of Harwich harbour. In sharp contrast to the busy urban centre of Ipswich to the west, the peninsula has an essentially rural character – a place apart that is a gently rolling terrain of arable farms and pockets of woodland with lonely marshes and creeks close to the shoreline. The Stour and Orwell Walk long-distance path follows both shores of the peninsula before ending at Cattawade close to Manningtree in Essex.

9 FRESTON & WOOLVERSTONE

Freston, a little way along the northern side of the peninsula, is sufficiently close to Ipswich to still have the imposing bulk of the Orwell Bridge in its sights and the distant thrum of the A14 in its ears. Nevertheless, this already feels very rural and slow-paced. There's a church here, St Peter's, which has an unusual war memorial in its churchyard, a life-sized *Peace* in the form of a young woman holding a laurel wreath aloft. It is unusual in that the figure is made out of wood, sculpted from oak in 1921 and restored on Armistice Day 2006. The churchyard stands at the south side of **Freston Wood**, an atmospheric ancient wood with gnarled pollarded oaks and many species of bird, flower and butterfly. If you come here in spring you'll be greeted by the delicious garlicky aroma and pretty white flowers of ramsons that cloak the bottom part of the wood in that season. Walk a little higher, towards the church, and the aroma morphs to the sweet hyacinth smell of bluebells that festoon the wood in late April and May.

Across the road that leads to the church, opposite The Boot pub, is a footpath that leads through woodland to Freston Park where **Freston Tower**, a six-storey, red-brick Tudor folly stands. Its precise history is uncertain but evidence suggests that most probably it was built in the 1550s by Thomas Goodling, an Ipswich merchant who bought Freston Manor in 1553 and who clearly liked to show off a bit. He also must have enjoyed having an unimpeded view of Ipswich and the River Orwell from his very own lookout tower – no Orwell Bridge in those days, of course. The tower is now owned by the Landmark Trust (www. landmarktrust.org.uk) who rent it out for holiday accommodation, a single room for each storey.

Woolverstone, the next village reached heading out along the peninsula, is home to Ipswich Girls' School which moved to its current premises at Woolverstone Hall in 1992. This is very much an estate village with no pub, shop or post office, but it does have a church, St Michael's, fronted by an avenue of neatly clipped yews, and down at the river there is a marina which has been the base for the Royal Harwich Yacht Club since World War II.

10 PIN MILL

A little way east of Woolverstone and close to the village of Chelmondiston, Pin Mill is probably the place on the peninsula that most know about. The waterfront pub here, the Butt and Oyster, is rightly very popular with sailors and Sunday-lunchers from Ipswich and beyond. Pub or not, though, the waterside hamlet here is an enticing spot. Pin Mill has always been very much centred on sailing and this was once the place where Thames barges came for repair and barges used to be unloaded here in the 19th century. The hamlet was also a centre for sailmaking and there used to be a maltings and a brickyard here too. Naturally enough given its waterside credentials, it is also one of those places deemed to be a former smugglers' haven. There is still has an active boatyard here, Harry King and Sons Ltd, and these days there is also a gallery and art studio, Pin Mill Studio (✆ 01473 780130 ⌂ www.thepinmillstudio.com) that runs workshops for adults and children in addition to watercolour painting days and photography courses – Pin Mill is nothing if not photogenic.

The hamlet also provided inspiration for the children's book illustrator Arthur Rackham, who kept his yacht *Selina King* anchored here in the late 1930s. The seafaring action in *We Didn't Mean to Go to Sea*, Rackham's tale of hapless child adventurers inadvertently sailing across to the Netherlands, begins here at Pin Mill at Alma Cottage close to the Butt and Oyster. It also features in his following book *Secret Water*.

Beyond the pub, heading east along the footpath through Pin Mill Plantation, a tract of woodland owned by the National Trust, you'll see lots of moored houseboats through the trees below, some in poor repair and apparently abandoned, others that look quite enticing. Many of these are converted Thames barges that have not seen the eponymous river for many a year. Continuing along here eventually brings you to Clamp House at Butterman's Bay, which takes its name from the schooners that used to transport dairy produce from the Channel Islands. A barge race, organised by the Pin Mill Sailing Club, has been held here every summer since 1961. From here you can retrace your steps or follow the path around the circumference of the wood back in the direction of Pin Mill.

If you have plenty of time and energy you could continue all the way to Shotley Gate, a wonderful walk alongside marshes full of ducks and wading birds. The contrast between the near-silent saltmarsh on the Shotley side and the frenzied commercial business of the container port on the other side of the Orwell is really quite remarkable. From Shotley Gate, there should be the occasional 98 or 202 bus back to Ipswich railway station via Chelmondiston, just half a mile from Pin Mill, but be sure to check first.

⟦⟧ FOOD & DRINK

Butt and Oyster Pin Mill Rd, Pin Mill IP 1JW ✆ 01473 780764 ⌂ www.debeninns.co.uk/ buttandoyster. A very popular waterside pub on the south bank of the River Orwell that is nearly always busy. The wonderful location counts for a lot and that is why people come here. The Adnams beer is fine but the food, while reasonable enough, is really nothing special.

11 SHOTLEY

Shotley, a mile short of Shotley Gate on the B1456, does not have much to recommend it other than one of the peninsula's few pubs, The Rose, but Church End just to the north of the village has the parish **church of St Mary's**, itself unremarkable but with a fascinating churchyard. Here you'll find the graves of sailors who served in two world wars, hundreds of them, many of them just young lads, as well as the tombstones of German sailors from World War I. There is also a memorial to the victims of a collision between two submarines. It's a sad and haunting spot, with the feeling of melancholia perhaps heightened further by hilltop views across to the lines of cranes of the Port of Felixstowe in one direction and Harwich docks in the other.

West of Shotley, **Erwarton Hall** has a particularly striking gatehouse, a splendid 16th-century Gothic edifice with six brick pinnacles like rockets ready for the launch and with something of the look of an oriental tomb. Sir Philip Parker of Erwarton Hall was Anne Boleyn's uncle and she is said to have often stayed at the hall. It is rumoured that after her beheading her heart was buried at Erwarton's St Mary's Church according to her wishes. This might appear an unlikely story but a small heart-shaped cask was discovered in an alcove of the church during restoration in 1838. On opening it contained a small quantity of black dust and it was subsequently reburied beneath the organ. There is a plaque in the church giving details of the story. Whatever the truth of the Anne Boleyn connection, there are obvious signs that link her name with the Erwarton area. The village's Queen's Head pub, now unfortunately closed for business, used to display a portrait of Anne Boleyn as its pub sign while not very far away, close to Beaumont Hall Farm, is a small wood called Boleyn's Covert.

Shotley Gate lies at the very end of the peninsula. Not an alluring place in itself, it was the home of HMS *Ganges*, a large training base for Royal Navy cadets, it is now more just a spot to watch ships come and go across the waters of Harwich harbour. HMS *Ganges*, which was originally a training ship in Harwich harbour but moved to a purpose-built onshore facility in 1905, finally closed in 1976 although it was used as a police training centre for some years afterwards. A small **museum** (✆ 01787 228417 ⌂ www.hmsgangesmuseum.org.uk) dedicated to the ship stands next to the marina entrance. The Harwich–Felixstowe Ferry also departs from near here. Shotley Gate has a pub should you need it, the Bristol Arms, and a reasonable bus service to and from Ipswich, but the best thing about the place really is its location and you are better off getting your boots on and heading away from the village. **Shotley Marshes**, immediately north of the village and reached by a footpath, is an expanse of low-lying farmland behind the river wall that is an important breeding site for wading birds like snipe and redshank as well as a wintering ground for flocks of Brent geese.

¶ FOOD & DRINK

Bristol Arms Bristol Hill, Shotley ✆ 01473 787200 ⏚ www.bristolarms.com. With real ale, decent food made with ingredients from mostly local suppliers and good views over Harwich harbour, this is a convenient port of call in the Shotley area.

12 HOLBROOK & STUTTON

Holbrook, on the south side of the peninsula roughly halfway, along is best known for its Royal Hospital School, the enormously tall tower of which can be seen for miles around. The school, which is in neoclassical style and the largest boarding school in East Anglia, was constructed here in 1933 as a school for Royal Navy children when the school was moved from its original base at Greenwich Hospital. Its 200-foot campanile tower can be seen from as far away as Ipswich.

The spread-out village of **Stutton** lies just west of Holbrook, and has fine pargeting on some of the cottages. Crowe Hall, one of six manor houses listed in the Domesday Book, lies just south of the main street surrounded by a long ornate wall. The parish church, St Peter's, lies some way east of the village. Once the houses would have clustered around the church but they were burned down in medieval times in an attempt to thwart the spread of plague. Whether this worked or not is uncertain as Pin Mill on the other side of the peninsula was one the last places in Britain to have an outbreak of plague recorded. The village has its own community shop (✆ 01473 328133) run by volunteers.

A road leads south of the village past Crepping Hall to Stutton Ness and the path that leads west along the river beach here to Stutton Mill is particularly lovely, passing fragments of woodland and sculptural dead trees. **Stutton Mill** at Newmill Creek is appealingly situated too, an isolated group of buildings shaded by willows next to an inlet. From here, the Stour and Orwell Walk continues west for its final leg to **Cattawade**, an unremarkable village at the head of the estuary.

13 ALTON WATER PARK

Alton Water Park 📞 01473 328268 🖰 www.anglianwater.co.uk. Open daily; Anglia Water.

Alton Water, close to both Stutton and Holbrook, is a reservoir popular with both windsurfers and sailors. This, the largest body of inland water in the county, is a good place for walks too, with footpaths around most of its eight-mile shoreline and a nature trail with bird hides. Ospreys, nightingales and grass snakes have all been seen here. Cycling is also a good option, especially along the southern shore where there is a surfaced cycle track. **Cycle hire** is available (📞 01473 328873 🖰 www. altoncyclehire.co.uk) at the visitor centre on the south side of the water between Stutton and Holbrook, where you'll find a tea room.

Tattingstone on the west side of Alton Water might be said to be where the Shotley Peninsula begins – west of this everything starts to feel rather more suburban as you get drawn into Ipswich's gravitational field. The village was split into two in the 1970s when the area was flooded to create Alton Water. A road bridge connects the two halves – plain old Tattington south of the water and Tattington White Horse (after the pub) on the northern side. Alton Hall, which used to stand in the village, was one of many properties to vanish beneath the water – a necessary sacrificial lamb to ensure Ipswich's future drinking water supply. Another building in the flood zone, Alton Mill, was dismantled completely and re-erected at the Museum of East Anglian Life at Stowmarket (see page 151). Tattingstone is home to the so-called **Tattingstone Wonder**, a folly dating from 1790 that is made up of a group of cottages with an added square tower and a Gothic flint façade. The story goes that Edward White, the incumbent squire, wanted to improve the view from his library window and so went about creating this architectural *trompe l'œil* in order to achieve the desired effect. From the front it really does look like a small parish church; from the rear it looks much more like three small cottages with a fake three-sided tower.

¶¶ FOOD & DRINK

White Horse, White Horse Hill, Tattingstone 📞 01473 328060 🖰 www.white horsetattingstone.co.uk. This nice country pub in a village just north of Alton Water has a good selection of cask ales and wines and traditional pub food including some vegetarian and gluten-free options. There is a small campsite at the rear of the building.

4

CENTRAL &
EAST SUFFOLK

This chapter covers the 'High Suffolk' plateau that rises south of the Waveney Valley. Let's not get too carried away with the words 'high' or 'plateau' though – as you might expect for East Anglia, it's pretty modest stuff. 'High Suffolk' may be overstating it a bit but compared with the rest of the county it is just that: a rolling plateau of arable farmland interspersed with villages and small market towns. A hundred years ago, this area was almost entirely devoted to agriculture and most of the land is still used for arable crops, although these days most local inhabitants are involved in pursuits other than farming. Despite the vast seas of golden wheat that turn some of these settlements into virtual islands in August, farming involves a very small workforce these days: agriculture may well be big business, but is no longer a big employer. Nevertheless, the towns and villages of this area retain plenty of connections with the soil, as do the people, and although village daily life may no longer revolve around the changing seasons, it still takes notice of them.

"Despite the vast seas of golden wheat that turn some of these settlements into virtual islands in August, farming involves a very small workforce these days."

GETTING AROUND

It's easy enough in a car. The main roads are the A12 and A14, both of which lead roughly north to south on either side of Ipswich. The A140 runs south from Norwich to Ipswich, dividing this area laterally. The A1120 is the major east-to-west route through central Suffolk and road signs identify this as a tourist route as it passes close to bone fide tourist draws like the Suffolk Owl Sanctuary at Stonham Aspel, Saxtead Green Post Mill and Framlingham Castle.

PUBLIC TRANSPORT

Central Suffolk tends to be best connected by public transport with Ipswich, the county's largest town, which isn't particularly central itself. The market towns of Stowmarket and Halesworth are minor transport hubs and have decent **bus** links with outlying villages, although many routes require going in and out of Ipswich, an inconvenient dog-leg.

The East Suffolk **train** line, connecting Lowestoft with Ipswich, has stops at Halesworth, Darsham, Saxmundham and Wickham Market along the way, all conveniently close to the area described in this chapter. Stowmarket lies on the main Norwich–Ipswich–London train line and so has frequent connections with Ipswich, Diss (just across the border in Norfolk) as well as a regular service to Bury St Edmunds to the west.

CYCLING

Cycling is good in parts, especially away from the A1120. The A12, A14 and A140 are all also to be avoided for obvious reasons. **National Cycle Route 1** and North Sea Cycle Route (✆ www.sustrans.org) pass right through the locale from Hadleigh in the Stour Valley via Ipswich and Woodbridge through Framlingham and Halesworth to Beccles in the Waveney Valley, while National Cycle Route 51 crosses the county from Ipswich to Bury St Edmunds. The 78-mile circular **Heart of Suffolk Cycle Route** loops through Debenham, Framlingham, Halesworth and the Waveney Valley. A reasonable number of connected bridleways can be used for off-road cycling too.

Cycle hire is available at Bicycle Doctor and Hire Service in Ipswich (✆ 01473 259853) and Byways Bicycles at Darsham near Saxmundham (✆ 01728 668764). The website ✆ www.cycle-route.com has plenty of route ideas for cycling in central Suffolk together with informative maps of the suggested routes. **Cycle Breaks** (✆ 01449 721555 ✆ www.cyclebreaks.com) based in Needham Market have a number of gentle, self-guided Suffolk cycle tours to choose from several of which are in central Suffolk or at least include the area as part of the itinerary. These tours offer quality bikes and support that includes accommodation bookings and luggage transfers.

WALKING

Pick your way around carefully and you'll find some worthwhile walking, especially along riverbanks. The **Gipping Valley River Path** follows the

TOURIST INFORMATION

Stowmarket Museum of East Anglian Life ☏ 01449 676800
⌕ www.southandheartofsuffolk.org.uk
Mid Suffolk District Council ⌕ www.midsuffolk.gov.uk
The South and Heart of Suffolk ⌕ www.southandheartofsuffolk.org.uk

route of the old canal towpath between Stowmarket and Ipswich passing Needham Market, Claydon and Sproughton along the way.

The **Thornham Estate** (⌕ www.thornham.org.uk) is large enough for half a day's walking, with a good network of publicly accessible paths through parkland, woodland and water meadows. There is also a surface path for pushchairs and wheelchairs.

HALESWORTH & AROUND

Halesworth, straddling the upper course of the River Blyth, is an attractive market town well worth a visit. In the town's hinterland lie several villages that each have a noteworthy church. This is countryside where it is easy to get pleasantly lost: narrow roads meander and change direction through delightful timeless countryside; villages are elusive and unsigned until you stumble right upon them. It's an area ripe for gentle exploration: perfect Slow territory.

1 HALESWORTH

🏠 **The Barns at Belle Grove, Brights Farm, Gypsy Hollow** and **Ivy Grange Farm Yurts** (see pages 215)

More or less equidistant from Beccles, Bungay, Saxmundham and Framlingham, Halesworth is a small market town tucked away in northeast Suffolk midway between the River Waveney and the coast. Halesworth was at one time the highest navigable point on the River Blyth but that was centuries ago and the river that flows through the town is pretty insignificant.

Small though it may be, the town has quite a distinct identity and a self-contained feel about it. A lot of this may be due to its location in the county – not quite in the Waveney Valley, not quite in the coastal strip, not quite 'High Suffolk' – which helps give the town its hard-to-pin-down character. Not that the town is isolated – it's on the main road between Bungay and the coastal A12 and also has a station on the East Suffolk rail line.

Having pride of place at the centre of Halesworth is **The Thoroughfare**, a shopping street lined with a charming hotchpotch of Victorian and Georgian buildings that appear fairly unspoiled and satisfyingly removed from any notion of 'clone town Britain'. In fact, the street is resolutely old-fashioned, with a miscellany of independent shops providing small-town needs like food, furniture, haberdashery, hardware and stationery. The 14th-century building at number 6 is especially worth looking out for as it has an intricately carved wooden beam that depicts figures from classical mythology and folklore. The Thoroughfare leads to the **market place** where there is another handful of shops and an art gallery. Market Day is Wednesday. Beyond the market place lie St Mary's Church with some 17th-century almshouses opposite, the gift of a local benefactor to provide for 12 poor single men and women of the parish. Rather remarkably, these were still in use as such right up until the 1960s. The Halesworth Art Gallery (✆ 01986 875367 ✆ www.halesworthgallery. co.uk) now occupies the upper floor of the almshouses building.

If you are at all curious about Halesworth's history, try the **town trail** which begins nearby on Angel Link close to the Angel Hotel, an old coaching inn. For the town trail just follow the sign of the duck. This will lead you along Steeple End, along Chediston Street where a policeman was brutally murdered in 1862, his murderer, John Ducker, being the last Suffolk man to be publicly hanged, then down Rectory Lane, better known locally as Duck Lane. After crossing the bridge and investigating the old brewery and malting buildings near The Cut the trail returns via the Town Park and The Thoroughfare to its starting point at the Angel. Duck signs, Duck Lane, John Ducker – is there a theme here?

The town's cultural scene is nurtured not just by the odd art gallery and a good bookshop, Halesworth Books (✆ 01986 873840), at 42 Thoroughfare but also by **The Cut Arts Centre** (✆ 01986 873285 ✆ www.newcut.org), which occupies some converted maltings just north of the centre. The Cut stages an impressive programme of events for such a small town and as well as a modern theatre and performance area there's also a good café and bar here. In addition to hosting regular film shows and musical performances, The Cut also provides a centre for workshops and community events. The arts centre is also the focus of the annual **Halesworth Arts Festival** (✆ www.halesworthartsfestival.

org.uk) in October, usually an eclectic mix of folk, jazz, classical, dance, theatre and comedy.

¶ FOOD & DRINK

There's not a huge amount to choose from in the town. The Thoroughfare has a couple of cafés including **Edwards** (✆ 01986 873763 🖰 www.edwardshalesworth.co.uk), at 59a and the **White Hart** pub (✆ 01986 873386) at number 10, which has the usual pub grub choices. The **Angel** (✆ 01986 873365 🖰 www.angel-halesworth.co.uk), also on The Thoroughfare, has bar food and Cleone's, an Italian restaurant. **Focus Organic** (✆ 01986 872995 🖰 www.focusorganic.co.uk) at 14 Thoroughfare has a good range of organic local produce and artisan bread.

Tilly's of Halesworth 10 Market Pl ✆ 01986 835899 🖰 www.tillysofhalesworth.co.uk. This 1920s retro-style café-restaurant located in a handsome Georgian building moved its operation wholesale from Southwold a while ago. On offer are a variety of breakfast choices, homemade food like fish platters and bubble and squeak from midday to dusk, and tiered teas – sweet, savoury or boozy – served in the afternoon.

2 WENHASTON

Just outside Halesworth in the direction of Blythburgh, Wenhaston is a pretty village close to the River Blyth. There are plenty of **walking** possibilities in the immediate surroundings of the village. One option would be to walk along the south bank of the river from here as far as Blythburgh and return on the opposite bank crossing the second bridge back to Wenhaston. Blythburgh has its magnificent Holy Trinity Church.

The Wenhaston Doom

The church of St Peter at Wenhaston is best known not for its architecture but for its rare 16th-century painting of the *Last Day of Judgment*. This was discovered during restoration work in the late 19th century when a wooden panel was taken down from above the chancel and accidentally left outside overnight in the rain. This fortunate neglect resulted in the panel's whitewash being dissolved away to reveal a bright painting beneath.

So-called 'Doom' paintings such as this are very rare because almost all were destroyed during the Reformation. It is likely that this example had long been whitewashed over and forgotten about as early as the mid 16th century, long before the despoilers of the English Reformation would have come to the church. Virtually all Doom (Day of Judgment) paintings were made directly onto walls so the fact that this example was painted onto wooden panels makes it quite unique.

The Wenhaston Doom is exceptional in its clarity and brilliance, better and brighter than any others in the country. A survivor of both the iconoclastic purges of the Reformation and well-meaning but heavy-handed Victorian restoration, it is a true medieval treasure. These days the Doom can be seen on the wall opposite the door of the church rather than in its original elevated position affixed to the chancel arch above the congregation. The outline of where the wooden figures of the Rood group of Christ, St John and the Virgin Mary would once have been attached can still be clearly made out.

3 BRAMFIELD

Heading south from Halesworth towards the A12 you pass through Bramfield, a tight cluster of houses and cottages around the church and pub. The church here, **St Andrew's**, is one of just 38 round tower churches in Suffolk. Unusually, this one has a tower that is completely detached from the rest of the building and always has been it would seem. The tower is actually older than the main body of the church, a lovely thatched building with a wealth of intriguing head stops in a range of styles from ghoulish to cartoon-like. There is also a terrified-looking Green Man playing peek-a-boo from behind oversized oak leaves. The somewhat gloomy interior has wall paintings and some beautiful rood screens too.

¶¶ FOOD & DRINK

The Queen's Head ☎ 01986 784214 🖰 www.queensheadbramfield.co.uk. This long-established dining pub with scrubbed pine tables, exposed beams and cosy open fires has good-value sandwiches, light meals and specials at lunchtime and more adventurous fare in the evening. Local meat features strongly, in particular steaks from Emmerdale Farm at nearby Darsham, although there are plenty of good vegetarian options too. It's child-friendly too with a special children's menu and an enclosed garden.

4 WALPOLE & HUNTINGFIELD

Heading southwest from Halesworth along the B1117 you soon come to **Walpole**, a small village with a church and post office. Just arriving at the village you will pass what looks like a fairly typical Suffolk farmhouse on the right of the road. What makes this stand out from the ordinary is the collection of gravestones in its front garden. The clue is there – this is not a house at all but **Walpole Old Chapel**, a farmhouse converted into a Puritan chapel in the late 17th century. If you want to look inside – naturally enough, it is somewhat austere – then timing is of the essence as it is usually only open on Saturday afternoons in spring and summer. The road continues past Heveningham Hall, the biggest stately home in Suffolk, to reach the village of the same name.

Before this a narrow road leads off right to soon arrive at **Huntingfield**, where there is a pub, the Huntingfield Arms, set rather idyllically on the village green and a most unusual church, **St Mary's**. The story of St Mary's is a very human tale of determination and perseverance. In the mid 19th century the rector's wife, Mildred Holland, took it on herself to repaint the hammerbeam roof of the church in its original 15th-century style – an enormously ambitious undertaking that took her seven years to complete. Between 1859 and 1866 Mildred Holland is said to have lain on her back for much of the time on top of scaffolding, painstakingly painting first the chancel and then the nave. It seems that she had no assistance whatsoever other than having the scaffolding erected for her by workmen and being given some advice on appropriate decoration from medieval expert E L Blackburne FSA. The cost of the whole undertaking is recorded as a little over £2,000, which was almost all paid for out of the rector's own pocket. The result is spellbinding, almost intoxicating: a ceiling of golden-winged angels, apostles and saints painted against a background of brilliant vibrant hues. To get the full psychedelic effect you will need to switch the church lights on, easy enough if have a pocketful of £1 coins to feed into the slot. You'll need quite a few though, as a pound does not buy you more than a few minutes of neck-cricking marvel time gazing up at the ceiling. Some, of course, will consider this fearless restoration job to be vulgar and garish – certainly, 'bright and colourful' does not really sum it up. Let us not forget that medieval churches would once have looked like this – bright colours on every available surface, unequivocal statements of faith and angels and apostles aplenty.

"The result is spellbinding, almost intoxicating: a ceiling of golden-winged angels, apostles and saints."

The other remarkable thing about the church interior is the font cover, a veritable indoor steeple that was installed as a tribute to Mildred Holland when she died in 1878 not so many years after completing her arduous labour of love. Both she and her rector husband William are buried in the churchyard close to the entrance gate.

¶¶ FOOD & DRINK

Huntingfield Arms The Street, Huntingfield ✆ 01986 798320. A decent village pub in a lovely rural situation, this has well-kept Adnams beer and good-value food that usually includes a choice of specials as well as a standard pub menu.

FRAMLINGHAM & AROUND

5 FRAMLINGHAM

⌂ **Abbey House** (see page 215)

'Fram', as most people tend to call it, is a lovely little market town that still functions in the way that a market town is supposed to, providing services to the villages that surround it. Voted the most desirable place to live in England some years back by *Country Life* magazine, you might think that this would be a rather smug place, but not at all. Framlingham really does not need to try too hard and so it doesn't – the town just goes about its business in the knowledge that while life may be pretty good here it is best not to shout about it too much.

What I find most appealing is that, unlike many other places of a similar size, the town still seems to have a strong sense of community.

"What I find most appealing is that, unlike many other places of a similar size, the town still seems to have a strong sense of community."

It's old-fashioned in an unselfconscious way and quite remarkably self-contained for a town of not much more than 3,000 souls. This is mainly the result of its serving a large rural hinterland, and local village folk, when not scurrying off to Ipswich or the supermarkets at Saxmundham, will probably choose to come here to do their shopping and pay their bills. Despite all of this, it has more of the character of a big village than a small town. Framlingham certainly embodies the spirit of Slow, although I doubt if many town residents have yet heard of the Cittaslow movement.

On top of all those virtues, the town has a couple of splendid sights – a well-preserved castle, the largest in the county, and a beautiful medieval church. Coming along the road from the direction of Dennington, the first thing you will see of the town as you round the bend at Church Farm will be the mock-Gothic spires of

Framlingham College, a large independent school. Arriving from the opposite direction, from Parham, is a little less auspicious, as you will pass a batch of warehouses and grain silos as you enter the town. Keep going though and you'll soon reach the **market square** with the church and castle positioned above it: on Tuesday market day and Saturday mornings most of the space is filled by stalls selling meat, bread, fruit and veg, clothes and bric-a-brac.

The Crown Hotel dominates the east side of the square and appears to be so firmly established that you might think that the square grew up around it – it didn't, though. There's a delightfully quirky secondhand bookshop on the south side alongside an Indian restaurant, a café, a butcher's and a deli. Queen's Head Alley leads onto this side of the square through a tiny alleyway. If you go through here, you'll see on the right a timber-framed house that was once an inn called the Blue Boar, an even older establishment than the Crown Hotel, where bears were once tethered outside while their owners slept within. The narrow archway itself is thought to be the original toll entrance into the town. Returning to the square, walk uphill past the Dancing Goat café and you'll soon arrive at the church and the impressive **castle**. Or you might want to seek out what is probably the smallest house in England: the **Check House** (at Mauldens Mill development) is now a domestic dwelling of the 'one up, one down' category that even the most imaginative of estate agents would have to describe as 'cosy and bijou'. It used to be the check house for the steam-powered mill that once stood here; later it became a betting shop.

St Michael the Archangel Church

This church contains the **family tombs** of the Howards, Dukes of Norfolk, who used to own the castle. After the Dissolution of Thetford Priory (see page 188), Thomas Howard, the Third Duke of Norfolk, rebuilt the chancel here as the new resting place for his family's bones. Thomas Howard was a lucky man as far as timing went. Uncle of both the wives Henry VIII had executed, Anne Boleyn and Catherine Howard, he continually plotted to gain influence through serving up his more desirable female relatives for the king's attention, and was himself eventually condemned to death, but this was commuted to imprisonment when Henry died on the day before the sentence was due to be carried out. His tomb, the most impressive of the group here, dates from 1554, the year before his son upped sticks and moved in with his new wife's family at Arundel in Sussex. Two kneeling, praying effigies sporting Elizabethan ruffs and neat beards guard the tomb on one side – these are his sons – while his daughters pray together above his head. Henry Fitzroy, a bastard son of Henry VIII, who died aged just 17, has a tomb with a frieze of reliefs from Genesis that was probably once part of Thetford Priory. Another tomb in black marble flanked by angels honours Robert Hitcham, the man who bought the manors of Framlingham and Saxtead from, the Second Duke of Norfolk, and bequeathed Framlingham Castle to Pembroke College, Cambridge with the instruction to build a poorhouse.

There's more to St Michael's than just tombs, spectacular though they may be. Jean Coles, a Fram resident who used sometimes to work as a guide in the church, drew my attention towards some of its other treasures. 'When I used to show visitors around I would always show them the tombs first because they are my favourites too. But then I would point them towards *The Glory* – it's a real focal point for the church.' *The Glory* is, in fact, a painting that sits in the reredos above the high altar: a bright, mysterious work that has concentric rings of light glowing mystically from its centre, rather like the background for one of William Blake's Old Testament pieces. 'It's a bit of a mystery, that picture. No-one knows who painted it, although we think it dates from the 18th century. It has got the letters 'IHS' in the middle of it and I'm told that signifies the name of Jesus.'

The other treasure is the church's **organ**, just one of three built by the craftsman Thomas Thamar that managed to survive the English Civil War – Oliver Cromwell had a bit of a grudge against ornate instruments like this, apparently. 'It was originally made in 1674 for Pembroke College, Cambridge,' Jean told me. 'But they gave it to the church in 1708 when they wanted to get something a bit more up to date for their chapel at the college. The case is even older, from 1630 or even earlier, and that actually has the arms of Pembroke College on it. We get organists coming from all over the country to play it – they really love its sound. They have to book it well in advance, of course, and they are only allowed half an hour each.'

Prospective organists might be humbled by knowing who has sat on the bench before them: Felix Mendelssohn is believed to have given lessons on this very same organ on his regular visits from London.

A stroll from Framlingham

✳ OS Landranger map 156 or Explorer map 212; start: Castle Street, Framlingham, grid reference TM286636.

A short, two-mile **circular walk** begins near the castle. This is a good way to see the castle from a variety of different viewpoints and it also gives a flavour of the surrounding countryside.

To start you follow the path down to the mere from the Castle Inn and enter the Suffolk Wildlife Trust reserve then follow the circular nature trail as far as the footbridge over the River Ore. Leave the trail here and cross the river and follow the left bank to a second footbridge before turning right onto New Road.

After about 500 yards, the road turns right at Great Lodge Farm; continue another 200 yards until you reach a footpath to the right. Follow this south along a field edge until you reach another footpath branching left.

Take this path, crossing another footbridge, until you reach the B1120 Badingham road, where you turn right and follow Castle Street back to the start.

Framlingham Castle

Framlingham Castle, Church St ☎ 01728 724189. Open mid-Feb to Oct daily, Nov to mid Feb weekends only; English Heritage.

Framlingham Castle lies just beyond the church on top of the hill, a domineering presence with a dozen hollow towers, a deep dry moat and sturdy, well-preserved battlements. It's a very special place for a walk around the walls, taking in the views of the village and the mere. Although fortifications existed here in Saxon times, the present castle dates from the 12th century, the work of Roger Bigod, the second Earl of Norfolk. Generations of Howards, whose graves lie in the church, were later incumbents of the castle before their move south to Arundel in 1555. More famously, Mary Tudor mustered her supporters and proclaimed herself queen while staying here in 1553. Her successor, Elizabeth I, subsequently made use of it as a prison for luckless priests before Pembroke College, Cambridge, took it over, demolished the existing inner buildings and built a poorhouse within its walls that remained in use until 1839. It now serves as a visitor centre and has a display that tells of the various struggles in the castle's history.

For children there's a specially devised audio tour and a set of giant games. Special family event days are held too, with ghost trails at Halloween, a time-traveller trail at half-term with clues to solve and prizes to win, and festive family fun trails on weekends leading up to Christmas. William A Dutt writes of rather more vigorous activity taking place within its walls back in 1744, when John Slack the Norfolk champion pugilist fought the Suffolk champion John Smith and won. John Slack went on to meet John James in Broughton, London – they all seem to be called 'John' – and defeated the London champion in less than four minutes.

Just beneath the castle is **Framlingham Mere**, a 33-acre lake that used to be much deeper than it is today. This is in the ownership of Framlingham College but is currently leased to Suffolk Wildlife Trust as a nature reserve for birds and water plants. It's a good place for moisture-loving wild flowers like ragged robin, marsh marigold and irises, and waders like snipe can often be seen here too. Looking at the rather puny River Ore that flows into the lake, it seems hard to believe that this same river once brought ships from the coast. The Caen and Northamptonshire stone used for constructing the castle would have come by this route.

¶| FOOD & DRINK

Of the few cafés around the market square, the **Dancing Goat** (✆ 01728 621434) at 33 Market Hill is as convenient as any, with good coffee and some sunny outdoor tables. **The Common Room** (✆ 01728 768238 ♐ www.thecommonroomfram.com) at 22 Bridge Street just down from the square is a good choice for cooked breakfasts and brunches. They are pretty flexible about making you whatever you want too.

Just outside the town along the Badingham road, the **Shawsgate Vineyard** (✆ 01728 724060 ♐ www.shawsgate.co.uk) produces dry and medium dry whites along with a red, a rose and two sparkling wines. There's a shop (Mon–Sat) and 90-minute Wednesday evening tours of the vineyard and production facilities can be pre-booked between May and mid-September. You can do a self-guided tour too – the shop will provide a vineyard map and information sheet. Experience Days give tours and tastings on most Saturdays and some Fridays between May and August. A special experience day for two that includes lunch is also on offer.

Castle Inn Castle St 🕿 01728 724033 🖱 www.castleinnframlingham.co.uk. Just before the castle entrance at the top of the town, this has a pleasant courtyard, Adnams ale, Aspall Cyder and decent pub grub at lunchtimes only.

Crown Hotel Market Sq 🕿 01728 723521 🖱 www.framlinghamcrown.co.uk. This long-established hotel on the market square has a lunch and evening menu that features rare-breed meat from local farmers, and Southwold fish.

Lemon Tree 3 Church St 🕿 01728 621232 🖱 www.thelemontreebistro.com. Just up from the market place, this bright bistro offers good coffee and light lunches made using local produce. There is also a good choice of wine by the glass.

Station Hotel Station Rd 🕿 01728 723455 🖱 www.thestationhotel.net. There's no longer a station here, nor a functioning 'hotel', but this shabby-chic establishment has been running as a pub since the 1950s. More a gastropub with a wood-fired pizza oven these days – it's not particularly child-friendly or the sort of place to come just for a drink – the Station serves imaginative food with a Mediterranean twist in a comfortable, homely setting and makes full use of locally sourced ingredients. There's a good selection of wines to choose from as well as tasty ales from the nearby Earl Soham Brewery.

6 DENNINGTON

Dennington, on the A1120 north of Framlingham, has all the essential ingredients: a good pub, an interesting parish church and a post office. In fact, the village has what is possibly the oldest post office in the country, which is no mean feat considering the widespread closures of country post offices over the last decade or two. It may be just coincidence but neighbouring Framlingham is also said to have two of the country's oldest pillar boxes, making this area a veritable Shangri-La for postal history anoraks. Most come to see the parish church though, or to have Sunday lunch in the pub.

The church of **St Mary the Virgin** is highly rated by those who make it their business to comment on such matters. It stands out from the crowd thanks to two unique features: a wooden pyx canopy over the altar, and the representation of a sciapod carved onto one of the bench-ends. A sciapod is a mythological desert creature that uses its one enormous foot to shade itself from the sun, an appendage that no doubt comes in useful for leaping too. Mentioned by Pliny in his writings, this is the sole English representation of this curious creature other than appearing as a minor detail on Hereford Cathedral's medieval world map, the Mappa Mundi. Other bench-ends represent creatures that are altogether more commonplace, although not in Suffolk – pelicans, tortoises, lions and even a giraffe with a twisted neck. The pyx, which is one of only four in England, is rather like a hanging spire and was used for storing the sacrament back in Catholic times. There are also some rather beautiful, and somewhat spooky, tombs belonging to the Bardolph family, delicately carved from ghostly alabaster and beautifully preserved.

¶¶ FOOD & DRINK

The Dennington Queen The Square, Dennington ℰ 01728 638241 ⌂ www. thedenningtonqueen.co.uk. Next door to the village church, this attractive timber-framed dining pub is highly rated locally for its imaginative pub fare. It is popular and often full on Sunday lunchtimes.

7 PEASENHALL

🏠 **Sheep Cottages** (see page 215)

This village lies further east along the A1120, a little beyond Badingham. The dead-straight stretch of road offers some lovely views southeast over the wheat fields towards the coast and even without consulting the map you can sense that this was once a Roman route. Peasenhall is a pretty village with a good smattering of Suffolk pinkwash and neat thatched roofs. The village derives its name from 'Pisenhalla' meaning 'a valley where peas grow'. On the back of this somewhat tenuous connection, the village instigated its very own Pea Festival in 2008 and it has since become an annual event. This takes place in July and includes such leguminous events as the World Pea Podding Championships, the East Anglian Pea Throwing Championships and the Great Pea Draw. The really enthusiastic can also enter the pea-eating competition – using chopsticks. No doubt, it is an admirably green event – you certainly get the impression that it does not take itself too seriously and that proceedings are pea- rather than po-faced. The dress code, although not compulsory, is of course green.

"The village instigated its very own Pea Festival in 2008 and it has since become an annual event."

ᐧ|ᐧ FOOD & DRINK

There's no longer a pub in the village, but **Weavers** is a good tea room and **Emmett's of Peasenhall** (✆ 01728 660250 🖰 www.emmettsham.co.uk), an old-fashioned food store and smokehouse, is highly regarded for its sweet-cured hams and bacon made from free-range Suffolk pork. They stock delicious Suffolk unpasteurised cheeses too, and the shop also has a small café with an Italian espresso machine.

Sibton White Horse Halesworth Rd, Sibton IP17 2JJ ✆ 01728 660337 🖰 www. sibtonwhitehorseinn.co.uk. A traditional village pub, just a mile from Peasenhall, that serves local, seasonal food, excellent real ales and a broad selection of wines.

Weavers Tea Room 2 The Knoll ✆ 01728 660548. A popular and cosy village café providing cream teas and good-value three-course lunches.

8 YOXFORD

🛖 **School Cottage** (see page 215)

Continuing east along the A1120 from Peasenhall, you pass through Sibton, virtually next door, before arriving at Yoxford. The village hugs the road as far as the junction with the A12 but it is nevertheless a rather quiet place. With an eclectic mix of building styles that blend attractively, the village has the face of something of an artistic centre, with a number of art shops and galleries alongside a couple of antique businesses. The small **Yoxford Arts Festival** (✆ 01728 668401 🖰 www. yoxfest.co.uk) takes place in August.

Holding a strategic location at the junction of two main roads, Yoxford was an important coach stop on the London to Yarmouth run in the days before steam power. You can see clear evidence of this at the church where a tall iron signpost points in three directions: Framlingham (10 miles), Yarmouth (30), London (93). The signpost stands tall for a reason – for coachmen to read from their high perch. When the railways came to the area in the 19th century, the village was promoted as a tourist attraction for well-to-do urbanites. 'Yoxford: The Garden of Suffolk' became the catchword, referring to the village's location between three country estates. This 'garden' label was hyped by newspaper journalists and also by some interested parties in the village wishing to cash in on the act. William A Dutt, writing in 1901, was clearly not impressed: 'It may be that injudicious advertisement has had something to do with the district's flattering designation, and that

"With an eclectic mix of building styles that blend attractively, the village has the face of something of an artistic centre."

if we had never heard of "Poppyland", Yoxford would have remained unknown and its mediocre charms unproclaimed.' This seems a little harsh, as it is quite a handsome village, with some lovely parkland close to hand.

Looking at adverts in the window of Horne's store on the main road probably tells you more about life in the village today than any number of historical accounts. With flyers for art exhibitions, tree surgery, holistic therapy and painting workshops, and small ads that give details of cockerels ('with bags of character'), boats, chicken huts and an 'ideal family horse' up for sale, you soon get a picture of what modern-day Yoxford is all about now that the Yarmouth stagecoaches have disappeared from the scene.

It's common knowledge that, rather like its pub, a village's post office serves as an important social centre, especially for the more elderly folk of the parish. This is especially true in Yoxford where the **post office** on the high street doubles as a tea room and dispenses cakes and cappuccino alongside postage stamps and pensions. Adrian, who runs the dual enterprise along with his wife, told me that, as with all post offices, nothing was certain and they might have to close in the future but 'with luck we'll be one of the rare eight hundred or so that remain'. He was philosophical about the future: the tea room part of the business was on a two-year lease and he sounded determined to keep this going at least. 'Maybe if the post office closes I'll have to extend the menu a bit.'

The Cockfield Estate lies just behind the village – the former family home of the Blois family who give their name to one of the village pubs. The estate takes its name from the Cokefeud family – a name to be conjured with if ever there was one. **Cockfield Hall** served as a high-class prison for Lady Catherine Grey, sister of Lady Jane Grey, in 1567 but she died soon after arrival and was buried in her own private chapel in the village's St Peter's Church. The hall, an impressive 16th-century brick building, has a rooftop forest of tall chimneys and crow-step gables. It is visible from the A12 but you can get a much closer look by following the footpath through the gatehouse just beyond Horne's store opposite the church. Follow the footpath for a short while through a dark wood with ancient yews and, after a small footbridge, the wood opens onto open parkland and a clear view of the hall with its large complex of stables and coach-houses all bearing similar architectural detail. On a visit to the village a few years back, the gatehouse was

A LITERARY DIVERSION –
HEROD'S TEMPLE IN SUFFOLK

In his rambling masterpiece, *The Rings of Saturn*, W G Sebald describes walking a stretch of Roman road in east Suffolk. Setting out from Yoxford, he walks for four hours across a sparsely populated landscape in which he sees nothing other than harvested cornfields and a sky heavy with clouds (Sebald's landscapes always seem to be strangely devoid of people).

He ends up at a remote moated house where he encounters Thomas Abrams, a remarkable farmer who has been building an accurate scale model of the Temple of Jerusalem for the past 20 years. Sebald describes Abrams as having spent years studying sources as obscure as rare tracts on Roman architecture and the Mishnah, part of the rabbinic talmud (roman) in order to pursue his obsession. Sebald discovers that Abrams's project has already attracted a number of interested parties: one morning the farmer found that the man who had parked his Rolls-Royce in his driveway was none other than Lord Rothschild.

It's a typical tangential Sebald tale – with singular, Sisyphus-like characters turning up in odd places – but who knows what schemes and obsessions are dreamed up in these isolated Suffolk farmsteads? It turns out that Abrams is, in fact, Alec Garrard, a friend of Sebald's, who has subsequently published an illustrated book, *The Splendour of the Temple* in which his 1:100 scale model is used to describe the history and architecture of the temple that existed between BC19 and AD70.

covered in scaffolding and builders were hard at work at the hall. 'They sold it off a couple of years ago,' a worker told me. 'I think the plan is to do it up and then put it up for hire.' He pointed out the fancy brickwork on the façade behind Horne's. 'That bit's not actually part of the estate. I think it was just added in the same style as the rest of the buildings so that wedding parties would be impressed when they arrived at the entrance to the hall.'

🍴 FOOD & DRINK

King's Head Brook St ☎ 01728 668781 🖰 www.kingsheadyoxford.com. A village pub with good beer and decent pub grub served all day.

Main's 26 High St ☎ 01728 668882 🖰 www.mainsrestaurant.co.uk. This small family restaurant in a former draper's shop has an imaginative menu that changes frequently depending on what is available. Local suppliers like Emmett's of Peasenhall, meat from J R Creasey's of Peasenhall and fish from Sizewell and Lowestoft feature strongly. Open Thu–Sat evenings only. On Saturday mornings there's a bakery here too, with handmade bread and croissants on sale. There's also a monthly bread-baking club in support of the community-minded Slow Sunday movement as well as 'Pauper's Nights' when a limited but less expensive three-course menu is on offer.

Post Office Tea Room High St ✆ 01728 668861. A post office not only open for business but which also doubles as a friendly tea room with teas, coffee and cakes (see page 142). There's also a small selection of deli goods on sale, free Wi-Fi, local papers and, it goes without saying, all your postal needs.

9 LAXFIELD

Laxfield is a couple of miles north of Dennington on the Stradbroke to Halesworth road. Its 16th-century timbered **Guildhall**, across the road from All Saints' Church, has a small museum devoted to local history. This is the village that William 'Smasher' Dowsing, the puritan iconoclast, hailed from. Dowsing's handiwork extended through much of Suffolk, such was his distaste for religious ornament and what he considered 'superstitious pictures'. There's still a Dowsing Farm in the parish. Religious fervour seems to be a tradition in Laxfield, as a century before Dowsing's church-smashing antics, a village man named John Noyes was burned at the stake here for his opposition to the Catholic faith, a brave if foolhardy stance to have during the reign of ex-Framlingham Castle resident, Queen 'Bloody' Mary. In fairness to the villagers, Noyes's neighbours all dowsed their fires on the day in protest … well, all but one.

¶¶ FOOD & DRINK

The King's Head Gorams Mill Lane ✆ 01986 798395 🖰 www.laxfieldkingshead.co.uk. Known to all and sundry – well, locals at least – as 'The Low House', this is an authentic old-school Suffolk country pub with low ceilings, settles, tiny rooms and narrow passageways. There's no bar as such, just a tap room that serves Adnams ales straight from the barrel. Nor will you find a juke box or television, as the King's Head prides itself on being a social pub with a sense of tradition. A blackboard menu flags up tasty, rustic, homemade dishes made with local seasonal produce and in summer you might find performing Morris dancers or a horse and trap parked outside.

10 SAXTEAD GREEN POST MILL

Saxtead Green Post Mill, The Mill House, Saxtead Green IP13 9QQ ✆ 01728 685789. Open April–Oct; English Heritage.

In Saxtead Green, 2½ miles northwest of Framlingham, this is a fine

THE REAL-LIFE AKENFIELD

Back in 1969, author Ronald Blythe published *Akenfield: Portrait of an English Village*, a classic account of Suffolk country life. The book was an evocative portrait of a rural community told through the eyes of its members, and described a farming economy that had not long made the transition from horses to tractors. *Akenfield* was an immediate best-seller that single-handedly took responsibility for disabusing city dwellers of some of the romantic notions they might have held about country life. *Akenfield* told it as it was: funny in parts but also gritty and unflinching, it spoke of almost unimaginable poverty and the hardship of rural working-class life from the Victorian era up until the 1930s.

There is no such real place as Akenfield, of course, but it isn't too difficult to deduce that the name is an amalgam of two Suffolk villages – Akenham, just north of Ipswich, and Charsfield close to Wickham Market. Indeed, Charsfield was where Ronald Blythe had carried out a series of interviews with locals in the summer and autumn of 1967 prior to writing his book. He spoke to young and old alike, documenting both the frustrations of youth and the bittersweet memories of senior villagers who were still able to remember events that seemed to belong to another age – picking stones by hand from fields and sewing children into their winter underwear.

The book was turned into a film in 1974. Rather than employ professional actors, authentic Suffolk villagers were used instead, a move that angered Equity, the actors' union. The Equity problem was circumvented by doing away with a formal script and having the characters improvising all of their dialogue based upon Blythe's 20-page 'transcript'. It was a neat solution – using locals rather than trained actors ensured authenticity. Ronald Blythe, a lay preacher in real life, played the village vicar. The film was shot over the period of a year in order to reflect the changing seasons, and at weekends only, so that village actors could attend to their usual professions during the week. Once again, the village of Charsfield had a part to play and this was one of several villages in the Wickham Market area, south of the River Deben, that was used as a filming location. Hoo, Debach, Monewden, Dallinghoo, Letheringham and Pettistree were the others.

Like the book before it, the film was also highly acclaimed for its rural realism, and it was watched by 13 million viewers on its first television showing – quite an achievement for a film with no cast, no stars and no formal script.

example of the type of Suffolk mill in which the whole body revolves on its base. It dates from 1796 but was completely rebuilt in 1854 following wind damage, then resurrected yet again between 1957 and 1960. The Saxtead Green post mill also appears on the sign of the 17th-century

Greene King pub, the Old Mill House (📞 01728 685064) just east of the mill. Another post mill survives in the village of Framsden, further west along the A1120 and south at the B1077.

If you look in the porch of the 15th-century towerless All Saints' Church in **Saxtead** village you'll see a set of stocks and a whipping post. The stocks bear the none-too-gentle warning to 'Fear God and Honour the King', which is hardly what one might call a progressive attitude.

11 EARL SOHAM

Earl Soham lies a mile or two further west, at a point where the A1120 once again regresses to its original Roman form of an unstinting straight line. It's a sprawling, laid-back place with nice old cottages set back from the road. The village is home to the **Earl Soham Brewery** (📞 01728 861213 🖥 www.earlsohambrewery.co.uk), which started life in an old chicken shed at the village's Victoria pub but now brews in an old forge building opposite the village green. The brewery produces a cross section of ales that give fellow producers Adnams and Greene King a run for their money and range from Victoria, a light 'session beer', to winter-only Sir Roger's Porter and Jolabrugg, a stronger, Christmas-only 'Yule Brew'.

⫴ FOOD & DRINK

Victoria The Street 📞 01728 685758. Close to the Earl Soham Brewery, this whitewashed local on the village green serves up hearty pub food and its very own excellent ESB Victoria Ale in its sparsely furnished bar. It has an open fire, board games and Queen Victoria-themed pictures.

12 PARHAM

🛇 **The Orchard Campsite** Wickham Market (see page 215)

Head south along the B1116 from Framlingham and you soon arrive in **Parham**, a village that gave its name to a World War II US Air Force bomber airbase located between the village and its neighbour, Great Glemham. The airfield has the **Parham Airfield Museum** (📞 01728 621373 🖥 www.parhamairfieldmuseum.co.uk) that stands as a tribute to the 390th Bomb Group that was based here. Between 1943 and 1945, over three hundred bombing missions were flown from the base using B-17 'Flying Fortresses', and the bandleader Glenn Miller performed in a hangar here in 1944. The museum is free but has fairly limited opening hours – mostly Wednesdays and Sundays in summer – so check first if you want to visit. For many years now there have been proposals for a wind farm on the airfield – Suffolk's first onshore wind farm – with plans for six turbines. Not surprisingly, this has stirred something of a local storm although nothing has happened as yet.

A wonderful late 15th-century timber-framed fortified manor house lies close to the village: **Moat Hall** is now part of a farm but used to be the residence of the Uffords, the former Earls of Suffolk, and later the Lords Willoughby. You can walk up here along a footpath from the village church of St Mary the Virgin and enjoy some sweeping views along the way.

WEST OF EARL SOHAM TO STOWMARKET

Continue west along the A1120 from Earl Soham and you'll soon arrive at Peats Corner, a junction where the B1077 leads south to Framsden, with a recently reconstructed post mill, and past Helmingham Park to Otley, where you'll see a splendid 15th-century moated manor house, rather like the one at Parham. **Framsden** is a small village that has a church with splendid 14th-century misericord carvings, a doggy-sounding pub, the Dobermann Inn (it used to be the Greyhound!), and a corrugated iron-village hall. What it is probably best known for though is **Fox Fritillary Meadow** just north of the village. This is a six-acre unimproved meadow, owned and managed by the Suffolk Wildlife Trust, that is the largest known site for snake's head fritillaries in East Anglia. It's undoubtedly a spectacular sight but you'll need to be exact with your timing if you want to see it in its full glory as the meadow is only open to the public on a single annual open event in mid- to late April.

Otley Hall (✆ 01473 890264 🖱 www.otleyhall.co.uk) is open for pre-booked group visits and for individuals as part of the Invitation to View scheme (🖱 www.invitationtoview.co.uk), with about seven dates available each year. The ten-acre gardens at the hall, which contain historically accurate recreations that include an orchard, herber, knot garden and nuttery, are worth a look in their own right and are open to the public every Wednesday between 11.00 and 17.00 during the summer months. The extensive gardens at **Helmingham Hall** (✆ 01473 890799 ⌂ www.helmingham.com) are also open to the public on summer afternoons (Tue–Thu and Sun) and the 400-acre park has herds of both red and fallow deer.

13 DEBENHAM

Debenham comes as a surprise from whatever direction you approach. It stands amid an enormous prairie of golden wheat stretching almost as far as the horizon – quite a contrast to the softer, wooded parkland further to the east around Yoxford. It's a peach of a village with something of the Lavenham about it, although far less of the touristiness. Its buildings range from magpie-timbered Tudor to Suffolk pink to solid Georgian brick, while the High Street has some charming gardens open to the street, where roses and hollyhocks reach for the sky in a clash of pinks. Scattered among some pricey-looking Tudor properties are a handful of old-fashioned shops that seem little changed from the 1950s, as well as a clutch of antique shops, galleries and gift shops. Given all the desirable properties on show lining the street, it comes as no surprise that a disproportionate number of estate agents have set up shop here too.

Many buildings in the village that are now private houses also used to be shops, as evidenced by large windows and house names that reflect the property's former function – the Old Cobblers House and so on. The Red Lion on the High Street is a 15th-century jettied building that once served as a guildhall; although it still has its sign, it no longer functions as an inn. Elsewhere, the most substantial medieval buildings on the High Street are the Old House at number 23, which incorporates both of its former neighbours 21 and 25, and number 37, a 16th-century jettied building. The ancient-looking Market Cross, which served as the village's market hall in the 17th century, gets its name from reputedly occupying the site of a former Anglo-Saxon cross. Now an architects' practice and art gallery, its first floor was converted for use as a school by Sir Robert Hitcham in 1668. Leading off from Market Cross at the northern end of the High Street, Gracechurch Street has another splendid parade of handsome half-timbered dwellings.

Offering a break from an almost relentless Tudor-beam theme on the High Street is a large neoclassical chapel dated 1905 that bears the legend 'The Ancient Order of Foresters' on its portico. It is now an antiques showroom and once featured as the same in the popular *Lovejoy* television series. For fans of the series, generally women of a certain age if truth be told, Debenham with its Tudor splendour, antique shops and well-heeled eccentricity, must represent something of a spiritual home. It's the sort of place where grandfather clocks, corduroy trousers and Morris Travellers blend into the scenery.

The River Deben rises nearby to give Debenham its name and, known as The Butts, runs as a prolonged ford through the village with the claim that it is the longest of its kind in Britain. The extensive tracts of arable land that surround the town are a relatively new thing: historical accounts suggest that most of the surrounding land was pasture in the 18th century but hedges were enthusiastically grubbed up and trees felled later in that century to make way for cereals. Now the heavy, but highly fertile, clay soils produce exceptionally high yields of wheat and barley. If anywhere in the region deserves the epithet 'Suffolk's breadbasket', it is probably here.

The **Cyder House** at Aspall Hall just north of Debenham (www. aspall.co.uk) has been producing its own Aspall apple juice, cyder and organic cyder vinegar since 1728 so the Chevallier family who have run the place for eight generations should know a thing or two about what to do with apples. Aspall cyder is made only from freshly pressed apples and the notion of stretching fermentations by eking them out with concentrates is anathema.

A surprising variety of apple types are used for cyder making: dessert apples such as Cox or Blenheim Orange for sweetness, cookers like Bramley for aroma and acidity, and a mixture of bittersweet apples that might include varieties like Médaille d'Or and Kingston Black to provide perfume, depth and body. The spelling of 'cyder' rather than 'cider' goes back to the 1920s when an earlier member of the Chevallier dynasty, John Barrington ('JB') Chevallier (1857–1940) considered the 'y' version indicative of the style he was producing at the time. It's not all about alcohol – there's organic vinegar and apple juice too. Aspall apple juice is cold-pressed from a mash made from pre-blended apples that hail from most of the country's prime apple locations – Cambridgeshire, Kent and the Wye Valley. Cox and Bramley form the base and these are supplemented by varieties such as Egremont Russett, Discovery and Crispin to achieve the right balance of flavour and acidity.

¶¶ FOOD & DRINK

At one time Debenham had nine pubs; now just two remain open, the **Angel Inn** at 5 High Street (✆ 01728 861700) and **The Woolpack** at number 49 (✆ 01728 860516). There's an excellent deli and butcher's, **Neaves of Debenham** (✆ 01728 860240 🖰 www. neavesofdebenham.co.uk), at the crossroads at 21 Cross Green, which stocks all manner of fresh and cured meats as well as olives, cheeses and other products it assures 'you won't find on supermarket shelves'.

Deben Rose 6 High St ✆ 01728 860190 🖰 www.debenrose.co.uk. A posh florist that doubles as a café serving teas, coffees and locally baked cakes and biscuits.

Teapot Pottery and Café Low Rd ✆ 01728 860475. There's a small, cosy tea room ensconced within this ceramic teapot emporium.

Vanilla Bake House 7 High St ✆ 01728 861582. A café with sandwiches, rolls and other locally sourced home-baked produce.

14 NEEDHAM MARKET

A small town just southeast of Stowmarket and close enough to the A14, Needham Market's pride and joy is its **church of St John the Baptist** which has a quite astonishing double hammerbeam roof that has been described as 'the culminating achievement of the English carpenter'; certainly Pevsner waxed lyrical about it in his *Buildings of England: Suffolk*, saying 'the eye scarcely believes what it sees, and has a hard if worthwhile job in working out how this unique effect could be attained'.

Wool combing became big business here in the 15th and 16th centuries until the arrival of the plague in the 1660s. Chains were fixed at either end of the village to prevent the disease spreading to other communities – a noble gesture that wiped out two-thirds of the town's population. Chainhouse Road in the town commemorates this event, as does another road known as The Causeway, a more palatable variant of 'the corpseway' that was used to move plague victims out of town for burial at the church in nearby Barking.

Meanwhile the **River Gipping**, which flows to the east, makes a rewarding strolling ground. The river was navigable in the medieval period and was used to bring stone for the building of the abbey at Bury St Edmunds. Then in the late 18th century, the river was canalised and a series of 15 locks were set up between Needham Market and Ipswich so that barges could navigate between Stowmarket and the coast. The towpath of what became known as the Stowmarket Navigation is still in place today and you can walk all the way to Ipswich from here, or even better, from Stowmarket. The **Gipping Valley River Path** is a 17-mile walk if done in its entirety from Stowmarket railway station to Ipswich docks, an interesting and peaceful route past locks and old watermills. It's a long way but the beauty of it is that both ends can be easily reached by train. Indeed, the Norwich–Ipswich–London railway line runs parallel to the canal for much of the way.

A **farmers' market** (✻ www.needhamfarmersmarket.org) takes place in Needham Market every Sunday (Jun–Oct 13.00–17.00).

15 STOWMARKET

It was not at all unusual for towns in East Anglia to be destroyed by fire in the medieval period – the lethal combination of open fires and overcrowding made this a common enough occurrence especially in the 16th and 17th centuries when buildings were largely built of wood. Stowmarket bucked this trend though and, rather than be razed by fire, it was instead accidentally blown up when a gun-cotton factory exploded in 1871 taking quite a lot of the town along with it. Despite this considerable setback, this remains central Suffolk's largest settlement, a pleasant enough market town (with a market on Thursday and Saturday) but with little of special interest.

What stands out here, though, is the **Museum of East Anglian Life** (✆ 01449 612229 ✻ www.eastanglianlife.org.uk), on a 75-acre site close to the town centre. Its location might be a tad unromantic – next to a large branch of Asda; you can park in the supermarket car park – but the museum, or MEAL as it likes to call itself, wonderfully encapsulates all things rural East Anglia, with a range of reconstructed old buildings giving a historic perspective on traditional life in the region. These include windpumps and watermills as well as agricultural buildings. You'll see displays of local trades and crafts like brewing and rope-making as well as agricultural machinery and a collection of rare-breed animals such as Red Poll cattle and Suffolk Punch horses. MEAL stages special children's activity days in summer that include egg hunts, pond dipping and Victorian days. An annual CAMRA beer festival takes place in the museum's Abbot's Hall barn each year with a heady choice of East Anglian real ales and ciders. Special events like 'Steam and Grease Sunday', focus on steam machines, and family-friendly printing days also take place periodically. A traditional music day takes place in July, and in past years the museum has also staged a Gypsy arts festival with international artists.

¶¶ FOOD & DRINK

Osier Café Museum of East Anglian Life ☎ 01449 672266. With home-cooked food and outdoor trestle tables for fine weather this is a convenient place for a drink and a snack while visiting the museum.

Great Finborough, Buxhall & Rattlesden

Just west of Stowmarket, along the minor roads south of the A14 is a handful of attractive villages, and with an intricate spider's web of footpaths linking them. The first village to be reached is **Great Finborough**, which has a pub, the Chestnut Horse, and a flint church with an exotic-looking spire, St Andrew's. John Peel, the BBC DJ and broadcaster, lived for many years in the village in a house he dubbed 'Peel Acres'. His grave (inscribed with his real name of John R P Ravenscroft and the first line of his favourite song, 'Teenage Kicks' by The Undertones) lies in the village churchyard, itself graced with fine views of the surrounding countryside. Every Easter Monday the village hosts a highly competitive event called the Bog Race, involving the men of the village and from nearby Haughley. The race starts and ends at the pub and, not surprisingly, a great deal of boisterous drinking generally takes place.

Buxhall lies a little further on, an attractive yet relatively ungentrified village that still mainly serves a farming rather than an incomer community. As well as a pub, The Crown, and a church it has a converted, capped tower mill. A couple of miles northwest of Buxhall is **Rattlesden** tucked away in a gentle valley, a gorgeous little place with rows of neat thatched cottages and the church of St Nicholas high on a rise above the village.

NORTH OF STOWMARKET

16 MENDLESHAM

Northeast of Stowmarket close to the A140, Mendlesham is well known locally for its cloud-scraping television and radio mast, an ugly beacon for miles around, but there's more to the village than just towering steel. The **church of St Mary** is large for a village of this size and highly unusual in being the last surviving Anglo-Catholic parish church in the county, where Mass is celebrated daily and the biggest event in the religious calendar is the Feast of the Assumption. Not surprisingly, the airy interior is filled with candles, icons, several altars and the persistent whiff of incense. For those with more interest in cudgel-wielding than Catholic ceremony, there's also a fine and fierce woodwose (see page 43) in the northern porch, and a village armoury in the room above it that contains armour dating from between the 15th and 17th centuries that was kept for use by villagers in the event of an insurrection. You're supposed to have an appointment to view the armoury, but you might just get lucky.

In the village itself, by the village sign, a **preaching stone** is said to have been used as a platform by mendicant friars in the 14th century and later by followers of the preacher John Wesley in the 18th. No doubt, it has also been put to use on occasion by the odd reveller delivering an opinionated rant on his or her way home from the village pub. A large street fair takes place in the village on May Day bank holiday.

¶¶ FOOD & DRINK

The Deli & Café Chilli Farm, Norwich Rd, Mendlesham ☎ 01449 766344 ⌂ www. thedeliatthechillifarm.co.uk. With local produce to the fore, this is a good place to stop for breakfast, brunch or lunch. The deli stocks a wide selection of specialist chilli products, as you might expect.

17 THE MID-SUFFOLK LIGHT RAILWAY MUSEUM

Mid-Suffolk Light Railway Museum, Brockford Station, Wetheringsett IP14 5PW ☎ 01449 766899 ⌂ www.mslr.org.uk. Museum open Easter and May–Sep Sun and bank holidays.

Wetheringsett is Mendlesham's neighbour just across the A140. This is the home of the Mid-Suffolk Light Railway Museum at the village's former Brockford station (there used to be a stop at Mendlesham too). The MSLR, or 'Middy' as it was known, was inaugurated in 1904 and had ten stations along a line that transported passengers between Haughley, north of Stowmarket, and Laxfield. Closure eventually came in 1951, by which time almost all of the passengers were children on their way to and from school. The museum was set up in 1990 and has displays of artefacts, photographs and rolling stock. You also get to take a short ride in one of the carriages, hauled by an Edwardian steam engine.

18 THE THORNHAM ESTATE & THORNHAM PARVA

Å Swattesfield Campsite, Thornham Magna (see page 216)

A little further north and you reach the villages of **Thornham Magna** and **Thornham Parva** just west of the A140. Thornham Hall sits between the two villages, the original hall having been demolished in the 1950s, and the Thornham Estate offers 12 miles of waymarked walks through parkland, woods and farmland and water meadows known as **Thornham Walks** (✆ 01379 788700 🖥 www.thornham.org.uk), with maps available for £1 from the information board at the main car park. Thornham Walks also incorporate a Victorian **walled garden** that can be reached by a surfaced path from the car park suitable for wheelchairs and pushchairs.

For those wanting more than informal self-guided strolls, Thornham Walks' staff are able to organise bespoke guided walks and environmental activities for groups and even 'environmental birthday parties'. With so much management work and maintenance needing to be done, volunteers are always welcome. Helen Sibley, one of two staff members who manage access to the walks, told me, 'We rely heavily on volunteer help. We have a regular volunteer day on the last Sunday of every month and every Tuesday, plus we have a team of probationers who work here once every other week and on Sundays. The Walks always require more volunteers and no experience is needed, just enthusiasm.' Helen went on to explain how the Thornham Walks came into being. 'The late Lord Henniker retired from the diplomatic service and became involved with a variety of grant-making trusts, helping people living in deprived areas of London. He and his wife retired to Thornham Magna in the 1970s, where there was a shortage of both local jobs and affordable housing, and together they began a programme of diversification of the Thornham Estate in order to try to alleviate some of these problems. Redundant farm buildings were turned into reasonably priced workshops for small businesses, others into offices and some into houses.

The estate had few rights of way at the time and the Hennikers were determined to open it up to the public. Twelve miles of waymarked walks were created and these became known as Thornham Walks, which are now enjoyed by thousands of visitors each year. Lord Henniker's final project was the derelict walled garden. The walls were restored and the garden was planted as a walled orchard with extensive glass houses.' The walled garden now serves as a centre for people with disabilities to learn horticultural skills.

Special events take place throughout the year at the Thornham Walks, such as dawn chorus birdsong walks, butterfly walks and fungi forages, also guided walks in the Upper Waveney Valley and mid-Suffolk. Some events, like scarecrow building and pond dipping, are specifically geared towards children's interests.

As its Latin suffix suggests, Thornham Parva is the smaller of the twin villages. 'Little thorny village' has very few houses but it does have a remarkable thatched Saxon church, **St Mary's**, which is renowned not so much for its tiny size, its thatched roof or circular Saxon window, but for its 14th-century retable (altarpiece) – the largest surviving example from the medieval period – which managed to outlive the iconoclast reformers of the 16th century by hiding away, more or less forgotten, in a stable.

Lord Henniker of Thornham Hall rediscovered the work in a pile of wood in 1927 and presented it to St Mary's Church where his brother was parson. The altarpiece, restored by a Cambridge University team, dates from around 1300 and shows strong Dominican influence with representations of eight saints witnessing the Crucifixion, one of whom, to give it a noteworthy East Anglian context, is local hero St Edmund. The Musée de Cluny in Paris has another piece that would once have belonged alongside this, but the two sections became separated at the time of Henry VIII's Dissolution. The pronounced Dominican style suggests that both pieces originated from Thetford Friary in Norfolk, a 13th-century Dominican stronghold that has since disappeared and now lies under the foundations of Thetford Grammar School. In the churchyard is the grave of Sir Basil Spence, the architect of Coventry Cathedral.

¶¶ FOOD & DRINK

Forge Tearooms Thornham Walks ☎ 01379 783035. Close to the beginning of the walks, near the car park.

Four Horseshoes Wickham Rd, Thornham Magna ☎ 01379 678777. An attractive thatched building with plenty of exposed woodwork, this dining pub serves traditional English favourites and European dishes along with a decent choice of real ales.

Thornham Coach House Thormham Estate ☎ 01379 783373
⌂ www.thornhamcoachhouse.co.uk. In a converted coachhouse on the Thornham Estate, this is open (Thu–Sun 10.00–16.00; dinner Fri and Sat evenings) for light lunches, coffee and cakes, with roast lunches on Sundays.

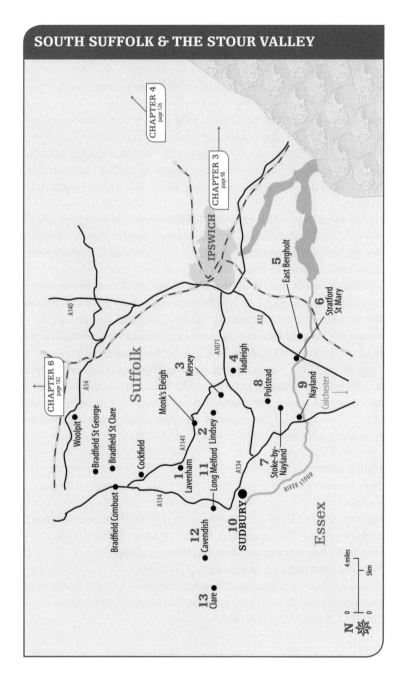

CHAPTER 4
page 126

CHAPTER 3
page 98

CHAPTER 6
page 182

IPSWICH

5
East Bergholt

6
Stratford
St Mary

A140

A12

A14

Suffolk

3
Kersey

A1071

4
Hadleigh

Monk's Eleigh

8
Polstead

9
Nayland

Colchester

A1141

2
Lindsey

Woolpit

Bradfield St George

Bradfield St Clare

Cockfield

1
Lavenham

11
Long Melford

A134

7
Stoke-by-
Nayland

Bradfield Combust

A134

10
SUDBURY

12
Cavendish

RIVER STOUR

Essex

13
Clare

N

0
0

4 miles
5km

5

SOUTH SUFFOLK &
THE STOUR VALLEY

This chapter covers the southern part of the county that includes the towns of Lavenham and Hadleigh and their hinterland as well as the Suffolk side of the Stour Valley (from East Bergholt and the Stour estuary in the east as far as Clare in the west) that stretches along the Suffolk–Essex border to the south.

In the south of the county, the Stour Valley is still very much a rural idyll, as the Stour babbles its way through fields of contented cattle and past improbably perfect-looking villages. A chocolate-box scene as painted by John Constable – and it was … many times over. It is not so much that Constable was a great painter – although he undoubtedly was – but *what* he painted. Though the healthy character of Constable's Suffolk has disappeared, the subject matter of many of his works is still easily identifiable almost two centuries later. This gives all of us a warm, fuzzy sense of continuity and tradition, and delights even those who do not normally have much time for paintings. Most of all, it somehow encapsulates the essence of rural England. The irony is that many who live here among the Stour Valley's timber-framed splendours are also those that have the most tenuous connections to the area – a classic incomers versus disgruntled locals dilemma. London and the Home Counties are sometimes just a little too close for comfort and the goose that laid the golden egg is in danger of being flattened beneath the wheels of a commuting 4x4. In the old days, geese would walk all the way to London from the area. There again, it was always just a one-way trip.

GETTING AROUND

It's easy enough in a car although meandering roads often mean that it takes longer to go from A to B than you might imagine. The main road leading to this part of the county from both north and south is the A12, which passes just to the west of Ipswich. The A1062 links the villages of the western part of the Stour Valley; the A134 connects Sudbury with Bury St Edmunds and Colchester across the Essex border; the A1071 connects Sudbury and Hadleigh with Ipswich; Lavenham is linked to Hadleigh and Bury St Edmunds by the A1171.

PUBLIC TRANSPORT

A useful **bus** route is the Beestons 236 service (Mon–Sat only) between Haverhill and Sudbury that passes through the villages of the western Stour Valley like Clare, Cavendish and Long Melford. Other services include the Chambers 374 bus that plies between Bury St Edmunds and Clare, the Beestons 90/91 between Ipswich and Sudbury via Hadleigh, and the Chambers 753/4/5 service between Sudbury and Bury St Edmunds via Lavenham. Sunday services tend to be non-existent.

For the Stour Valley, the most useful **railway** station is at Manningtree, which although lying just within Essex is close to East Bergholt, Flatford Mill and the long-distance Stour Valley Path. Manningtree lies on the main Norwich–Ipswich–London line and usually has trains every hour during the day. Sudbury has a branch line from Marks Tey in Essex from where there are connections to London.

CYCLING

Cycling is good in parts, especially away from the main routes that are best avoided. **National Cycle Route 1** and **North Sea Cycle Route** (⌂ www.sustrans.org) pass right through the locale from Hadleigh in the Stour Valley via Ipswich and Woodbridge to Beccles in the Waveney Valley, while **National Cycle Route 51** crosses the county from Ipswich to Bury St Edmunds. In the Stour Valley is part of the **National Byway** (⌂ www.nationalbyway.org), still in development in the region, running from Sudbury along the river west. Another option is the 69-mile **Painters' Trail** (⌂ www.dedhamvalestourvalley.org), which tours Constable Country in Dedham Vale. The website ⌂ www.dedhamvalestourvalley.org has several cycle routes with maps of the Stour Valley that may be downloaded for free. A reasonable number of connected bridleways can be used for off-road cycling too.

Escorted tours of the area are offered by Cycle Breaks (✆ 01449 721555 ⌂ www.cyclebreaks.com) and UK Cycling Holidays (✆ 01379 644818

TOURIST INFORMATION

East Bergholt Flatford, Flatford Lane ☎ 01206 299460
Hadleigh The Library, 29 High St ☎ 01473 823778
Lavenham Lady St ☎ 01787 248207
Sudbury The Library, Market Hill ☎ 01787 881320
Dedham AONB and Stour Valley Project ⌂ www.dedhamvalestourvalley.org

⌂ www.ukcyclingholidays.co.uk) who have a number of itineraries on offer. Cool Pedals (☎ 01206 325224 ⌂ www.coolpedals.co.uk) in Colchester is the nearest place to the Stour Valley for **cycle hire**; it can also provide trail guides for day cycling routes in south Suffolk.

WALKING

Pick your way around carefully and you'll find some worthwhile walking, especially along riverbanks. The Dedham Vale AONB and Stour Valley Project (⌂ www.dedhamvalestourvalley.org) gives a good selection of suggestions for walks in the Stour Valley area and has free downloadable guides on its website. One long-distance footpath passes through the area: the 60-mile **Stour Valley Path**, part of the European Path E2, begins at Cattawade near Manningtree in Essex and loosely follows the River Stour valley west through Sudbury to eventually reach Newmarket. John Harris's Walking in Suffolk website (⌂ www.walkinginsuffolk. co.uk) features a wealth of links to downloadable maps and walk guides.

LAVENHAM, HADLEIGH & AROUND

A little way north of the Stour Valley, this area has at its centre one of the most celebrated villages in the county. Many visitors that come here restrict themselves solely to Lavenham but the surrounding countryside is highly attractive in its own right and there is plenty more to be discovered along the quiet lanes of this corner of Suffolk.

1 LAVENHAM

🏠 **Lavenham Priory**, **Milden Hall** and **The Swan** (see pages 216)

The cherry liqueur in the Suffolk assortment box, Lavenham is the village that has showed up on a thousand calendars, jigsaws and chocolate boxes. With wobbly timber-framed cottages, flower-bedecked gardens and thatch galore, it's even more overwhelmingly gorgeous than the many lovely villages that grace the Stour Valley just south of here. Its beauty makes it almost unreal: the only things that do not seem to be half-timbered are the smart cars lining the cobbles – although you might see the odd Morris Traveller doing its best to complement the vernacular. Like a very rich, celebratory meal, too much exposure might induce a little artery thickening but as a once-in-a-while experience Lavenham is unparalleled – just don't even think of building a bungalow here, or opening a kebab shop.

Lavenham grew fat and rich on the medieval wool trade and by the early 16th century had become the 14th-wealthiest town in the country, a sort of medieval Knightsbridge, paying more tax than York or Lincoln. Prosperous merchants invested their fortunes in real estate and what would have been considered very desirable properties for the time. Then as now, close-studded timbers spoke of affluence, albeit for rather different reasons; living in a plastered cage of medieval woodwork did not come cheap. A decline in the town's fortunes came with the 16th century, thanks to undercutting by newly arrived Dutch weavers from Colchester, but it was this decline and the transferral of the weaving industry elsewhere that have managed to keep Lavenham so beautifully preserved. If it had had access to the new-fangled waterpower used in the west and northwest of England, or had been near a coalfield, its buildings would very likely never have survived so intact.

"With wobbly timber-framed cottages, flower-bedecked gardens and thatch galore, it's even more overwhelmingly gorgeous than the many lovely villages that grace the Stour Valley."

With an astonishing total of 361 listed buildings in the village, there is little point in my directing you to more than one or two: you can just potter around the rest at will. Although they've been meticulously restored, it seems remarkable that some of the timber-framed buildings are actually still standing given the eccentric tilt to the horizontal that some of them have. Some of the wobbliest houses, like the almost cartoon-like 'Cordwainers', can be seen at the corner of the High Street and Market Lane.

The all-white and quite spectacular **Guildhall** dominates the market square across from the Angel Hotel. This was the headquarters of the town's powerful Guild of Corpus Christi, and it's a hugely impressive

ART IN THE LANDSCAPE

In Suffolk, modern art can sometimes be found in the unlikeliest of places: alongside reed beds, on shingle beaches, beside woodland paths, in church stained-glass windows and on village signs.

1 Barbara Hepworth's unfinished Family of Man sculpture set alongside the reed beds at Snape Maltings. (PV) **2** Willy Lot's cottage at Flatford Mill on the River Stour, a famous subject of Constable's paintings. (LM) **3** This shell sculpture at Aldeburgh, made by local artist Maggi Hambling, bears a line from the libretto of Britten's *Peter Grimes* opera that was set in the former fishing town. (DF)

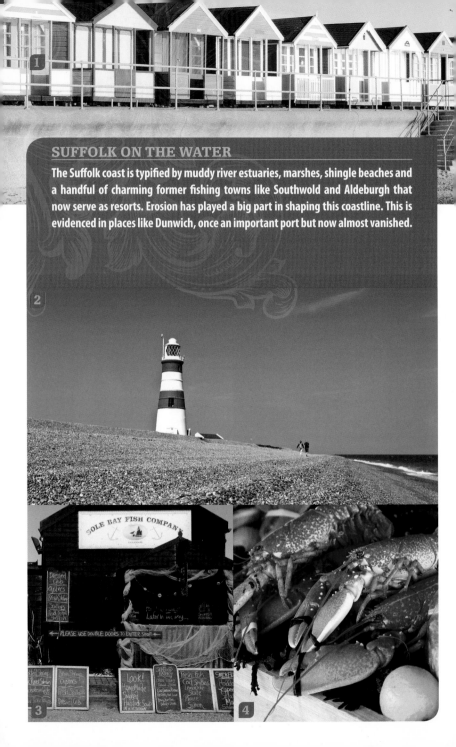

SUFFOLK ON THE WATER

The Suffolk coast is typified by muddy river estuaries, marshes, shingle beaches and a handful of charming former fishing towns like Southwold and Aldeburgh that now serve as resorts. Erosion has played a big part in shaping this coastline. This is evidenced in places like Dunwich, once an important port but now almost vanished.

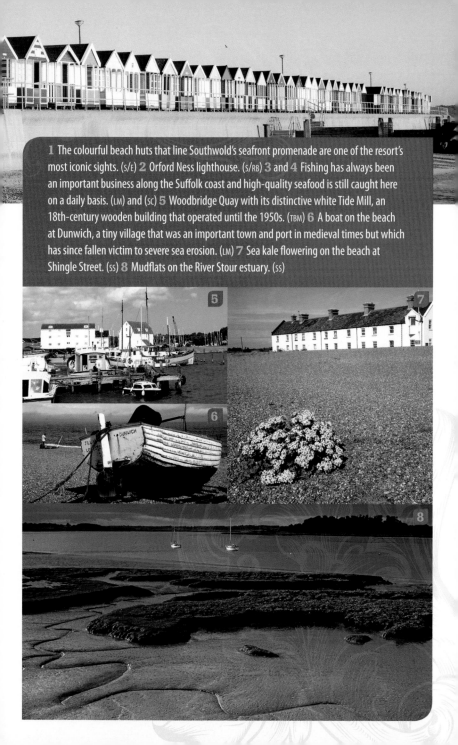

1 The colourful beach huts that line Southwold's seafront promenade are one of the resort's most iconic sights. (S/E) **2** Orford Ness lighthouse. (S/RB) **3** and **4** Fishing has always been an important business along the Suffolk coast and high-quality seafood is still caught here on a daily basis. (LM) and (SC) **5** Woodbridge Quay with its distinctive white Tide Mill, an 18th-century wooden building that operated until the 1950s. (TBM) **6** A boat on the beach at Dunwich, a tiny village that was an important town and port in medieval times but which has since fallen victim to severe sea erosion. (LM) **7** Sea kale flowering on the beach at Shingle Street. (SS) **8** Mudflats on the River Stour estuary. (SS)

Belle Grove

★ ★ ★ ★ ★

In a tranquil corner of rural Suffolk, we are excellently placed for exploring the coast including Southwold, Walberswick & Aldeburgh. Enjoy & explore that special combination of sky, sun, sea, dunes and marshes that has long attracted walkers, artists, musicians & writers. Not to mention the great foodie opportunities!

EXCEPTIONAL
EXOTIC
EXTRAVAGANT

Five star retreat near timeless Suffolk Heritage Coast

www.belle-grove.com

f telephone 01986 873124

16th- and 17th-century building that is whitewashed all over, beams and all. Now it serves as a National Trust museum (see below).The **Angel Hotel** on the other side of the square became the centre of a controversy in 2013 when its owner, celebrity chef Marco Pierre White, repainted the 1420 building in a Barbara Cartland-esque shade of pink that offended locals claimed was neither authentic nor appropriate. Such are the priorities of Lavenham. After bitter accusations that the Angel now 'looked like blancmange', the famously grouchy chef reluctantly agreed to repaint it the correct shade of pink after consultation with English Heritage. This was not the first time the chef had ruffled feathers in the village: when he first took over the Angel he refused to serve lager, claiming this encouraged the wrong kind of clientele.

The market square itself has some very fine Georgian houses to complement the Tudor and if you look down the steep street alongside the Angel, you'll see the lush folds of the valleys beyond. The town's church of **St Peter and St Paul** is, as you might expect, large and exceptionally grand. It was rebuilt in the late 15th century by a consortium of local families, who were no doubt willingly converting their wool-wealth into what might be termed 'medieval fire-insurance' – a generous gift to God to avert any possibility of a fiery afterlife. The flint tower seems enormous, 140 feet high and visible for miles, while the interior is lavish, with a chantry dedicated to St Catherine and St Blaise, who, martyred by being 'combed to death' by the emperor Diocletian, ended up becoming the patron saint of the wool trade.

To keep things real and bring a bit of muddy-booted rusticity into town, a **farmers' market** is held in the village hall on the morning of the fourth Sunday of each month. This has all manner of local products like bread from Sparling and Faiers, pork products from Clavering Pigs and free-range eggs from Manor Farm. Sometimes the falcons, owls and hawks from Lavenham Falconry (✆ 01787 249744 ⌂ www. lavhammewsfalconry.com) are on display outside – a rare opportunity to ruffle the feathers of a real-life raptor.

The Guildhall

Market Sq ✆ 01787 247646. Open Apr–Oct daily, Mar Wed–Sun, Nov weekends only; National Trust.

Otherwise known as the Guildhall of Corpus Christi, one of five guilds in the town, this dramatic white building is the jewel in the crown of

LAVENHAM ON THE SILVER SCREEN

If the village seems to be something of a living museum or film set then it will not come as any surprise to learn that Lavenham has featured as a backdrop for period dramas like Stanley Kubrick's *Barry Lyndon*, Michael Reeves's *Witchfinder General* and even Pasolini's *The Canterbury Tales* in the past. In the case of *Witchfinder General*, a witch-burning scene was shot in the market square, the same location as real burnings in the past.

Most famously the village was used in recent years as a stand-in for Godric's Hollow, the fictitious West Country village birthplace of both Harry Potter and his headmaster, Albus Dumbledore, and made an appearance in the film *Harry Potter and the Deathly Hallows, Part 1*. Any modern buildings caught messing up the magical Potter aesthetic were digitally edited from the final print, although there probably wasn't much to do given the homogeneity of the architecture here. The 'Potters' Cottage in Godric Hollow', a grade1-listed 14th-century building known as the De Vere House, has since become the second most-photographed doorway in the UK after 10 Downing Street. The house changed hands for a little less than £1 million in 2012. Lavenham's timber-framed other-worldliness certainly makes a convincing setting for schoolboy wizardry action – if you were looking to catch a game of Quidditch anywhere in England then this would probably be the first place you'd look. It almost goes without saying that episodes of *Lovejoy* were also filmed in the village in the past.

Lavenham's Tudor heritage. The guildhall was built around 1530 but by the end of the following century it was in use as a jail, a use which continued until the end of the 18th century when it was closed before later serving as a workhouse and almshouse. During World War II the building received evacuees and served as a restaurant and nursery before coming into the National Trust's care in 1951. As well as the timber-framed main hall, the first floor has an exhibition of Lavenham's wool-trade history and building tradition. You'll also find a tea room, a gift shop and a courtyard garden.

¶¶ FOOD & DRINK

Angel Hotel Market Pl ✆ 01787 247388 ⌂ www.wheelersangel.com. Lavenham's oldest inn, overlooking the splendid market place and guildhall, this has been renovated and refurbished by Marco Pierre White as part of the Wheeler's of St James franchise. All food uses locally sourced ingredients where possible. Both à la carte and bar menus are offered; there's a comprehensive wine list and Suffolk ales on handpump.

The Greyhound High St ✆ 01787 247475. The closest it gets to a straightforward drinking pub in Lavenham. This has good beer and decent standard pub food too.

Munnings Tea Room Gable End, 29 High St 📞 017860 519368 🖰 www.
munningstearoom.com. A smart traditional tea room serving good sandwiches and full
afternoon cream tea.

The Swan High St 📞 01787 247477 🖰 www.theswanatlavenham.co.uk. Various dining
options are available here: light lunch and bar bites in relaxed surroundings or top-range
fine dining in full medieval style in a high-ceilinged room with a minstrels' gallery.
Afternoon tea in the lounge, garden or brasserie here is quite special too. They even have
'deconstructed Black Forest gateau' – very postmodern. See also *Accommodation*, page 216.

Tickled Pink Tea Room 17 High St 📞 01787 248438. Said to be haunted, this cosy tea
room in a 16th-century timber-framed cottage serves all manner of snacks, cakes and
sandwiches.

2 LINDSEY

The countryside around Lavenham is rolling and picture-postcard
pastoral, especially along the narrow country lanes that lead off the main
A1141 to Hadleigh. If you turn right after Monks Eleigh the chances are
that after negotiating a few single-track roads that seem to go nowhere
you'll end up in the hamlet of Lindsey.

Similar to Worstead in Norfolk, this tiny village is associated with a
variety of cloth and Lindsey gave its name to a coarse cloth made of
linen and wool known as linsey-woolsey. It's hard to credit it with such
importance in the past given what you find on the ground – a tiny and
very attractive cluster of thatched cottages with a modest rustic church
that has no tower.

Head south from the village and at Rose Green veer east to discover
some barely visible earthworks and, hidden behind a hedge, the thatched
12th-century **chapel of St James**, now in the care of English Heritage.
The chapel was formerly the chantry of Lindsey Castle, of which the
aforementioned earthworks – effectively, just a trace of motte and bailey
– are now the only reminder. The chapel is not really visible from the
road and so quite easy to miss. You can park at the small lay-by next to
the English Heritage sign and then go through the gate that leads to the
entrance. Inside, it is bare but highly atmospheric.

Tracts of ancient woodland can also be found in the area. **Groton
Wood**, managed by the Suffolk Wildlife Trust, a couple of miles south
of Rose Green, is noted for its coppiced small-leaved limes and wild
cherry trees.

North of Lindsey, the village of **Monks Eleigh** is home to **Suffolk Heritage Orchards** (The Hall, Church Hill ✆ 01449 740478 ⌂ www. suffolkheritageorchards.co.uk), where George Hodgkinson, a retired City shipping lawyer, grows a bewildering number of old varieties of apples, greengages and plums. These include the apple varieties St Edmund's Pippin from Bury St Edmunds and Sturmer Pippin from Sturmer near Haverhill, as well as Coe's Golden Cop, a classic Suffolk plum. They produce four types of apple juice too and have a regular stall at Wyken Vineyards (see page 204) farmers' market each Saturday when apples and plums are in season.

¶ FOOD & DRINK

Bildeston Crown High St, Bildeston ✆ 01449 740510 ⌂ www.thebildestoncrown.co.uk. The sister pub of the Lindsey Rose, this hostelry east of Monks Eleigh and a few miles north of Lindsey and Kersey dates from 1529 and makes the most of the ancient beams, open fires and flagstones. Very much a pricey (and award-winning) gastropub with an ambitious evening tasting menu but a reasonable-value set menu is available too; a range of Suffolk real ales are on offer.

Lindsey Rose Lindsey Tye ✆ 01449 741424 ⌂ www.redroseinn.co.uk. With open beamed partitions and rich red décor, this 15th-century food-oriented inn has a set menu on weekdays, light bites Monday to Saturday and traditional roasts on Sunday. All dishes use the freshest, most seasonal and most local ingredients available including meat from the Rose's own farm.

Swan The Street, Monks Eleigh ✆ 01449 741391 ⌂ www.monkseleigh.com. With an imaginative menu that will satisfy traditionalists as well as foodies, this bistro-like gastropub has a good range of wines and Adnams on handpump. There's a good-value set menu Tuesday to Saturday and at Sunday lunchtimes. Local produce like Suffolk asparagus and Red Poll sirloin steak feature strongly.

3 KERSEY

Like its neighbour Lindsey, the village of **Kersey** has given its name to a type of cloth and 'kersey' describes a lightweight, coarse broadcloth of the sort used in military uniforms. Although the cloth was made in many other places it probably originated here. Kersey is widely regarded as one of the county's most photogenic villages. With an assortment of timbered weavers' cottages strung along its high street, a large wool-trade church and a quaint water splash at the bottom of the hill, it is a delightful scene on arrival from the north. The only thing that detracts

SUFFOLK PINK

Suffolk cottages are typified by their pastel pinkwash, a colour not generally common elsewhere in the country. Historically, the distinctive colour is said to be the result of adding pig or ox blood to traditional lime whitewash, the exact shade varying considerably according to the quantity added and because of natural pigments in the daub beneath. Sometimes juice from sloe berries was also added to produce a richer tone – there are some who argue that blood was never used and it was solely juice and red ochre that was used to create the colour.

Whatever the truth of this, these days the colour is far more standardised and widely available, blood-free, from Dulux and other proprietary paint manufacturers. The correct colour is important to both villagers and local authorities, and certainly not any shade of pink will do as chef Marco Pierre White discovered to his cost when he repainted his hotel in Lavenham (see page 162).

Interestingly, it would appear that Suffolk pink is a relatively new tradition, and the colour-washing of external walls was not widely practised until the late 19th century. Constable's Suffolk landscapes of the early 19th century show white or off-white plastered buildings, with not a hint of 'Suffolk pink' to be seen. So for true 'heritage' Suffolk read white, not pink.

from Kersey's Hovis-advert wholesomeness is the line of Range Rovers and their ilk parked along the street. Blame the Tudors – they were never very forward thinking when it came to 21st-century parking arrangements.

Edit this unavoidable modernity from your mind's eye and Kersey is indeed gorgeous. With pinkwashed cottages, pargeted walls, time-hardened beams and thatched roofs on show, it's an assembly that shouts out iconic Suffolk. The hill that dips down to the ford and then rises sharply up the other side to the church at the top is perhaps more archetypal Dorset but does set the scene off beautifully. Cue Hovis music … or the *Lovejoy* theme tune.

The ford at the bottom of the hill – a tributary of the River Brett and usually a damp squib of a thing that is just deep enough to wet your tyres – has a footbridge to one side of it. Next to this stands River House with a huge Elizabethan door. Just up from here is the village pub, The Bell, with bright hanging baskets prettifying its already handsome magpie-beam exterior. Across the ford at the top of the hill stands the church of **St Mary's**, which as so often in former wool towns and villages seems supersized in terms of a village of this size's needs.

¶¶ FOOD & DRINK

Bell Inn The Street ☎ 01473 823229 ⟨ www.kerseybell.co.uk. A lovely old inn dating from the 14th century that offers a choice of real ales, Aspall Cyder and locally sourced homemade pub food. Good-value daily specials and Sunday roasts.

4 HADLEIGH

East of Lavenham, halfway to Ipswich, Hadleigh is a small town set in gently rolling countryside. The River Brett flows through the town, rather wider here than it is at Lavenham and Monks Eleigh upsteam. From Hadleigh the river flows due south to reach its confluence with the River Stour near Stratford St John.

Like Lavenham, this compact market town has plenty of timber-framed wool-trade buildings, although Hadleigh is much less of a museum piece and more an everyday lived-in sort of place. Despite a considerable expanse of new estates north of the centre close to the A1071 bypass there's much of interest in the compact centre and it is worth making a diversion to look at the town's three-storeyed 15th-century Guildhall that once served as a poorhouse.

The most rewarding area for a stroll is along High Street, Queen Street, Church Street, Angel Street and Benton Street, which have a plethora of eye-catching old houses, some with pargeting. The **church**, as with all these wool towns, is very grand and St Mary's is the only large church with a spire in the county. The exterior bell is also Suffolk's oldest and inside the church you'll find a painting, *Head of Christ*, by Maggi Hambling, who was raised in Hadleigh – a far less controversial work than her Aldeburgh steel seashell sculpture (see page 46). There's a fine modern stained-glass memorial window too in memory of the parish's former rector, John Richard Betton. The aforementioned **Guildhall** complex (⟨ www.hadleightownhall.co.uk) lies on the south side of the graveyard. It currently serves as offices for the town council and an events centre; guided tours are available by prior arrangement. **Market day** in the town is on Friday morning.

A well-publicised campaign – 'Hands Off Hadleigh' – has been fought against Tesco for many years in the town – the supermarket chain first applied for planning permission to build in Hadleigh back in 1987. Until now, several applications and appeals later, they have been unsuccessful, although Tesco's world-domination strategy seems to have something of the samurai spirit about it and the company always seems to get what it

BOXFORD'S LIONESS & THE WALL OF DEATH

Just west of Hadleigh, the old weaving village of Boxford was once the home of George 'Tornado' Smith (1908–71), the son of a former landlord of the village's White Hart pub, who is acknowledged as being one of the first Englishmen to perform the gravity-defying 'Wall of Death' on a motorcycle in this country in the early 1930s. As well as taking his act to the Essex coastal resorts, Smith would also perform the feat in the pub garden for the amusement of the villagers.

To spice up his already quite spectacular act, he also sometimes carried a lioness in his sidecar. The lioness, Briton, who was taken for walks through the streets of Boxford, now lies buried in the pub garden; there's even a plaque to her memory.

wants in the end. For the time being though, it is Morrisons that has the sole supermarket franchise in the town.

A pleasant stroll along the **River Brett** can start from the medieval Toppesfield Bridge, the oldest working bridge in Suffolk, from where there is a signed riverside walk. An alternative here is to turn left to climb up to the wooded Broom Hill nature reserve and on to reach Constitution Hill. Another enjoyable walk leads along a **disused railway track** that passes through Raydon Great Wood and serves as an alternative detour for National Cycle Route 1.

¶¶ FOOD & DRINK

Angel Delights Tea Room 85 High St ℰ 01473 828191 🖱 www.angel-delights.com. A traditional tea room with delicious cakes, quaint décor and bone china cups and teapots.
The George 52 High St ℰ 01473 822151 🖱 www.thegeorgehadleigh.co.uk. A former coaching inn with decent honest pub grub made mostly using local produce and Suffolk ales on tap.
The Hadleigh Ram 5 Market Pl ℰ 01473 822880 🖱 www.thehadleighram.co.uk. No longer a pub as such, this upmarket town-centre restaurant offers a wide-ranging menu and extensive wine list.

Wolves Wood

This RSPB reserve, three miles east of Hadleigh just north of the main Ipswich road, is a remnant of ancient woodland that is managed by traditional coppicing. The dawn chorus is said to be quite something here in spring, with up to 20 species of bird singing, including garden warblers and nightingales. In the summer months, butterflies and dragonflies abound in the rides around the ponds. A one-mile nature trail leads from the car park. Dogs are not allowed.

THE STOUR VALLEY: EAST BERGHOLT TO SUDBURY

Working east to west along the Stour Valley, Suffolk's southern border with Essex, I begin with what is one of Suffolk's best-known villages, East Bergholt, before following the valley west through Nayland to Sudbury.

5 EAST BERGHOLT

Forever remembered as John Constable's birthplace, East Bergholt, and Flatford Mill in particular, are major honeypots for visitors to Suffolk. East Bergholt is both a beginning and an end: for walkers, the **Constable County Trail** starts here and passes past Flatford Mill and across the Stour on its way to Dedham in Essex. Flatford village is also the last place along the river's Suffolk bank before it widens to an estuary at Manningtree, although you might argue that the bridge at Cattawade, where the Stour starts to become tidal, has this honour.

East Bergholt is a largish village, just north of the river but close enough to Essex to have a Colchester postcode. Although the village also deserves a place in history for its tradition of Protestant radicalism in the 16th century, it is, of course, the painter John Constable who has really put the place on the map by not only being born here but also immortalising numerous local views in his paintings. His place of birth was demolished years ago and now just a plaque marks the site – but you can see a memorial window to the artist and his wife in the tower-less church of **St Mary** (with its unusual 16th-century wooden bell house, apparently constructed when the church ran out of money for the proposed bell tower) next door. If you venture down the high street towards the Red Lion, you can also see Constable's first studio next to a garage and engineering workshop. The cottage opposite the pub has a sign that says 'Dealer in Hatts' and another that says 'Ye Olde House', just in case you weren't sure. There's a handy bus stop by the pub with services to Colchester, Ipswich, Manningtree and Hadleigh.

Many visitors to East Bergholt head straight to **Flatford** by the river, down a narrow, leafy lane that follows a one-way system, a sensible

EAST BERGHOLT
& JOHN CONSTABLE (1776–1837)

As a schoolboy, Constable would have crossed the Stour and walked through the meadows from East Bergholt to the grammar school in the Square at Dedham. One of his earliest paintings is of the headmaster, who encouraged his pupil's artistic potential, though it is hard now to imagine that Constable's masterly landscape paintings were once so little appreciated that he sold only 20 in England in his lifetime, and had to wait until the age of 52 to be elected to the Royal Academy.

As a young man he loved to paint the details around his home of Flatford Mill – 'willows, old rotten planks, slimy posts and brickwork' – subjects so far from the more fashionable subjects of brooding forests, mountains and medieval ruins that they were scarcely considered picturesque at all. At the same time he was disinclined to emulate fellow Suffolk artist Thomas Gainsborough (see page 176), born some 50 years before and whom he much admired, in using his landscapes as the backgrounds to portraits of fashionable folk: he preferred (and was criticised for) showing farm workers and animals going unselfconsciously about their daily business in a real setting. As his own brother commented, 'When I look at a mill painted by John I see that it will *go round*, which is not always the case with those by other artists.'

Constable returned to East Bergholt each summer, renewing his happy associations with the place: 'I love every stile and stump, and every lane in the village,' he remarked. It was here that he developed his very individual techniques for painting directly from nature: he was probably the first artist to sketch in oils in the open air, and he influenced many successors including the French Impressionists of the late 19th century. Constable's towering trees in full leaf and huge skies with rolling, stormy clouds are still a very recognisable part of the late summer scene.

precaution given the numbers that come here. At the end of the lane are a large car park and a path down to the river where you'll find a small Constable museum, a tea room and, a little further along, **Flatford Mill** itself and **Willy Lot's cottage**. Both the mill and the cottage are immediately identifiable from the paintings.

The best view of the mill is from across the river, so cross over on to the Essex bank and walk a little way along it. You are unlikely to be alone, especially in summer, especially on a Sunday. **Rowing boats** for hire can be found at the bridge alongside, quite likely, aspiring artists with easels doing their own take on the Constable theme. Pollarded willows and cud-chewing cows in the fields help complete the bucolic setting.

It is only a two-mile walk from here into **Dedham**, which has a fine wool-trade church and **Castle House**, an art museum (✆ 01206 322127 🖰 www.siralfredmunnings.co.uk) dedicated to the work of Sir Alfred Munnings in the artist's former home, where there is also a tea room and gardens.

¶¶ FOOD & DRINK

Bridge Cottage Tea Room Flatford ✆ 01206 298260. A conveniently placed riverside tea room next to the footbridge and close to Willy Lot's cottage.

Essex Rose Tea Room High St, Dedham ✆ 01206 323101. Across the river in Essex, this is a good place to stop for a snack, homemade cakes or afternoon cream tea.

Red Lion The Street ✆ 01206 298332. This village pub has well-kept local beers, decent pub grub and 'huffas' (large filled rolls) at lunchtimes.

6 STRATFORD ST MARY

This village, which featured in many of Constable's paintings, is the most southerly village in Suffolk (although Landguard Point near Felixstowe lies slightly further south). It lies along the old London coaching road and so used to be a popular stop for herders marching their geese, turkeys and cattle south to market at London. Such was the volume of trade here in the past that the largest of the village's four inns was reputed to have extensive stabling for up to 200 horses, while another had 20 acres of pasture for cattle passing through. The trade has now gone, of course, but the through road remains – the frenetic A12, which unhappily divides the bulk of the village from its church. Stratford St Mary is certainly a pretty village, with plenty of splendid half-timbered Tudor buildings, but you cannot quite escape the rumble and swish of lorries and cars speeding past on their way to and from Colchester. These days, three pubs remain – The Swan, The Anchor and The Black Horse.

¶¶ FOOD & DRINK

Hall Farm Straford St Mary C07 6LS ✆ 01206 322572 🖰 www.hallfarmshop.co.uk. A combined farm shop, delicatessen and butcher's, close to the village's St Mary's Church and which has won several food awards. This has an excellent choice of quality local meats, free-range poultry, home-grown seasonal vegetables, freshly baked bread and all manner of deli items. A café serves meals and snacks made with seasonal local produce from the farm shop.

7 STOKE-BY-NAYLAND

🏠 **Gilly Parva** (see page 216)

Continuing west, either by road or on foot along the Stour Valley Path, you soon arrive in Stoke-by-Nayland, set away from the river on top of a hill. The church of **St James** here, with its 120-foot tower, is a beacon for miles around and Constable featured it in a number of his paintings, although not necessarily in exactly the same landscape.

One of his most famous paintings, *Stoke-by-Nayland Church*, features the church illuminated beneath a dramatic rainbow. An earlier visitor, the puritan William 'Smasher' Dowsing, was less enthusiastic about art and destroyed countless 'superstitious' pictures within the church along with some 15th-century glass. Someone, perhaps Dowsing, perhaps another puritan, has also done their best to damage the alabaster tomb of Lady Anne Windsor, leaving a chipped nose and broken hand.

"The church of St James, with its 120-foot tower, is a beacon for miles around and Constable featured it in a number of his paintings."

The village is peaceful and highly good-looking, glowing with Suffolk pink; the churchyard is a lovely spot to watch the swallows and house martins that swoop around the tower. A footpath leads between some handsome timbered houses opposite and, if you ignore the sign pointing to 'Cherry Wood', you can continue across the tops of fields and enjoy a view down to the valley below. Seen from here, you realise that Stoke-by-Nayland is quite an elevated village by East Anglian standards. If you retrace your steps and then follow the sign and footpath down to the valley, you'll eventually end up in Nayland, albeit by a rather circuitous route.

🍴 FOOD & DRINK

The Crown Park St ☎ 01206 262001 🖥 www.crowninn.net. With low-ceilinged, rambling rooms, The Crown offers a seasonal menu combining traditional and contemporary. It has an outstanding wine list, Adnams ales in the bar, and a sunny terrace for warm weather.

8 POLSTEAD

Just north of Stoke-by-Nayland, on the other side of the shallow valley of the River Box, a tributary of the Stour, is Polstead. The village is infamous as the location of the **Red Barn Murder** of 1827 in which a local farmer's boy, William Corder, murdered his lover. The story captured

A walk in Constable Country

✳ OS Explorer map 196; start: Manningtree station, grid reference TM094322.

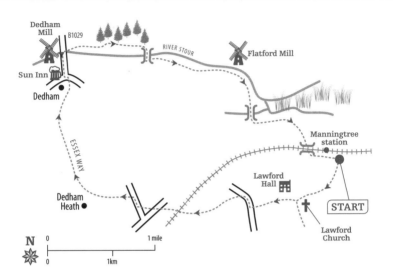

This seven-mile walk sneaks into Essex. Actually that's an understatement: most of it is in Essex, but it sums up the gentle charms of the Stour Valley so well that it's well worth the stray over the county border. Also, despite its requiring quite a bit of field-crossing, the southern part of the route follows the Essex Way, which is mostly waymarked (it's still a good idea to take the OS map).

the imagination of the people thanks to its publication in the penny dreadfuls and when Corder was later caught and subsequently hanged at Bury St Edmunds, his execution attracted a huge audience. Given the macabre tastes of the time, this wasn't the end of it: his skin was used to bind a copy of the trial proceedings (which can be seen along with his scalp in Moyses Hall Museum, Bury) and souvenir hunters squabbled over pieces of the hangman's rope, which sold for a guinea an inch, and even chipped away the victim's tombstone. A melodramatic play based on the events, *Maria Marten or The Murder in the Red Barn*, remained hugely popular throughout the mid 19th century and was resurrected as a 1935 British film.

The route starts at Manningtree station, and heads out through the car park on the south side, where a rising path leads up to Lawton church. Here you join up with the Essex Way, which traces an intricate and nicely varied route past Lawford Hall, a Georgian-looking pile concealing an Elizabethan core, and over the Shir Burn and railway to reach Dedham. In this gorgeously handsome village street, you can take a look at the fine wool trade church of St Mary's and perhaps also visit **Castle House** (✆ 01206 322127 ⁂ www.siralfredmunnings. co.uk), the former home of painter Sir Alfred Munnings and now an art museum open to the public on three or four afternoons a week in summer; it has the largest collection of Munnings' paintings anywhere.

Dedham has plenty of places to stop for a drink or a bite to eat, although they tend mostly to be rather upmarket: Essex Rose Tea Room (✆ 01206 323101) on the high street is a good choice, or for something smarter and more formal, Dedham Boathouse (✆ 01206 323153 ⁂ www.dedhamboathouse) or the **Sun Inn** (✆ 01206 323351 ⁂ www.thesuninndedham.com), which although a distinctly elegant (and much-liked) dining venue is also a place where you can just pop in for a pint of Adnam's or one of the other regional brews on offer.

Leaving Dedham, head north on the B1209, past Dedham Mill and over **Dedham Bridge**; follow the Stour Valley Path along the famous water meadows of **Dedham Vale** immortalised by Constable; kingfishers make the occasional appearance, and snipe and redshank frequent the marshes. Recross the river just before Flatford Mill and follow the St Edmund Way back to Manningtree station.

A more cheerful association is the small sweet cherry variety, known as **Polstead Black,** that used to grow here and which is thought to have originally been brought to the area by Romans. Cherries are commemorated in several place names around here: Cherry Meadow, Cherry Farm, Cherry Billy's Lane; and there used to be a cherry fair too, on the village green each July. Cherry growing is, alas, no longer big business, although some local gardens still have their own Polstead Black cherry trees. There used also to be an ancient oak tree in the village – the **Gospel Oak** – that was considered to be the oldest tree in Suffolk at around 1,300 years old and the scene of Saxon worship back in the 7th century when it may have been planted by St Cedd or one of his followers. The oak collapsed in 1953 but its remains can still be seen between St Mary's Church and Polstead Hall near the war memorial. St Mary's Church is distinguished in not only having a beautiful location but also in being the only surviving medieval stone spire in Suffolk. The pub on the village green, the Cock Inn, dates from the 17th century, although the original pub was next door. The Cock Inn once served as premises for the local assizes and the Red Barn murder inquest took place here. Alongside all this talk of long-standing tradition, it's worth mentioning that the **community shop** on the green next to the village hall is the oldest in Suffolk and second oldest in England, dating from 1984. The shop also doubles as the village post office, open mornings only. You can buy local **apple juices** here, made from Polstead apples at nearby Willow Farm, which also has its own farm shop (℡ 01787 211883) at Polstead Heath north of the village.

"The community shop on the green next to the village hall is the oldest in Suffolk and second oldest in England."

ᵢ FOOD & DRINK

The Cock Inn The Green ℡ 01206 263150. This old village inn has real ale, an open fire and decent pub food. It is closed on Mondays.

9 NAYLAND

Down in the valley itself on a lovely stretch of the Stour, Nayland is another fine village of timbered and colour-washed cottages. It's not quite Lavenham but it's not that far off in visual appeal, with timber-framed and pinkwashed cottages every way you look.

Across the Nayland Bridge, a footpath along the opposite bank follows the river west past a weir – part of the Stour Valley Path that leads to Wissington, with its Norman church, where the path crosses into Essex. As a reminder that you are still in Constable Country, St James's Church has an altarpiece by the artist: *Christ Blessing the Bread and Wine*.

ᵢ FOOD & DRINK

Anchor Inn 26 Court St ℡ 01206 262313 ⌂ www.anchornayland.co.uk. This traditional, yellow washed pub has a delightful setting next to the bridge over the River Stour. There's plenty of local produce on offer like home-reared lamb, duck, pork and beef, and a range of real ales that include Adnams and other guest ales. A 'beer ballot' allows the bar customers to vote on which beers they want the pub to serve – all very democratic!

THE STOUR VALLEY: SUDBURY TO CLARE

Continuing west along the Stour Valley, Sudbury, Long Melford, Cavendish and Clare come in fairly fast succession. Sudbury is by far the largest of these.

10 SUDBURY

🏠 **Mill House** (see page 216)

The largest of the wool towns in this part of Suffolk, Sudbury is a busy place, with traffic streaming through its centre and local shoppers competing for parking spaces in the central square below the church. Despite the town's glorious wool-trade past and its later artistic connections Daniel Defoe was not at all impressed with what he found at Sudbury when he visited here in the early 18th century, 'I know nothing for which this town is remarkable, except for being very populous and very poor.' Clearly he came to the town prior to what must have been a considerable revival as the town is a wealthy-enough-looking place today, with plenty of showy civic buildings and solid private dwellings on show.

Among a rich mix of architectural styles Georgian buildings tend to dominate. One fine example of these is **Gainsborough's House** (see page 176), the solid 18th-century house that now serves as a museum to the town's most famous son, Thomas Gainsborough, born here in 1727. A prominent bronze **statue** to the artist, palette and paintbrush in hand, stands at the top of the market square next to the imposing tower of the **church of St Peter**.

One of three medieval churches in the town centre, St Peter's was built as a chapel of ease to **St Gregory's Church**, which stands some distance away close to the river. St Peter's is no longer used for religious purposes but it still has a role to play in town life serving as an occasional venue for concerts, craft fairs and farmers' markets. The market square next to the church hosts a twice-weekly market on Thursdays and Saturdays.

The third of Sudbury's churches, **All Saints'**, can be found a little way south of the centre. The churchyard here has a large mausoleum to the Gainsborough family, who were wealthy merchants in the town long before Thomas took up a paintbrush, although Thomas himself is buried in London.

THOMAS GAINSBOROUGH, LANDSCAPE ARTIST

Although he is generally better known as a society portraitist, Thomas Gainsborough started his career as a Suffolk landscape artist and his early works such as *Cornard Wood* (now in the National Gallery), with its waving trees and stormy sky, were a great influence on the younger artist John Constable (see page 169).

Gainsborough remained fond of including landscapes as backgrounds to his portraits: in *Mr and Mrs Andrews*, also in the National Gallery, the fashionably dressed sitters are off to one side of the painting, while their newly harvested cornfield – at the Auberies, a farm estate near Sudbury – glows equally prosperously alongside them.

It is easy to escape Sudbury's gentle bustle. As well as the river stroll outlined below there is also a very pleasant 3½ mile **meadow walk**, the first part of the longer **Gainsborough Trail** that starts at Friar's Meadow and follows the old railway track over the river to reach a pumping station before following the river north through water meadows to arrive at Brundon Mill where the trail rejoins the old railway track that is followed south back to the starting point. The trail is signed with waymarks 6+and you have a reasonable chance of seeing wildlife like kingfishers, grass snakes and water voles along the way.

Gainsborough's House

46 Gainsborough St, CO10 2EU ✆ 01787 372958 🖱 www.gainsborough.org. Closed Sun.

This museum and art gallery occupies the house where the artist was born and fittingly the walls are filled with his paintings, both commissioned portraits of the gentry and local landscapes painted at various times in his career. Although the collection does not include masterpieces like *The Blue Boy* and *Mr and Mrs Andrews*, which are on display elsewhere in leading art galleries, this is the largest collection of Gainsborough paintings on show in any one place, and the setting of the house where the artist grew up provides added poignancy. Its Gainsborough memorabilia include his books and studio cabinet on which he would grind colours, as well as personal items like his swordstick and pocket watch. Special exhibitions, printmaking workshops and lectures are held here. There's also a café and gift shop close to the visitors' entrance.

The walled garden has as its centrepiece a 400-year-old mulberry tree that was planted during the reign of James I who used to encourage the planting of such trees with the aim of establishing a silk industry in England. Unfortunately, the king was unaware that it was the white mulberry tree that fed silkworms, not black mulberries like this one, which supplies edible fruit. The tree still produces a fine crop most years.

The tourist information centre has a **Town Trail** that describes the town's buildings, and the **Talbot Trail**, a series of small bronzes to follow around the centre of town, tells of Sudbury's past.

A stroll beside the **river** is hard to beat on a fine summer's afternoon. Continue down Gainsborough Street past the museum and you'll soon arrive at a footbridge across the River Stour from where you can wander south down to Ballingdon Bridge or north to Brundon Mill. At the Quay, south of Friars Street, you can take river trips on the *Rosette*, an electric boat run by the River Stour Trust (✆ 0845 8035787 ⌂ www. riverstourtrust.org; Easter–Oct, Sun and bank holidays). These go downriver to Cornard, where there is a visitor centre, and on to The Swan at Great Henny.

¶¶ FOOD & DRINK

Sudbury has a decent choice of pubs, restaurants and cafés. The suggestions listed below tend to stand out from the crowd in one way or another. **Sudbury Farmers' Market** takes place at St Peter's, Market Hill, on the last Friday of the month.

The Angel 43 Friars Gate ✆ 01787 882228 ⌂ www.theangelsudbury.co.uk. The Angel is one the town smarter restaurants, offering reasonable value set menus and à la carte mains featuring seasonal local produce. There's a garden for summer dining.

The Brewery Tap 21 East St ✆ 01787 370876 ⌂ www.thebrewerytapsudbury.co.uk. Sudbury's only free house, this has a choice of eight real ales on tap as well as snacks that include gammon baps, pork pies and homemade Scotch eggs. You can also order cooked food from a nearby take-away and the pub will provide plates and cutlery.

Granary Quay Lane ✆ 01787 313000. A tea room run by the River Stour Trust; open Easter until the end of October on Sundays and bank holidays and Wednesday afternoons in August. Proceeds go to restoration and conservation of River Stour Navigation.

Secret Garden Tea Room 21 Friars St ✆ 01787 372030 ⌂ www.tsg.uk.net. A quality tea room with a strong French theme and a blackboard with daily specials. Local seasonal produce is used as much as possible, and work by local artists and photographers is usually on display on the walls.

11 LONG MELFORD

As you head north from Sudbury, Long Melford is almost like a continuation of the same place: a long, linear village of thatched Suffolk pink with more than a few antique shops and booksellers lining the high street. **Melford Hall** (open Wed–Sun; closed during winter), an Elizabethan country house belonging to the National Trust, lies north of the village next to a large open green that was the site of a Whitsun horse fair, the largest in East Anglia, in the 19th century. Beatrix Potter was once a regular visitor to the hall and Elizabeth I stayed here in 1578.

The village's **Holy Trinity Church**, an enormous 15th-century Perpendicular edifice brimming with medieval stained glass, lies north of the green – you need to get quite close before it reveals itself fully. Here is living proof that Long Melford was once one of the very richest places in the land thanks to the success of the wool trade. The church contains chapels to three of its wool tycoon benefactors – the Cloptons, the Cordells and the Martyns – and with an attached Lady Chapel, it's effectively two buildings in one – more like a cathedral than a parish church. Simon Jenkins gives it a five-star rating in his book *England's Thousand Best Churches*, the only church in Suffolk to rate so highly.

Kentwell Hall & Gardens

Long Melford CO10 9BA 📞 01787 310207 🖰 www.kentwell.co.uk. Open Easter to end Sep; mid-Jul to end Aug daily, rest of year Sat and Sun; discounts available with online booking.

A little way north of Long Melford's Holy Trinity Church, Kentwell Hall is a grand moated Tudor mansion complete with a brick rose maze and a walled garden containing a herb garden, a potager and a large variety of espaliered apples and pears. The extensive grounds hold ancient yews and cedars, a shrubbery, a ha-ha wall and a three-quarter-mile-long avenue of lime trees. An unhurried wander through the **grounds** reveals an ice house, a camera obscura and even an 'alchemist's hut' tucked away in a clump of yews. In the **rare-breed farm** based in the old dog kennels by the moat, you'll find Norfolk Horn sheep, Longhorn cattle and Suffolk Punch horses.

The hall and gardens host plenty of **special events** like Tudor re-enactment days, Dickensian evenings and musical performances.

ⵆ FOOD & DRINK

Black Lion The Green 📞 01787 312356 🖰 www.blacklionhotel.net. On a corner of the village green, this 17th-century inn has classy dining in either a smart restaurant with antique fittings or a more informal front restaurant. For a special treat, it's the place to come for the ultimate cream tea.

Crown Inn Hall St ✆ 01787 377666 🖰 www.thecrownhotelmelford.co.uk. A free house with a fine selection of ales and a daily changing seasonal menu with contemporary British cuisine, as well as sandwiches or baguettes in the bar. The large courtyard garden is ideal for al-fresco dining.

Tiffin's Tea Emporium Drury House, Hall St ✆ 07854 355098 🖰 www.tiffins-tea-emporium.co.uk. The place to come for homemade cakes scones and, naturally, tea, of which you have a bewildering number of varieties to choose from – all loose-leaf, of course.

12 CAVENDISH

Cavendish, due west of Long Melford further along the Stour Valley, is exceptionally pretty and, understandably, perhaps just a little bit given to vanity, with neatly grouped thatched pink cottages facing a large village green with the church juxtaposed behind them. Dotted along the high street are a handful of smart eating places, a pub above the green and an antique shop or two.

The village was not always so peaceful. During the Peasants' Revolt of 1381, John Cavendish, who came from the village, killed the rebel leader Wat Tyler with his sword at Smithfield in London. Irate local peasants decided to take their revenge on Cavendish's father, Sir John Cavendish, who was lord of the manor in the village. Sir John attempted to plead for sanctuary at **St Mary's Church** while hanging onto the door handle but was finally caught up with at Bury St Edmunds where he was beheaded by the mob. The very same handle supposedly hangs from the door of the village church today. Both Sue Ryder, who founded her international charitable organisation, the Sue Ryder Foundation, here and Leonard Cheshire, her husband, the World War II pilot who set up homes for disabled people, are buried in the village.

🍴 FOOD & DRINK

Bull Inn High St ✆ 01787 280245 🖰 www.thebullcavendish.co.uk. A traditional English pub with Adnams beers and reasonably priced standard pub fare.

13 CLARE

🏠 **Cobbles** (see page 216)

Another fine medieval wool town, this is perhaps my favourite of all the places along the Stour Valley. Particularly striking is the 15th-century **Ancient House** (🖰 www.clare-ancient-house-museum.co.uk) which has luxuriant white pargeting (see page 117) like the sugar icing on a fancy cake. A date of 1473 on the wall no doubt refers to the date of the house itself rather than the pargeting, which would be at least a couple of centuries later. The house now serves as a **museum** with local history displays and exhibits from archaeological digs in the area.

Directly opposite is the church of **St Peter and St Paul**, a fine Perpendicular building in which Henry VIII and Catherine of Aragon have bespoke pews bearing their crests. On the wall next to the porch a sundial dated 1790 is inscribed 'Go about your business', which might be interpreted as 'Back to work, peasants, now that you have paid your respect to God'. I found that the sundial seems to tell the time with uncanny accuracy (once you allow for correction to British Summer Time), as does the chiming clock on the tower. Inside the porch is a Green Man boss and, even more mysteriously, above the entrance to the church, an upside-down figure that some consider to be a rare example of a Green Woman.

The **town centre** is compact and businesslike, and wears its history lightly. Daniel Defoe, writing back in the early 18th century, described Clare as 'a poor town and dirty' but neither of these adjectives applies today. Thankfully, neither can Clare be described as a museum piece, which some of the settlements further east along the Stour Valley are in danger of becoming as locals move out and Home Counties money moves in. This is commendable when you consider that Clare has the third-largest number of listed buildings in Suffolk (after Bury St Edmunds and Lavenham) and has somehow managed to hang on to its identity without polishing it up for the tourist market. This is no Tudor Disneyland. Walking up the high street past the Swan Inn you will find all the outlets and amenities you'd expect in a self-contained and not particularly touristy market town: an independent bookshop, Harris and Harris Books (✆ 01787 277267 🖳 www.harrisharris.co.uk), a couple of antique shops and an old-fashioned ironmongers, the sort of place you can buy individual nuts, bolts and door hinges. Around the corner, surrounding the market place on Market Hill is a traditional butcher's and what appears to be the town's liveliest pub, the Bell Hotel.

"Clare has the third-largest number of listed buildings in Suffolk and has somehow managed to hang on to its identity without polishing it up for the tourist market. This is no Tudor Disneyland."

A couple of minutes' walk from the town centre, **Clare Castle Country Park** has the stone remains of a 13th-century Norman castle keep on top of a mound overlooking the town. A footpath spirals up to the top and, although there is not that much to see in terms of historic remains, it is worth the climb for the view south over the rooftops of Clare back to the church of St Peter and St Paul, and north across the valley into the sheep-grazed fields of Essex beyond. Clare's former railway station stands within the inner bailey of the castle; a small display on the town's railway history is inside a former goods shed. The park also serves as the gateway for a 3½-mile waymarked circular walk as well as a shorter historic town trail.

If you return to the entrance of the country park and take the footpath that leads down to the river by the antique shop you'll soon come to the entrance to **Clare Priory** (✆ 01787 277326 ⌂ www.clarepriory.org. uk) after crossing the river (the Essex border diverts around this so you are actually still in Suffolk). Clare Priory was founded in 1248, the first house of Augustinian friars to be set up in England. As with most other religious houses it was suppressed by order of Henry VIII in 1538 and it was not until 1953 that Augustinians returned. Today it serves as a retreat centre for a mixed community of friars and lay people. Access is free but limited to the priory grounds and a walled garden which includes a ruined 13th-century church nave as part of its structure. It is a strikingly peaceful spot, its isolated benches dotted between the apple trees offering the perfect setting for quiet reflection.

⫙ FOOD & DRINK

Bell Hotel Market Hill ✆ 01787 277741 ⌂ www.bellhotelclare.co.uk. A 16th-century coaching inn with a seasonal menu. Two bars serve local ales and bar snacks; there's also a separate garden room/conservatory menu, and slightly more formal dining in the 'Tudor' restaurant.

The Cock Callis St ✆ 01787 277391. Very much a local pub that serves decent good-value bar meals. There's a large beer garden at the back.

Number One Delicatessen and Café 1 High St ✆ 01797 278392 ⌂ www. numberonedeli.co.uk. With a central location in Clare, this combined deli/café has decent snacks, good breakfasts (up until 14.30) and tasty quiches and salads.

A1065

A134

Norfolk

THE
BRECKS

PEDDARS WAY

A1075

CHAPTER 2
page 68

A11

4
LAKENHEATH FEN
RSPB RESERVE

2
Brandon

3
Santon
Downham

1
THETFORD

THETFORD
FOREST

5
Elveden

Suffolk

A1065

A11

6
Mildenhall ●

A134

11
Wyken Hall

9 ●
West Stow
Anglo-Saxon Village

7
BURY ST
EDMUNDS

A143

10 ●
Pakenham

A14

12 ●
Woolpit

8
Ickworth
House

13
● The Bradfields

CHAPTER 4
page 126

CHAPTER 5
page 156

14
● Cockfield

15
● Hartest

0   4 miles

0   5km

N

6

WEST SUFFOLK &
THE BRECKS

This chapter covers two distinct regions: Breckland, the arid, sandy heath and forest region that straddles the county boundary in the northwest of Suffolk, and the western region of the county that lies immediately south of this and has Bury St Edmunds at its centre. Both regions have historical interest well beyond what one might expect. Thetford, Breckland's largest town just over the border in Norfolk, was once home to the monarchs of East Anglia and the seat of a bishopric. Brandon nearby has long been a centre for flint mining, an industry that dates back to Neolithic times. Bury St Edmunds is a place apart, the capital and burial site of the Saxon King Edmund. The area south of Bury St Edmunds is home to some of Suffolk's most enchanting countryside, a rural landscape of rolling farmland, sleepy tucked-away villages, narrow country lanes and high hedgerows – an area ripe for Slow exploration. Although focusing primarily on Suffolk, this chapter will occasionally make brief inroads into Norfolk in order to get a fuller understanding of what the Breckland region has to offer.

"This area is home to some of Suffolk's most enchanting countryside, a rural landscape of rolling farmland and sleepy tucked-away villages – an area ripe for Slow exploration."

GETTING AROUND

Both of the main towns of this region lie on major trunk roads: Thetford on the A11, which connects London with Norwich, and Bury St Edmunds on the A14, which links the Midlands with Felixstowe. South of Bury St Edmunds, the A143 leads to Haverhill and the A134 to Sudbury.

PUBLIC TRANSPORT

This is far from wonderful but it is usually possible with careful planning to just about get to where you want providing you do not wish to travel on a Sunday. The main towns, at least, can easily be reached by bus or train. Thetford stands on the Norwich to Cambridge rail line and has a regular **rail service** with Greater Anglia (www.greateranglia.co.uk) to both cities – almost hourly during the day. Some Cambridge trains will stop at Lakenheath for the RSPB reserve at weekends – just one in each direction on a Saturday, three each way on Sundays. Bury St Edmunds has regular rail links to Ipswich, and to Cambridge too, although no direct service to Norwich: you need to change at Stowmarket. Trains to Ely link with national services north and south.

Surprisingly, there are no direct **bus services** between Ipswich and Bury St Edmunds – to travel between the two requires a change in either Diss (in Norfolk) or Stowmarket. Simonds bus service 304/338 runs fairly regularly between Bury St Edmunds and Diss via Ixworth, Stanton and Redgrave in the Waveney Valley. Between Stowmarket and Bury St Edmunds there a few buses a day with Mulleys Motorway service 386, via Rattlesden and Bradfield St George. There's a decent service between Bury St Edmunds and Mildenhall with Mulleys Motorways service 355 and Stephensons of Essex service 16, and also between Bury St Edmunds and Newmarket with the latter service. Coach Services buses 84 and 332/333 run frequently between Bury St Edmunds and Thetford, while service 86 continues on to Mildenhall. The Stagecoach in Cambridge 11 service operates throughout the day between Bury St Edmunds and Newmarket, continuing to Cambridge.

Local services also run from the larger towns to outlying villages. The Coach Services 200/201 service between Thetford and Mildenhall, calling at Santon Downham, Brandon and Lakenheath along the way, is especially useful for the Brecks, while Chambers 374 service between Bury St Edmunds and Cavendish and Clare via Hartest and Boxted is a convenient – and scenic way – way to reach the Stour Valley. Unfortunately, there are no buses on Sundays for any of these services.

CYCLING

Given a general lack of traffic and quiet roads, the Brecks have plenty of potential for cycling. Thetford Forest has lots of off-road choices too. For those who want to go farther afield, Sustrans National Cycle Route

13 (📞 0845 1130065 🖱 www.sustrans.org.uk) connects Thetford with National Cycle Route 1.

The Brecks website (🖱 www.brecks.org) has plenty of information on Thetford Forest Park cycle trails as well as downloadable maps. More information on cycle trails can be found at the Forestry Commission website (🖱 www.forestry.gov.uk). You can also buy a cycling pack from tourist information centres that details five **easy routes** in the Brecks suitable for family cycling. These tend to be theme-based; for instance a Flint-Hunters' Explorer Trail.

Thetford Forest Park has three waymarked forest trails of varying difficulty that start from the High Lodge Forest Centre, where bike hire is also available at Bike Art (📞 01842 810090 🖱 www.bikeartthetford. co.uk). Harling Drove, just north of Thetford over the Norfolk border, is a fairly long easy route through the heart of Thetford Forest, suitable for both cyclists and walkers.

HORSERIDING

There's scope to abandon two wheels for four legs in the Brecks region too and the potential for riding is probably the best in East Anglia. Horseriders have free access on all Forestry Commission freehold land. The Thetford Forest area also has stables where horses may be hired, such as Forest Park Riding and Livery Centre at Brandon (📞 01842 815517), which also organises riding lessons and 'own a pony' days. There is even scope for experienced riders to bring their own horse to the region – a list of 'horse-friendly' bed and breakfast accommodation is available from the Brecks Tourism Partnership website (🖱 www.thebrecks.org), although much of this tends to be in Norfolk.

WALKING

There's some excellent walking to be had. In the Brecks, one obvious choice for **long-distance** hikers is the **Peddars Way**, which begins in Suffolk at Knettishall Heath just south of the Norfolk–Suffolk border before crossing west Norfolk to reach The Wash at Holme-next-the-Sea. Other long-distance routes that spend more time in Suffolk are **St Edmund Way** (Brandon to Flatford via Thetford and Bury St Edmunds – 81 miles) and **Iceni Way** (Knettishall Heath to Hunstanton via Brandon and the Fens – 83 miles). Shorter routes in the west of Suffolk include the 13-mile **Lark Valley Path**, which leads from Bury

𝒊 TOURIST INFORMATION

Bury St Edmunds 6 Angel Hill ✆ 01284 764667 ⊕ www.visit-burystedmunds.co.uk
Thetford Belmont House, 20 King St ✆ 01842 751975 ⊕ www.explorethetford.co.uk
Brecks Tourism Partnership ⊕ www.brecks.org

St Edmunds to Mildenhall, and the ten-mile **Little Ouse Path** between Thetford and Brandon.

You can walk anywhere you like on **Forestry Commission land** and numerous circular walks are waymarked from all the main parking areas. Thetford Forest High Lodge has four waymarked forest trails, and Knettishall Country Park has four trails through heath, woodland and along riverside. Further suggestions for shorter walks are made in the appropriate places in this chapter.

For those who prefer somebody else to deal with the organisation side of things, Suffolk Walking Holidays (✆ 01787 580591 ⊕ www.suffolkwalkingholidays.co.uk), based at Great Cornard near Sudbury, offer a fully supported self-guided walking holiday with accommodation along the route of the St Edmund Way.

THE BRECKS & THETFORD FOREST

Although Breckland borders the pancake-flat region of the Cambridgeshire Fens to the west, it really could not be more different. Breckland, in contrast to the fertile black soil found in the Fens, has light, sandy soil that is far less ideal for intensive farming. The word 'breck' comes from a word that means land that becomes quickly exhausted. It's the closest thing that Britain has to a desert and this is really not so far-fetched, as the rainfall is the lowest in the country, summer temperatures can be among the highest, and winter frosts, the hardest. The sand that covers the chalk was originally wind-blown, but trees have since been planted to stabilise the soil. Back in the days before such enlightened ideas, when large estates sought to maximise their profits by introducing sheep, the sand blew freely around causing untold damage, depleting thin topsoil in one place and covering up fertile land in another.

Naturally, what is a shortcoming today was actually a boon in the distant past. In Neolithic times, Britain's very first farmers were drawn to the region because Breckland's light soil was easy to work with their limited stone tools, and because there was no dense forest needing to be cleared with nothing other than brute strength and a hand axe. The region had a plentiful supply of flint too, the machine steel of the Neolithic Age.

With careful farming, Breckland became reasonably prosperous and **Thetford**, its capital, became an important regional capital in the Anglo-Saxon period. It was later, in the medieval period, when the real damage was done. Sheep were introduced to the land in large numbers and allowed to roam freely, overgrazing and damaging the soil with their hooves. In other parts of Suffolk and Norfolk, sheep may have brought fortune but here they just heralded disaster. Breckland became increasingly depopulated as a result – the area is still sparsely populated today – and rabbits and pheasants became the land's only bounty.

The vast **Thetford Forest**, flanking the A11 around Thetford itself, is a recent innovation, planted by the Forestry Commission after World War I to provide a strategic reserve of timber. The forest area spans both Suffolk and Norfolk, and the county boundary, largely defined by the course of the Little Ouse River, passes right through it. In the Norfolk Brecks, much of what is not forest goes to make up the **Stanford Battle Area**, established in 1942, and marked on OS maps as 'Danger Area', where the army practise manoeuvres and test ordnance. Vast stands of Scots and Corsican pine may be what most people immediately associate with Breckland these days but it is a very recent trend.

Step back just a hundred years in time and you would see only sandy heathland, gorse and rabbits – lots of rabbits. It almost goes without saying that this is a part of East Anglia that many speed through without stopping. Consequently, it is not as well known as perhaps it deserves to be. Outside the few towns, Breckland's distinctive habitat is a prized haven for wildlife: it is home to several species of plant, insect, bird and mammal that are found almost nowhere else in the country.

"Step back just a hundred years in time and you would see only sandy heathland, gorse and rabbits – lots of rabbits."

It may seem perverse to start a chapter on West Suffolk in Norfolk but I do this purely because Thetford lies at the very heart of the Breckland region, historically, politically and geographically.

1 THETFORD

Sometimes dismissed as a 'London overspill town', Thetford tends to get overlooked. While it is true that it does have some large and unlovely housing and industrial estates built for an influx of workers from the south in the 1960s, this is just part of the picture. Thetford was hugely important before the Norman invasion and even held the bishopric of East Anglia before Norwich did. Whether or not Thetford was the royal seat of Boudica, the Iceni queen, is highly uncertain but it was certainly an important centre during the late Iron Age and early Roman period. In Anglo-Saxon times, Thetford became the home of the East Anglian monarchs and seat of a bishopric, and later King Canute made the town his capital too in 1015, half a century before the Norman Conquest. Despite the religious focus being transferred to Norwich after the conquest, a Cluniac priory was established here in the 12th century that lasted until the Reformation.

"Head straight to the centre and you encounter some striking medieval architecture and a heady sense of history."

Ignore the outskirts and head straight to the centre and you encounter some striking medieval architecture and a heady sense of history. The bus station is right in the centre next to the Little Ouse River. It's reached by way of the same narrow medieval street that has the Thetford Grammar School. Beyond the lacklustre shopping precinct just across the river from the bus station, the town centre has a good assortment of medieval and Georgian buildings in timber and flint. The best of these is the **Ancient House**, now the Museum of Thetford Life (✆ 01842 752599), in White Hart Street, a 15th-century timber-framed building that is also the base for the town's **tourist information centre**.

The stonework of the town's Norman **castle** is long gone but the motte remains to provide a satisfying mound to climb up and get a view over the town. There is rather more to see at the site of the **Cluniac priory** west of the centre by the river. This was founded in 1103–04 by Richard Bigod to become one of the largest and richest priories in East Anglia. The priory was torn down after the Dissolution but there are still some impressive flinty remains and even bits of original tile flooring in places. The towering remains of the arch of the massive presbytery window are particularly striking.

Nearby, **Thetford Grammar School** dates back to Saxon times, was re-founded in 1566 and is still active today. Its most famous ex-pupil is **Thomas Paine** (1737–1809) – who had the distinction of being involved in both the French Revolution (where he only escaped execution by a whisker) and the American War of Independence; he was one of the original signatories to the Declaration of Independence and invented the term 'United States of America'. Born in the town (as Thomas Pain; the 'e' was added later when his squiggly signature was misinterpreted as Paine), he attended the school between 1744 and 1749 before going on to be apprenticed to his father as a corset maker. Paine's gilt **statue** by Sir Charles Wheeler, President of the Royal Academy, stands outside the King's House, with the radical thinker clutching a copy of his revolutionary book *Rights of Man* upside down. Why he holds the book upside down is open to speculation. Tourist information at the Ancient House can give details of a **Tom Paine Trail** through the town and the occasional guided tours.

Tom Paine aside, Thetford's other associations include the television series *Dad's Army*, much of which was recorded in and around the town. A Dad's Army tourist trail highlights spots that became the fictional Sussex town of Walmington-on-Sea. In 2010 the Thetford Society erected a bronze statue of Captain Mainwaring (the Arthur Lowe character) seated on a bench next to the River Ouse by the bus station. There's a Dad's Army museum (✆ 01842 751975 ⬧ www.dadsarmythetford. org.uk) at the back of the Guildhall on Cage Lane if you are interested. Nearby, and reached by means of a footbridge, **Maharajah Duleep Singh**, the former squire of the nearby Elveden Estate (see page 195) a little further down the A11, has a very fine equestrian statue set among the shady willows of **Butten Island** in the midst of the Little Ouse River.

Outside the town, some good **walks** are to be had around Thetford. The most obvious route is along the **Little Ouse Path** that links Thetford with Brandon, most of which follows an old towpath. It's about ten miles of easy walking in total and if you are up to this you could walk all the way then catch a bus or train back from Brandon. Even if you walk just a short distance along the river path past the abbey ruins you get a sense of being in open countryside despite the proximity of the town's council estates.

▮▮ FOOD & DRINK

Bell Hotel King St ✆ 01842 754455. This 15th-century inn, right in the heart of town, was where the *Dad's Army* cast and crew used to stay. The hotel, now part of a national chain, tends to make the most of this association as well as its reputation for being haunted but serves decent enough pub food and Greene King ales.

The Dolphin 35 Old Market St ✆ 01842 762406. A 17th-century inn in the historic centre, with a log fire for cold winter days and a beer garden for summer. It has a choice of cask ales and a menu that features steaks, grills and specials cooked with meat provided by local suppliers.

2 BRANDON

West of Thetford on the southern, Suffolk bank of the Little Ouse, is Brandon. If the presence of Grimes Graves, a little way north back over the Norfolk border, is not enough to attest that the town was once central to an important **flint industry**, then just take a look at the buildings. The flint trade was big business as far back as the Neolithic period and returned to prominence with the invention of the musket and the need for gun flints. It is interesting to reflect that, given the area's USAF and RAF bases, the war industry has long played a part in the region and, in addition to forestry, much of Brandon's present-day economy is focused upon servicing the nearby airbase at Lakenheath. Brandon is not a tourist town by any stretch of the imagination.

Brandon's flintknappers had their work cut out back in Napoleonic times when the town grew quite prosperous through supplying the essential parts for the British Army's muzzle-loaders. Virtually all the shots fired at Waterloo would have involved Brandon flint to spark them off. The invention of the percussion cap saw the demise of this trade but, according to John Seymour, flintknappers were still active in the town in the 1960s, when he witnessed men in leather aprons chipping away in the back yard of the Flintknappers Arms pub – where else indeed? You can get a good idea of the town's flintknapping past by visiting the **Brandon Heritage Centre** (✆ 07882 891022 ⚲ www.brandonheritagecentre.org; open weekends and bank holidays only) on George Street.

"Brandon's flintknappers had their work cut out back in Napoleonic times."

The Little Ouse River used to be of far more importance here back in the days when Brandon served as the port for nearby Thetford. These days, forestry rules supreme and it is articulated lorries and the A11, not boats and water, that are the means of distribution for Brandon's produce.

Brandon is home to the **Brandon Brewery** (✆ 01842 878496 ⚲ www.brandonbrewery.co.uk), a small independent brewery that produces a variety of bottled and cask beers with colourful names like Gun

Flint, Molly's Secret, Old Rodney, Slippery Jack and even Grumpy Bastard. There's a shop on site and you can also sample the produce and get a tour if you phone in advance. The brewery is doing its bit for the environment in providing a herd of Breckland Highland cattle with spent malted barley for an occasional special treat. Apparently the cattle, which it would seem are far more conservation-conscious grazers than sheep, are very fond of the grain – who can blame them? – and can always be tempted back from wild, overgrown areas with generous helpings of the stuff.

Brandon Country Park

Bury Rd, Brandon ✆ 01842 810185 ⌂ www.brandoncountrypark.co.uk. Park and visitor centre open daily; free entry.

Just a mile or so south of Brandon, this used to be the grounds of a country house that is now a private nursing home. The park has three waymarked forest walks, an 'intermediate' cycle trail, a tree and history trail, an orienteering course, a restored Georgian walled garden and a visitor centre. It's well set up with picnic areas too, one beside a lake, another in an old orchard. A very Gothic-looking mausoleum to Edward Bliss, the original owner of the estate, can be seen alongside the red walking trail not far from the house. Naturally enough, given that this is Brandon, knapped flint features heavily in its construction.

Thetford Forest & High Lodge Forest Centre

Thetford Rd, Brandon ✆ 01842 815434 ⌂ www.forestry.gov.uk/highlodge; Forestry Commission.

A little way east of Brandon, along the B1107 to Thetford, this offers free entrance to cyclists and walkers arriving without a car. There's an information point with leaflets and maps, a picnic area and a café serving homemade, locally sourced food. Four waymarked walks of varying length explore the forest area from the visitor centre, and the four cycling routes include a family route as well as more challenging mountain-bike rides. **Cycle hire** is available from Bike Art (✆ 01842 810090 ⌂ www.bikeartthetford.co.uk). Go Ape! (✆ 0843 2497684 ⌂ www.goape.co.uk) also based in the park provides adventurous zip-wire and tree-top activities for children. The centre also organises special summer wildlife events such as dusk nightjar rambles and moth expeditions.

⍾ FOOD & DRINK

Flintknappers 1–3 Market Hill, Brandon ☎ 07432 551500 ⌂ www.
theflintknappersbrandon.co.uk. This is nothing fancy – just an old, town pub with standard
bar meals – but convenient enough if visiting the town.

3 SANTON DOWNHAM

Halfway between Thetford and Brandon along the Little Ouse River,
this small village mostly revolves around the sawing and carting of the
forestry business – the headquarters of the East England office of the
Forestry Commission is based here. Don't let this put you off though –
Santon Downham really deserves a look. Tucked away deep in the heart
of the forest, the village is little more than a handful of cottages, a wide
green and a small flint church at its eastern end. The village effectively
occupies a small clearing in what is the largest forest in England. Tall
dark pines are never far from sight – this is definitely Hansel and Gretel
territory. There are no facilities in Santon Downham – no pub, shop or
café – but the village makes an ideal setting-off point for a stroll along
the bank of the Little Ouse or a walk in the forest, or, best of all, both.
The thing to do is bring a picnic or packed lunch with you as you'll have
no trouble finding a peaceful spot to enjoy it.

Before forestry took over the area the village was part of the Downham
Estate, which was at one time owned by Charles Sloane, who later became
Lord Cadogan. Downham Hall was demolished in
1925 and most of the buildings in the village date
from just after this, constructed as homes for forestry
workers. The exception is the flint-built parish **church
of St Mary**, which is mostly Norman with some later
additions. Sometimes referred to as the 'Church in the
Forest' for fairly obvious reasons, this has a curious
figure carved above its south door that may or may not
depict a wolf (or perhaps a lion) with what appears to
be a lily sprouting from its tail. The carving is ancient,
worn and undeniably mysterious, but its symbolism is anybody's guess.

*"Tall dark
pines are
never far from
sight – this
is definitely
Hansel
and Gretel
territory."*

Like all of the Brecks, the soil around here is very light and sandy,
and before being stabilised by the planting of conifers in the early 20th
century had a tendency to blow around quite a lot, especially after
overgrazing by rabbits. Extreme sandstorms were not unknown in the
past. Records show that the village was almost completely overwhelmed

by sand in the late 17th century when cottages were buried and the navigation of the river so dramatically affected by drifting sand that its course was altered considerably (and by definition that of the boundary of the Suffolk–Norfolk border).

For an enjoyable **walk** of a couple of miles along the valley of the Little Ouse, turn left out of the Forestry Commission car park and walk downhill and you'll soon come to a bridge across the river to the Norfolk bank. Cross over and take the track on the right parallel to the river to soon arrive at a picnic spot and a car park close to a footbridge that leads back across the river. You can cross here and follow the St Edmund Way between paddocks and then right along a road to climb gently through thick forest to return to the village. Before you cross the bridge, you might first want to continue a little further along the Norfolk side to reach **All Saints' Church** adjacent to Santon House. This miniature flint church exudes quaintness, with an equally tiny octagonal tower; although no longer in use, it is usually open. Constructed in 1628 from materials salvaged from demolished buildings the building was adapted in the mid 19th century. Curiously, because it once belonged to the parish of Santon Downham, this is the only church in Norfolk that ever belonged to a Suffolk diocese, that of St Edmundsbury.

4 LAKENHEATH FEN RSPB RESERVE
IP27 9AD ✆ 01842 863400; RSPB.

This recently created RSPB Reserve lies just north of Lakenheath on the road to Hockwold cum Wilton and is accessible from a railway station on the Norwich to Cambridge line. The reserve has a wonderful array of birdlife that includes honey buzzards, hobbies, bitterns and those most exotic of birds, golden orioles. Cranes have bred here recently too – the first time in 400 years in the region – and it's also a good place to see cuckoos, which are commonly heard but generally hard to see. The reserve, created from 740 acres of carrot field just over a decade ago, has reverted into a typical fen landscape of reedbeds and grazing marshes.

Speaking of golden orioles, I recall that it used to be possible to see these gorgeous, rather exotic birds swooping across the Cambridge train line somewhere in this vicinity. This was back in the days when they bred in the poplar plantations that lined the tracks. I never did see them from the train but I did once travel to the plantation with birder friends, where we were charmed by the birds' fluting calls and astonished to discover that a brilliant yellow-and-black colour scheme is actually good camouflage for the dappled light of poplars. The trees eventually disappeared as they ended up – quite literally – as matchwood. It's good to know that the birds are back.

There's a visitor centre and loos, and a number of guided walks and child-friendly events are put on throughout the year. A number of **trains** on the Norwich–Cambridge line stop here at Lakenheath station at weekends, one each way on Saturdays, three each way on Sundays. It's a request stop so you'll need to tell the conductor in advance and flag down the appropriate approaching train when leaving. A footpath links the station with the RSPB visitor centre and there's a convenient cycle link to the Hereward Way. Getting here in the week without a car is more problematic as the nearest working station is Brandon nearly five miles away. The on-demand Suffolk Links Brecks Bus (✆ 01638 664304) can be used to reach the reserve from Brandon or Thetford but you need to book it at least by noon the day before (bookings must be made Mon–Fri 08.00–16.00). Alternatively there is a bus service to Lakenheath village every two hours or so from Mildenhall, Brandon and Thetford but it is still a three-mile walk from the village to the reserve.

Lakenheath itself is dominated by RAF Lakenheath, the home of the largest US Air Force fighter base in Britain. A near nuclear accident took place here in 1956 at the height of the Cold War when a B-47 bomber crashed into a storage igloo containing three nuclear warheads. It was a close thing but thankfully (to put it mildly!) no detonation occurred. If it had, then it is very doubtful that there would be a bird reserve in the area today, even more than half a century later, or even a village at all. The village that gives the base its name is not particularly attractive and very much given over to the everyday needs of a USAF base. What it does have is the large medieval **church of St Mary**, which has wall paintings of St Edmund and, like Mildenhall, still bears scars from the Civil War with its vandalised corbel angels. Life was evidently tough for angels in the mid 17th century in northwest Suffolk.

5 ELVEDEN

Situated close to a crossroads a little way south of Thetford, to most people this used to be little more than a sign on the A11 and an inconvenient bottleneck for traffic. It used to be an accident black spot too before traffic-calming measures were introduced. Some will tell you that there have been more people killed on the A11 since World War II than there are names on the obelisk-like war memorial south of the village. All this changed in 2013 when, after years of planning delays, numerous media campaigns, a massive amount of soil-shifting and tarmac-laying, the spending of many millions of pounds and a huge amount of disruption, the A11 at Elveden was finally bypassed by a dual-carriageway so that travellers between London and Norwich could make the journey a little quicker than before and Norfolk businesses could reap the benefits of improved accessibility.

Elveden is a small estate village centred upon **Elveden Hall**, a somewhat bizarre private residence. The estate (⌁ www.elveden.com), which has the largest arable farm in the country, is in the possession of the Earl of Iveagh but the hall itself was emptied of its contents in 1984 and stands empty. You can just about get a glimpse of the hall from the rear of the village churchyard and make out its green dome. The hall was the home of Maharajah Duleep Singh, a deposed Sikh prince from the Punjab who was exiled to England for his part in the Sikh Wars during Queen Victoria's reign. He purchased the estate in 1863 and refurbished the Georgian hall in lavish Moghul style using Italian craftsmen. An equestrian statue of the maharajah stands in Thetford and, although he died in Paris in 1893, his surprisingly modest grave lies in the churchyard of Elveden's St Andrew and St Patrick Church. Elveden Hall passed into the hands of the Guinness family after Duleep Singh's death and the first Earl of Iveagh went even further, building a new wing and adding a replica Taj Mahal to the complex. Since its interior was emptied in 1984, Elveden Hall has become much used as a film set: it has appeared as a location for *Tomb Raider*, the Bond movie *The Living Daylights* and Stanley Kubrick's *Eyes Wide Shut*. The bad news is that the hall is not open to the public.

St Andrew & St Patrick Church

A bit of a Victorian–Edwardian Gothic extravaganza this one; with a double apse, a long cloister that connects a priest door to the bell tower and some lovely modern stained-glass windows that include a memorial window to Maharajah Duleep Singh. He transformed the original Victorian church of St Andrew on taking over the estate, ploughing money into it for its beautification. When the estate passed into the hands of the Guinness family, the first Earl of Iveagh built an entirely new church alongside that effectively created a south aisle. Naturally, in the turn-of-the-century world of the landed gentry, church attendance was compulsory for all estate workers, even Nonconformists (the Guinness family did not employ Catholics). The church is kept firmly locked but you can make an appointment to look inside by phoning Mr and Mrs Ede at ☎ 01842 890607.

¶ FOOD & DRINK

Alfresco Courtyard Elveden Estate ☎ 01842 898068 ⌂ www.elveden.com. An outdoor café and restaurant (with seats inside for less clement weather) set in a stable courtyard surrounded by estate shops. Snacks, light bites and main courses using meat from the estate. The estate shop has a delicatessen that sells estate game and venison and over 20 varieties of British cheese.

6 MILDENHALL

I have passed through this town numerous times on the coach trip between Norwich and London. To be honest, it always felt like a bit of an unnecessary detour. Mildenhall has long been an air-force service town – a large RAF airbase just up the road is used by the US Air Force – and the town seems so resolutely focused on performing this function that it has little truck with any unnecessary frills. The town has something of a listless air about it – the fate perhaps of towns that are dominated by a military base of one sort or another. Historically though, Mildenhall was important as a market town long before man took to the skies, and it was also the place where a large Roman hoard – the Mildenhall Treasure, now kept in the British Museum in London – was discovered in 1945.

Connoisseurs of medieval church architecture will want to check out **St Mary's Church**, which has one of the largest porches in Suffolk and a splendid hammerbeam roof of carved angels that are said to be riddled with shot left by trigger-happy puritans during the Reformation.

BURY ST EDMUNDS & AROUND

Immediately south of the Brecks region the landscape changes to become more undulating with mixed farming and pockets of deciduous woodland here and there. At the heart of this region lies Suffolk's third-largest town, Bury St Edmunds, an ancient place that was once one of the royal towns of the Saxon kings.

7 BURY ST EDMUNDS

🏠 **Angel Hotel**, **Ickworth Hotel** and **The Old Manse Barn** (see pages 216–17)

One of several jewels in Suffolk's crown and, according to the 19th-century writer William Cobbett, 'the nicest little town in the world', Bury St Edmunds has received much admiration over the years for its special character and, as well as Cobbett, has been lauded by other literary luminaries such as Charles Dickens and Daniel Defoe. Even the name, Bury St Edmunds, has a timeless, quintessentially English appeal that something more humdrum like Ipswich struggles to achieve. Much of the town's history is encapsulated in its very name: St Edmund, that sainted hero of the Anglo-Saxons, was, in fact, buried here and his subsequent canonisation brought almost cult-like status ... and pilgrims. Bury St Edmunds is a place of great historical interest, of course, but its one-time draw as a medieval pilgrimage centre is just part of the picture.

Bury remains affluent and well-to-do today and, even without its St Edmund connections, the town has an undeniable appeal with its unhurried, old-fashioned pace and rich array of Georgian and Victorian architecture. It is quite a mysterious place too, filled with architectural nooks and crannies and occasional murky historical cul-de-sacs.

If you arrive by car and park at the old cattle market, the first thing you'll come to is the relatively new shopping centre, The Arc, opened in 2009, which has a futuristic Debenhams store that looks a little like a cut-price version of Birmingham's silver-buttoned Selfridges. It is a bold design that may not be to everyone's taste but keep going past the glitzy new shops and you'll soon arrive at the **Butter Market** and neoclassical **Corn Hall**. The rectangular square around the Corn Hall is filled with traders and shoppers on Wednesday and Saturday market days and is the best place in town to buy fresh fruit and vegetables. Beyond this along Abbeygate Street lie the Abbey Gardens and Cathedral on Angel Hill. The helpful **tourist office** opposite the gardens next to the Scandinavia Café can help with recommendations and orientation.

"The town has an undeniable appeal with its unhurried, old-fashioned pace and rich array of Georgian and Victorian architecture."

St Edmund's Abbey is little more than an appealing ruin these days, having been destroyed at the time of the Dissolution, but the pleasant **Abbey Gardens**, created in 1831 with flower beds and ornamental trees, provide a restful space to wander in and contemplate the time when the site may have been the East Anglian equivalent of Glastonbury. The ornamental beds are lovingly tended and are some of the most colourful plantings I have ever seen – even on a cloudy day you might require a pair of sunglasses. The River Lark flows through the gardens – a river as picturesque as its name suggests. A momentous historical event took place at the abbey here in 1214 on St Edmund's feast day when a gathering of barons and the Archbishop of Canterbury swore on St Edmund's shrine that they would force wayward King John to accept the Charter of Liberties, a document that led the way to the creation of the Magna Carta. **St Edmundsbury Cathedral**, with its intricate, angel-bedecked hammerbeam roof, started life in the 15th century as the Church of St James and was only granted cathedral status in 1914 – to form one of a quartet of cathedrals in East Anglia alongside Norwich, Ely and Peterborough. In keeping with the myth of the protective wolf, the bishop's throne has details of wolves guarding St Edmund. The cathedral was extended in the 1960s and commemorated with a fanfare specially composed by Benjamin Britten. A Gothic-style tower was added as part of a millennium project in 2005.

"In keeping with the myth of the protective wolf, the bishop's throne has details of wolves guarding St Edmund."

St Mary's, the sister parish church just to the south, with another hammerbeam roof, poppyhead pews and 11 pairs of flying angels, is even finer according to the discerning eye of Simon Jenkins, who describes St Mary's as being 'left like Cinderella up the road, rather forlorn'. The church's stained glass is probably its most immediately striking feature, especially the west window, which is the largest in any English parish church and was paid for by local landowners in thanks for a bumper harvest in 1854. The chancel arch has a window in the form of a pilgrim's badge that shows Edmund being killed with arrows. For a modern take on the Saxon king's martyrdom, head for the Risbygate Street roundabout where you can see a modern sculpture of woven stainless steel that depicts Edmund trussed in captivity, punctured by Viking arrows.

Modern-day, secular Bury St Edmunds owes as much to brewing as to anything else and the **Greene King Brewery** has stood in the town since 1799. There's a museum and a shop on site, and brewery tours can be arranged (01284 714 297 www.greeneking.co.uk). The brewery is also the landlord of what claims to be Britain's smallest pub, **The Nutshell**, just off the market place on The Traverse close to the Victorian Corn Hall. There's a desiccated cat on display here that was found bricked up behind a wall during building repairs; you cannot really miss it as it dangles from the ceiling like a ham in an Andalusian bar. It's a black cat but certainly not a very lucky one. I will admit to initially being sceptical about the pub's claim to be the smallest in the country. I remember The Vine in Norwich also being rather 'bijou' (as an estate agent might put it) but The Vine, a tiny Thai restaurant these days, is a veritable coaching inn in comparison with The Nutshell. The Nutshell was not always just a pub: in the late 19th century it was also billed as a 'Museum of Art and Curiosities', with a display of old musical instruments, works of art in ivory and cardboard and cork models of local buildings. It still has its offbeat items – as well as the dead cat, there are historical photos, a vast array of currency notes, a few miscellaneous animal heads and an aeroplane propeller to look at while you are supping your pint at the bar, elbows drawn in. Less is more, as they say, but sometimes more is less.

The Greene King Brewery, which did admirably to maintain its real ale business through the lean times of the 1970s, has grown in recent years to become the largest British-owned brewery in the country. However, it has its critics for its active acquisition policy of taking over smaller breweries and their pub estates, ironically resulting in less choice of real ales for the consumer.

If small breweries are your preference then you might be better off seeking out Greene King's main local competitor, the **Old Cannon Brewery**, opened in 1999, has a range of its own ales like Hornblower, Rusty Gun and Gunners Daughter. The Victorian building that houses the brewery-pub was the home of an earlier Cannon Brewery that closed during World War I. The premises now also multi-task as a brasserie, a bed and breakfast and a venue for 'stitch 'n' bitch' sessions.

Returning from thoughts of beer to architecture once more, the **Moyse's Hall Museum** (✆ 01284 706183 ⌂ www.moyseshall.org) on Cornhill at the top of Butter Market is widely believed to be one of the oldest stone-built domestic buildings in the country. Built sometime around the end of the 12th century, it is something of a mystery why it was constructed of imported flint and limestone rather than the cheaper and far more readily available wood normally used. It was probably done as a show of wealth, and quite a lavish one considering that materials had to be brought from quarries far away. It's a now museum, with interesting Bronze Age, Anglo-Saxon and Roman exhibits, but has served as a prison, a police station and a workhouse in the past. The collection relating to the notorious Red Barn Murder at nearby Polstead (see page 171) is well worth seeing for those who have a taste for the macabre.

The town has a fair number of literary connections. A century or so before William Cobbett visited the town, Daniel Defoe came here to stay at the Cupola House, a former 17th-century inn on The Traverse. **Charles Dickens**, too, spent time at the ivy-covered Angel Hotel and even gave it a mention in *The Pickwick Papers*. This Georgian landmark has had more recent celebrities staying there too, most notably Angelina Jolie, who used the hotel as her base while filming *Tomb Raider*.

Another well-known Bury St Edmunds landmark that is considerably less refined (although you cannot say the same thing about its product) is the BSC **sugar beet factory** on the A14. This is the biggest of its type in the country and in season – around midwinter – is the destination for hundreds of clanking lorries delivering beet from the frozen fields of west Suffolk and beyond. Sugar beet is hardly the most beautiful of crops and its processing machinery is anything but lovely too. So, if you detect a slightly cloying smell in the air during your visit then this is its source (if you can detect hops or malt then that is the Greene King Brewery, of course). In fairness, the factory, which has its own power station on site supplying local homes, is a town icon in its own way, a reminder that for all its quaint museum-piece qualities and rarefied medieval atmosphere, this is a major market town in agribusiness country.

¶¶ FOOD & DRINK

Angel Hotel 3 Angel Hill ☎ 01284 714000 ⬩ www.theangel.co.uk/eaterie. The revamped bar and restaurant at this Bury institution serves food created from local ingredients that include venison from the Elveden Estate. Quite reasonable prices considering the quality. See also *Accommodation*, page 216.

Baileys2 5 Whiting St ☎ 01284 706198 ⬩ www.baileys2.co.uk. In the medieval grid of streets in the centre of town, this coffee shop and tea rooms offers breakfast, light meals and nibbles, all home-cooked using local produce where possible. Excellent homemade biscuits, cakes and puddings, and imaginative sandwiches and salads. Also plenty of gluten-free options.

Bury Beer House 1 Tayfen Rd ☎ 01284 766415 ⬩ www.burybeerhouse.co.uk. A challenge to the Greene King hegemony in town, this has at least eight cask ales from its

A WOLF, A CORPSE, PILGRIMS & WITCHES

Edmund came to East Anglia from Germany in the mid 9th century to become the King of East Anglia, the last Saxon king before Danish and Norman rule. The Danes, always keen to have things their own way, tortured and killed Edmund in 870 because of his refusal to disavow Christianity. The story goes that his head went missing after his death until it was discovered 40 days later lying between the protective paws of a wolf (a wolf is represented on the town crest in remembrance of this). Once his head had been seamlessly reunited with its body, Edmund's corpse was buried at a place called Haegelisdun – possibly modern-day Hoxne – but was dug up 30 years later to be taken to the monastery of Beodricsworth, which later became known as St Edmundsbury in his honour.

In 1032, the monastery was granted abbey status by the Christian Dane, King Canute, and St Edmundsbury Abbey became an important place of pilgrimage following Edmund's canonisation. St Edmund was the patron saint of England for many years but somewhere along the line he was replaced by St George, a historical figure who, if truth be told, may be little more than a myth and has more connections with Turkey and Palestine than with England.

The Normans enlarged the abbey church and the surrounding town, Bury St Edmunds, developed around it to become a prosperous trade and weaving centre. In the 17th century, the town found fame as a centre for its witch trials, in particular that of the year 1645, in which the self-proclaimed Witchfinder General, Matthew Hopkins, saw to it that 18 people were executed in a single day. Bury's prosperity continued through to the 18th century, although the town failed to be caught up in the Industrial Revolution in the same way that Ipswich did in the Victorian age.

own Brewshed Brewery on handpump, in addition to cask ciders, draught stout and even lager. No proper meals but bar snacks like deep-fried whitebait and crispy fried brawn with piccalilli are available.

Harriet's Café Tearooms 57 Cornhill ✆ 01284 756256 ⥿ www.harrietscafetearooms. co.uk. A good choice for afternoon tea, with old-fashioned service and surroundings that, although perhaps a little self-conscious, is charming nevertheless. A live pianist is often present to provide a musical background.

The Nutshell 17 The Traverse ✆ 01284 764867. You may well be tempted to have a drink in what the *Guinness Book of Records* claims to be the smallest pub in Britain (see page 199). There's a choice of Green King ales of course, but no food – it's far too small to have a dining area or even much elbow space. Don't attempt to swing a cat, especially the one hanging above the bar.

Old Cannon Brewery 86 Cannon St ✆ 01284 768769 ⥿ www.oldcannonbrewery.co.uk.

A Victorian brewhouse-pub with excellent beer and modern pub food, a five-minute walk from the centre.

8 ICKWORTH HOUSE

Horringer IP29 5QE ✆ 01284 735270. Rotunda open mid-Mar to end of Oct Thu–Tue, Italianate gardens, park, woods and children's playground open all year; National Trust.

Amid sugar beet fields a few miles outside Bury in the village of Horringer, Ickworth House is an extraordinary rotunda of a house that is now in the ownership of the National Trust. It was built at the beginning of the 19th century by the fourth Earl of Bristol and Bishop of Derry as a storehouse for his art collection and estranged wife and family; but some of the intended works of art never arrived because they were taken by Napoleon. Notwithstanding this setback, a collection was amassed that includes Gainsborough, Titian and Hogarth paintings as well as a vast array of Regency furniture. The exhibition in the basement beneath the rotunda depicts 1930s life in domestic service at Ickworth.

The surrounding park, open throughout the year, was landscaped by Capability Brown between 1769 and 1776, although the basic design goes back to around 1700 when the first Earl of Bristol carved out the landscape to his own requirement after the original Ickworth Hall was demolished in 1701. A herd of deer was introduced in 1706. Also seek out the Italian-style garden with its terrace walk created in 1 821, the walled kitchen garden and the Victorian stumpery that contains a large fern collection and stones from the Devil's Causeway in Northern Ireland.

9 WEST STOW ANGLO-SAXON VILLAGE

Icklingham Rd, West Stow IP28 6HG ✆ 01284 728718 ⏚ www.weststow.org. Open daily; a Bury St Edmunds Heritage ticket allows entry to both this and to Moyses Hall in the town.

This lies seven miles northwest of Bury St Edmunds, signposted from the A1101. Excavations here in the 1960s revealed the remains of the buildings from an Anglo-Saxon settlement as well as a cemetery with over one hundred graves. A reconstructed wooden village has been erected on part of the site, constructed using the technology and techniques of the Anglo-Saxon period. It's all fascinating stuff, with costumed Anglo-Saxon villagers played by knowledgeable enthusiasts occupying the village at the busier times of year. Even if the idea of interpreters spelling out the history for you is anathema, it is undeniably a great hands-on way for children to learn about the past. Numerous special re-enactment activities in summer are mostly geared towards children, along with demonstrations for all ages of Anglo-Saxon pursuits like fletching and flintknapping.

West Stow Country Park beyond the car park, visitor centre and village, with its mixture of heath and woodland, is a good place for a picnic or a walk along the River Lark.

EAST OF BURY ST EDMUNDS

The A14 that thunders through Bury St Edmunds continues east to bypass Stowmarket on its way to the coast. It is worth avoiding this busy highway if you can and instead make use of the lesser roads that lead to all sorts of worthwhile villages and hidden-away places. The destinations described below are all fairly close to Bury.

10 PAKENHAM

Just six miles northeast of Bury, Pakenham glows with pride in being the last parish in England to have a windmill and a watermill both working. The 2003 village sign will remind you of this just in case you weren't aware. There's even a book, *Pakenham – Village of Two Mills* by N R Whitwell, which you can read in full on the village website (⌂ www.pakenham-village.co.uk) if your eyes are up to it. The **windmill**, which is black-tarred and dates from 1830, was still in use up to the 1950s. It underwent full refurbishment of its sails in 2000 but, although the sails still turn, it no longer grinds. In contrast, the **watermill** (☎ 07585 899633 ⌂ www.pakenhamwatermill.org.uk), a gleaming

"The windmill underwent full refurbishment of its sails in 2000 but, although the sails still turn, it no longer grinds."

white building built in 1814, is still fully functional; it's open for visitors at weekends and bank holiday afternoons, and on Thursdays between Easter and the end of September. The watermill, which despite its name is actually located closer to Ixworth than to Pakenham, holds milling demonstrations on the first Thursday of the month and every Sunday afternoon in summer. You can buy stoneground wholemeal flower from the mill shop and several farmers' markets and food halls in the area. There's also a tea room.

Pakenham village, which has plenty of pretty thatch, also has an unusual cruciform **church**, St Mary's, with a stubby octagonal tower and a lovely stone font that has carvings of unicorns and pelicans.

For windmill aficionados, **Bardwell Windmill** (✆ 01359 251331; open daily), just north of Ixworth, dates from the 1820s. The mill is still undergoing restoration and regular events such as steam threshing days are put on in order to raise funds.

¶¶ FOOD & DRINK

The Six Bells Inn The Green, Bardwell IP31 1AW ✆ 01359 250820 ⌂ www. sixbellsbardwell.co.uk. This 16th-century country inn in Bardwell village, just north of Ixworth and the A143 Bury to Diss road, featured in *Dad's Army* and there's a photograph of the cast in the bar. The food is fairly standard pub fare with meat, poultry and vegetables mostly locally sourced. Closed at lunchtimes on weekdays.

11 WYKEN

On the other side of Ixworth, a couple of miles to the east, **Wyken Hall** is an Elizabethan manor house central to an ancient estate and 1,200-acre farm that has Shetland sheep and a herd of Red Poll cattle as well as a seven-acre vineyard. **Wyken Vineyards** (⌂ www.wykenvineyards. co.uk), planted in 1988 on the site of what is thought to be a Roman vineyard, has won several awards for its white wines – Wyken Bacchus was winner of English Wine of the Year in 2009. **Wyken Hall Gardens**, a pleasing blend of topiary, herb gardens, rose beds, perennial borders and fruit trees, surround the house. They are open from Easter until the end of September every day except Saturday, when a **farmers' market** is held here.

The vineyard restaurant, the Leaping Hare (see below), is highly rated, and its shop, the Wyken Hare Country Store, is full of crafts, pottery, books, clothing and naturally wines.

¶¶ FOOD & DRINK

The Leaping Hare Wyken Vineyards, IP31 2DW ✆ 01359 250287 ⌂ www. wykenvineyards.co.uk. Open daily for breakfast, lunch and afternoon tea, and on Friday and Saturday evenings for sumptuous three-course meals, this well-regarded restaurant is located in a 400-year-old timbered barn on the estate. Ingredients are sourced from as nearby as possible – beef and lamb from Wyken's own farm, game from the estate, fruit and veg from the kitchen garden.

A CHURCH WALK IN CENTRAL SUFFOLK

Back in 2008, Hilary Bradt spent a considerable amount of time sniffing out Suffolk churches on an epic Land's End to Lowestoft bus journey, together with Janice Booth whose *Green Children of Woolpit* box is on page 207. Here's a brief description of how they spent their day in the Woolpit area.

'We'd already done a wonderful church walk near Bury. Then it was our last day, with some final churches to visit and footpaths to walk. We'd selected Beyton, Hessett and Woolpit, linked by lanes and paths. All were special: Beyton for its round tower and carved pew-ends, Hessett for its wonderful 14th-century murals showing the Seven Deadly Sins and tradesmen's tools (a warning not to work on Sundays) and Woolpit – wonderful Woolpit – which was so crammed with angels you felt the whole church might take to the wing.

We sat on a bench at the village pump and waited for the bus for Stowmarket. The sun was warm, there were no cars, few people and even the pub was sleeping. At that moment, I would have been happy to travel this way for ever, just catching the next bus to wherever I fancied. The feeling didn't last, however. By the time we reached Diss, having stopped to explore Eye, we'd seen the last bus of the day leave for Beccles without us.'

12 WOOLPIT

The name Woolpit is a bit of an odd one, and nothing to do with the wool trade. It first appeared in a document in 1005, long before the wool trade started to flourish in the region. One suggestion is that it may derive from the Old English *wulf pytt* (a pit for trapping wolves).

Woolpit was a place of pilgrimage in the medieval period, with pilgrims coming to pay their respects to the Shrine of Our Lady of Woolpit that was probably housed in what is now the vestry of the village's Church of St Mary – there's still a well called Our Lady's Well in a field just northeast of the church. The early 16th century and the Dissolution brought an end to the pilgrimage trade, so the village shifted its economy to the more prosaic pursuit of manufacturing bricks. Woolpit's first brick kilns and pits were recorded in 1574, and by the 18th century, a large number of villagers were employed in three pits here. This brick industry's unique selling point was that it produced a very distinctive and elegant type of brick known as 'Woolpit white'. Many of the village's buildings are built of these 'whites' but many thousands more – millions probably – left the village to be shipped to provide fancy brickwork elsewhere. The local clay is not exactly white but it is paler than usual, and the subsequent pale brick became highly sought after and widely used locally. It is even rumoured that Woolpit whites were used in the construction of George Washington's first White House. You can browse a permanent display on Woolpit brickmaking in the village's small **Woolpit and District Museum** (✆ 01359 240822 🖥 www.woolpit.org/museum), on the upper floor of a 17th-century timber-framed cottage.

As Hilary Bradt attests (see box, page 205), Woolpit's **church of St Mary** really is quite exceptional. Its double hammerbeam roof has a whole squadron of angels, and there's also a magnificent Tudor eagle lectern and what writer Simon Jenkins describes as 'a church within a church' – a sumptuous two-storey porch. The spire, with its flying buttresses, is a Victorian replacement.

¶¶ FOOD & DRINK

Swan Inn The Street ✆ 01359 240482 🖥 www.woolpitswan.co.uk. A traditional 15th-century coaching inn in the centre of the village that serves local ales and daily specials.

SOUTH OF BURY ST EDMUNDS

You have a choice of roads to take heading south out of Bury towards the Stour Valley. The A134 through Bradfield Combust follows the route of a Roman road for a while before meandering in a distinctly un-Roman manner to reach Long Melford. The A143 from Bury passes through Horringer and past Ickworth Hall before passing through of some of Suffolk's highest land to arrive at somewhat unprepossessing Haverhill, an overspill town rather like a smaller version of Thetford in Norfolk but without the latter's rich history. Threading between these two main routes, the ultra-quiet B1066 leaves the market town behind to plunge through some of west Suffolk's most overlooked countryside passing delightful villages like Hartest tucked away in folds of the landscape along the way.

13 THE BRADFIELDS

West of Woolpit and closer to Bury St Edmunds, the Bradfields consist of three appealing villages: **Bradfield St George**, **Bradfield St Clare** and **Bradfield Combust**. All are sprawling parishes with narrow, twisting lanes that lend themselves perfectly to bicycle outings. Bradfield St Clare is another candidate for the actual site of St Edmund's martyrdom, although it is best not to mention this to

THE GREEN CHILDREN OF WOOLPIT

Janice Booth

A wrought-iron sign in Woolpit village centre shows a wolf, a church and two children. The wolf and the church are easy to interpret, but the children are part of a more curious tale.

Sometime in the mid 12th century, so the story goes, harvesters found two frightened children crying in a field: a girl of about ten years old and a boy who was younger. They wore strange clothes, spoke in an unknown language and their skins were green. Although clearly famished, initially they refused all food – until offered some raw beans. They seized on these with great delight and tried to open the stalks, thinking that was where the beans lay. When villagers split the pods and gave them the beans inside, they ate them greedily.

They were taken to the home of Sir Richard de Calne, who cared for them. Gradually their green colour faded. The boy was always sickly and soon died, but the girl survived to normal adulthood and eventually married.

When she had learned enough English, she explained their origins: she and her brother had come from a land of perpetual twilight, where the sun never shone and the people (Christians) were green. Far away across a broad river, they could see another land that glowed with light, but their people did not travel there. In one version of the legend, she claims they were swept up by a whirlwind; in another, she and her brother wandered into a cave, mysteriously drawn by the distant sound of bells, when they were tending the family's sheep, and after many days lost in the dark passages they emerged at Woolpit.

The main sources of the legend are Ralph, Abbot of Coggeshall, and William Newburg, both contemporary chroniclers probably born within a decade or so of the alleged event but writing about it some years after. It's not impossible that one copied details from the other. The words they put into the mouth of the girl are improbably complex for a child who knew no English before she was ten; but both claim that the children spoke a strange language, and were green.

The colour might perhaps be explained by vivid green clothing – its vegetable dye could have run and stained their skin – and/or the sickly pallor of anaemia.

As for the language, could they somehow have come from across the English Channel? Or, language apart, were they linked to the old legend of the Norfolk man who was appointed guardian to his wealthy brother's two children, whom he then tried to murder in order to gain their inheritance? Having failed, he later abandoned them in Wayland Wood near Watton in Norfolk and they're said to be the original 'Babes in the Wood'. Choose your own theory!

A similar event allegedly occurred seven centuries later, in Spain, but descriptions of it are suspiciously like those of the Woolpit tale.

The legend is well covered on ⏚ www. anomalyinfo.com, among other websites.

anyone in Hoxne (see page 92). The parish of Bradfield St George is the setting for *Corduroy* by the Suffolk country writer Adrian Bell (father of journalist Martin Bell) who named it Benfield St George in his semi-fictional account of Suffolk rural life. 'Corduroy' is quite an apt term to describe the gentle green furrows and folds of this landscape in spring.

Bradfield Woods (✆ 01449 737996 🖱 www.wildlifetrusts.org/reserves/bradfield-woods) nearby, close to Felsham Hall, has been coppiced traditionally for firewood and hazel rods since the 13th century. Some of the ash coppice stools in the wood are thought to be over 1,000 years old. These woods once belonged to the abbey of St Edmundsbury but these days are managed as a nature reserve by the Suffolk Wildlife Trust. As with most ancient woodland, it is a wonderful refuge for wildlife, with a broad variety of plants, plenty of migrant songbirds like garden warblers and blackcaps, woodland mammals such as stoats and badgers, and scarce white admirals among its 24 species of butterfly.

Spring is probably the perfect time to visit when the coppiced areas are awash with flowers like early purple orchid, bluebell and wild garlic, and the newly arrived birds are in full song. The chances of hearing nightingales singing are very good at this time of year even though their numbers have declined in recent years. Three coloured trails lead along the rides – you can pick up a trail guide from the visitor centre or by the noticeboard.

ⵏ FOOD & DRINK

Fox and Hounds Felsham Rd, Bradfield St George IP30 0AB ✆ 01284 386379. A Victorian pub with a dining area and an above-average selection of Suffolk real ales.

14 COCKFIELD

South of the Bradfields, just off the Bury to Sudbury road, Cockfield is composed of nine small hamlets widely spread out around the central village of Cockfield with its 14th-century St Peter's Church. Each of the hamlets takes its name from the green that it lies next to – Colchester Green, Buttons Green and so on. Great Green, a little way northeast of the main village of Cockfield, more than lives up to its name in having an enormous triangular green as its focal point. Another of the hamlets, Parsonage Green, has a literary connection as Robert Louis Stevenson wrote *Treasure Island* while staying at the Old Rectory here.

As elsewhere in the less populated parts of Norfolk and Suffolk, ghosts of the recent past lurk here in the form of a disused US Air Force airfield from World War II. Lavenham airfield close to Smithwood Green was the base of the 487th Bomb Group from 1944 to '45 and B-24 Liberators and B-17 Flying Fortresses rumbled out of here on their way to bombing targets in Germany. Part of the airfield taxiway now serves as a public footpath. With scattered greens, moated farmhouses and gently undulating terrain, this is a marvellous area to spend awhile exploring on foot, although Lavenham just down the road to the south might prove to be just too much of a temptation.

¶¶ FOOD & DRINK

Three Horseshoes Stow's Hill ✆ 01284 828177 ⌂ www.3horseshoes.net. A long, thatched 14th-century building with exposed beams and a crown-post roof that is one of the oldest pubs in Suffolk. As well as Adnams ale and at least one guest beer, there's homemade British pub food like steak and ale pie. Closed Mon and Tue.

15 HARTEST

🏠 **Appleby Cottage** (see page 217)

It takes a while to reach Hartest whichever way you arrive at the village. The village lies on the B1066 midway between Long Melford and Bury but if you come here from Shimpling to the east you will arrive at the village green after careering down Hartest Hill, considered by some to be the steepest descent in all Suffolk. Relative isolation such as this has certainly not led to neglect: Hartest is a highly attractive village of brightly painted cottages and other desirable real estate clustered around a village green. For pure good looks, it gives Kersey a run for its money as the perfect rural Suffolk idyll.

"For pure good looks, it gives Kersey a run for its money as the perfect rural Suffolk idyll."

The first impression that the village makes is that of a mix of the traditional, the plain old-fashioned – the village garage at the top of the green looks to be straight out of the 1950s – and the gentrified. In the last category, the village local, The Crown, has clearly been rebranded as a stylish gastropub for the discerning visitor. But, if the pub looks as if it might have ideas above its station, it might well be because the building was formerly Hartest Hall, the seat of the squire in these parts.

The upper part of the village green has a curious large granite boulder known as the **Hartest Stone** sitting on it, a glacial erratic dumped unceremoniously in the vicinity during the last ice age. The stone is said to have been hauled here on a wooden sledge from a field on top of nearby Somerton Hill on 7 July 1713 by 'twenty gentlemen and twenty farmers' and a team of 45 horses – no mean feat as this was quite some distance even if it was largely downhill. The stone was relocated to celebrate the Peace of Utrecht and the Duke of Marlborough's victories in the War of Spanish Succession. Rumour has it that after the stone had been successfully shifted to its new location an 'erotic debauch' took place among the villagers. In July 2013, celebrations in the village paid tribute to the 300-year anniversary of the stone, with bell-ringing, maypole dancing, and a deputation from Somerton asking for the stone to be returned. A symbolic 'stone' was then collected from a barn at Place Farm and taken to Hartest to be paraded around the green. No erotic debauch, though.

South of the village at the top of a hill on the Shimpling road, **Giffords Hall Vineyard** (✆ 01284 830799 ⊕ www.giffordshall.co.uk) is a medium-sized vineyard that produces a range of English wines from grape varieties that include Bacchus and Pinot Noir. Planted in the late 1980s, the vines are now fully productive; the 2011 vintage received several awards. Unaccompanied tours are possible anytime in summer and private tours can be arranged on request. A vineyard shop and small café are open throughout summer, closing for harvest but reopening around Christmas (11.00–16.00, closed Mon).

¶¶ FOOD & DRINK

The Crown The Green ✆ 01284 830250 ⊕ www.thecrownhartest.co.uk. A gently upmarket village pub owned by the Brewshed Brewery in Bury St Edmunds, with real ale, an extensive wine list and various food options: bar snacks, sandwiches and 'grazing boards' to share as well as full meals with the emphasis on local produce.

UPDATES WEBSITE

You can post your comments and recommendations, and read the latest feedback and updates from other readers online at ⊕ www.bradtupdates.com/suffolk.

ACCOMMODATION

The places to stay listed below have been selected for their good location and because they embrace the Slow mindset, either in terms of their overall feel or because they embody a 'green' approach. Prices for hotels vary considerably, but two people sharing a room in a B&B can expect to spend around £60–80 per night. Holiday cottage prices also cover a wide range, depending on capacity, season and location. Of course, school holidays and especially August mean peak prices. There is plenty to be said for visiting out of season in order to save money. Campsites run the gamut from no-frills to luxurious 'glamping' options.

The accommodation selection here is just a small assortment of selected places. These have been ordered according to geographical area. The list is not meant to be in the least bit exhaustive but rather just a small personal selection.

The hotels, B&Bs and self-catering options featured in this section are indicated by 🏠 under the heading for the town or village in which they are located. Campsites are indicated by 🛆.

1 THE SUFFOLK HERITAGE COAST
Hotels

The Crown and Castle Market Hill, Orford IP12 2LJ 📞 01394 450205 🖱 www.crownand castle.co.uk. A smart and stylish hotel with a gorgeous location in Orford, this is probably best known for its excellent Trinity restaurant. The Crown and Castle has 21 very comfortable rooms with plenty of style; the ten luxurious garden rooms each have their own terrace.

The Ship St James St, Dunwich IP17 3DT 📞 01728 648219 🖱 www.theshipatdunwich. co.uk. A nice old pub with rooms close to the beach at this fascinating seaside village, The Ship has 15 comfortable rooms; some are newly converted, all come with traditional furniture and old-fashioned iron bedsteads.

The Swan Market Pl, Southwold IP18 6EG 📞 01502 722186 🖱 www.adnams.co.uk. Right in the heart of the Suffolk coast's most elegant resort close to the seafront, this has tastefully decorated guest rooms.

B&B

Arch House Aldeburgh Rd, Aldringham IP16 4QF ☎ 01728 832615 ⤍ www.archhouse-aldeburgh.com. Close to Aldeburgh and Snape Maltings, this has colourful stylish bedrooms and a drawing room with a log fire in winter. There's a sunny outdoor terrace for summer use. Dinner from organic locally sourced produce can be provided on request.

Self-catering

Admiral Cottage Rectory Rd, Blaxhall IP12 2DP ☎ 07802 878172 ⤍ www.snapecottages.co.uk. In a village close to Snape Maltings, this fully refurbished and well-equipped cottage sleeps four. The steep stairs may not suit the less mobile.

Aldeburgh Cottage High St, Aldeburgh IP15 5DQ ☎ 01728 638962 ⤍ www.aldeburghcottage.co.uk. Stylish self-catering close to the beach in a restored Victorian cottage that combines period features with clutter-free contemporary style.

Martello Tower Aldeburgh ☎ 01628 825925 ⤍ www.landmarktrust.co.uk. A converted Martello tower, this one near Aldeburgh, the most northerly in England, sleeps four.

The Balancing Barn Near Walberswick ⤍ www.living-architecture.co.uk. A highly unusual modern building that appears to defy gravity. Accommodating up to eight people, this has ultra-modern interior decoration and a top-of-the-range kitchen.

The Dune House Near Thorpeness ⤍ www.living-architecture.co.uk. Another very unusual modern dwelling in the Living Architecture collection, this beautiful Norwegian-designed house is right on the edge of the sea nestled among dunes. It sleeps nine.

Campsites

Harbour Camping & Caravan Park Ferry Rd, Southwold IP18 6ND ☎ 01502 722486 ⤍ www.waveney.gov.uk. Right by the beach and Southwold harbour just south of the town, this council-owned site with a basic but adequate toilet and shower block has straightforward family camping at a moderate price.

USEFUL WEBSITES

Suffolk Bed and Breakfast (⤍ www.suffolkbedandbreakfast.co.uk) has details of a large number of properties that can be searched for online according to location. **Best of Suffolk** (⤍ www.bestofsuffolk.co.uk) has a large number of B&Bs to choose from and you can search by size and facilities. **Suffolk Secrets** (⤍ www.suffolk-secrets.co.uk) and **Suffolk Cottage Holidays** (☎ 01394 389189 ⤍ www.suffolkcottageholidays.com) are other options that offer plenty of choice, as are the Suffolk entries for **Country Cottages Online** (⤍ www.countrycottagesonline.net/england/cottages-in-suffolk) and **Heritage Hideaways** (☎ 01502 578278 ⤍ www.heritagehideaways.com).

Mill Hill Farm Caravan & Campsite Westleton Rd, Darsham, Saxmundham IP17 3BS
📞 01728 668555 (no website). Good-value with 30 pitches reasonably close to the coast.

2 THE WAVENEY VALLEY
Hotel
Waveney House Hotel Puddingmoor, Beccles NR34 9PL 📞 01502 712270 🖱 www.
waveneyhousehotel.co.uk. In a lovely position overlooking the River Waveney close to
the town centre in Beccles, this attractive riverside hotel has ten tastefully furnished,
comfortable rooms.

B&B
Buckland House Halesworth Rd, Ilketshall St Lawrence NR34 8LB 📞 01986 781413
🖱 www.buckland-house.co.uk. A homely B&B hidden away in the Saints country south
of Bungay, this 18th-century cottage was once a Methodist meeting room. Modern,
individually styled rooms and an extensive breakfast menu made with local produce.

Self-catering
Fritton Lake Woodland Lodges Church Lane, Fritton NR31 9HA 📞 01493 488666
🖱 http://frittonlake.somerleyton.co.uk. A choice of 45 eco-friendly lodges scattered around
the mature woodland and lake of the Somerleyton Estate in northeast Suffolk. There's a
choice of sizes but all come with great views, open-plan living area and fully fitted kitchens.

Campsite
Outney Meadow Touring & Camping Park Outney Meadow, Bungay NR35 1HG
📞 01986 892338 🖱 www.outneymeadow.co.uk. Very close to Bungay in the Waveney
Valley, this campsite is part-sheltered by trees and has canoe and bike hire available.

3 SOUTHEAST SUFFOLK
Hotels
The Crown Thoroughfare, Woodbridge IP12 1AD 📞 01394 384242 🖱 www.
thecrownatwoodbridge.co.uk. Thoroughly refurbished, with ten stylishly modern yet
comfortable bedrooms, this chic boutique-style hotel is now the smartest place in town.
Kesgrave Hall Hall Rd, Kesgrave, Ipswich IP5 2PU 📞 01473 333741 🖱 www.kesgravehall.
com. A little way east of Ipswich and convenient for visits to that town, this boutique hotel
has a choice of 23 rooms that range from standard to super-deluxe.

B&Bs
Church Farm Church Rd, Kettleburgh, Woodbridge IP13 7LF 📞 01728 723532 🖱 www.

churchfarmkettleburgh.co.uk. This 450-year-old farmhouse in an idyllic setting overlooking the Deben Valley has just four rooms. Excellent breakfasts include local honey, sausages and fish and home-produced eggs.

Dorincourt Guesthouse Undercliffe Rd West, Felixstowe IP11 2AH ☎ 01394 270447 ⌖ www.dorincourt.co.uk. This large Victorian villa overlooking Felixstowe's promenade has four good-value rooms, some with a sea view.

Self-catering

Teachers House Shottisham Rd, Alterton, Woodbridge IP12 3DE ☎ 01728 638962 (no website). Once the teacher's house for the former village school, this is near Woodbridge on the Bawdsey Peninsula close to the River Deben and the sea. It sleeps up to four.

Treacle Pot Cottage Mill Lane, Trimley St Martin, Felixstowe IP11 0RP ☎ 01394 275367 ⌖ www.suffolk-holiday-cottages.co.uk. Sleeping up to four, this cosy 19th-century cottage two miles from Felixstowe was once the local sweet shop.

Freston Tower Near Ipswich ☎ 01628 825925 ⌖ www.landmarktrust.co.uk. This six-storey Tudor folly is available for rent through the Landmark Trust if you fancy living vertically for a while. It sleeps four and the sitting room at the top offers wonderful views over the River Orwell.

Martello Tower Y Bawdsey, near Woodbridge ☎ 01394 389189 ⌖ www. suffolkcottageholidays.com. Very expensive but undoubtedly a unique experience, this converted tower is completely refurbished and comes with all mod cons. Sleeps five.

Campsites

Forest Camping Limited Tangham Campsite, Butley, Woodbridge IP12 3NF ☎ 01394 450707 ⌖ www.forestcamping.co.uk. In the heart of Rendlesham Forest, this 90-pitch site is ideal for UFO spotters, cyclists and forest walkers. It is also convenient for the coast just a few miles away.

Mill House Camping Mill Hill, Earl Soham, Woodbridge IP13 7RP ☎ 01728 684312 ⌖ www.themillhouse.net. This small family-run site is on an eight-acre rare breed smallholding in east Suffolk, five miles from Framlingham. Basic facilities and no electricity but there's a campfire circle and cooking fires and barbecues are permitted.

Secret Meadows White House Farm, Hasketon, Woodbridge IP13 6JP ☎ 01394 382992 ⌖ www.secretmeadows.co.uk. Secret Meadows offers expensive boutique-style camping in luxury lodge tents with four-poster beds, Gypsy caravans or a 'Hobbit box' – a wooden horsebox truck with a Middle Earth theme. Organic towels, complimentary handmade soap and a welcome basket are all part of the package.

Suffolk Yurt Holidays Ufford Rd, Bredfield, Woodbridge IP13 6AR ☎ 0790 7964890 ⌖ www.suffolkyurtholidays.co.uk. Five spacious hand-crafted yurts set in wildflower meadows surrounded by ancient trees. Each yurt has a fridge and wood stove and can accommodate either four adults or two adults and up to four children. Separate eco-friendly shower block, kitchen and safari-style eating area.

4 CENTRAL & EAST SUFFOLK
B&Bs

Abbey House Monk Soham, Framlingham IP13 7EN ☎ 01728 685255 🖱 www.abbey-house.net. Situated in a small village between Framlingham and Debenham, Abbey House is a former Victorian rectory surrounded by trees. The spacious, comfortable bedrooms look out onto the garden and there is a heated outdoor swimming pool for guests' use.

Brights Farm Bramfield, Halesworth IP19 9AG ☎ 01986 784212. A B&B with homely, nicely furnished rooms on a 250-acre working organic farm. There's a guest lounge and maps of the local area for walking enthusiasts. Self-catering accommodation is also available.

Self-catering

The Barns at Belle Grove Bell Grove Farm, Halesworth IP19 8QU ☎ 01986 873124 🖱 www.belle-grove.com. Five converted barns, each with a different character, fitted out with sumptuous textiles, rugs and reclaimed wooden fixtures. With wood-burning stoves and under-floor heating powered by solar panels, each barn has its own private garden area. See advert, colour page 16.

School Cottage Yoxford IP17 3EU ☎ 01728 638962 🖱 www.bestofsuffolk.co.uk. A cosy mid-terrace cottage sleeping just two. The small sitting room has a wood-burning stove and there's a raised decked sitting area in the garden

Sheep Cottages Bruisyard Rd, Peasenhall IP17 2HP ☎ 07768 693548 🖱 www.sheepcottages.co.uk. Two 16th-century cottages – Black Sheep and White Sheep – that have been refurbished in a simple, modern style to create a contemporary uncluttered feel.

Gypsy Hollow Valley farm, Butts Rd, Westhall, Halesworth IP19 8RN 🖱 www.gypsyhollow.co.uk. B&B in a Gypsy caravan in the peaceful grounds of a farmhouse, with a separate summerhouse, spa and kitchen area.

Campsites

Ivy Grange Farm Yurts Butts Rd, Westhall, Halesworth IP19 8RN ☎ 07802 456087 🖱 www.ivygrangefarm.co.uk. A glamping site that has yurts with double beds, fairy lights, wood-burners and hand-painted furniture. Facilities include woodland showers, a safari-style kitchen and a communal barn with table tennis and table football.

The Orchard Campsite 28 Spring Lane, Wickham Market IP13 0SJ ☎ 01728 746170 🖱 www.orchardcampsite.co.uk. A friendly family campsite with a relaxed atmosphere and a good choice of tent pitches – in woodland, next to a pond or in a meadow. There's a landscaped barbecue area and a campsite shop with an off-licence. Open fires are encouraged and firewood can be provided. Pre-erected tents are also available, and there's a Gypsy caravan for hire too.

Swattesfield Campsite Gislingham Rd, Thornham Magna IP23 8HH ✆ 01379 788558 🖱 www.swattesfieldcampsite.co.uk. A small, low-impact campsite in the Waveney Valley where you can either bring your own tent to pitch or rent a boutique bell tent or log cabin.

5 SOUTH SUFFOLK & THE STOUR VALLEY
Hotel
The Swan Lavenham CO10 9QA ✆ 01787 247477 🖱 www.theswanatlavenham.co.uk. This timber-framed 15th-century inn with rooms is in the heart of the celebrated wool town of Lavenham. Expect luxurious surroundings, oak beams, open fires and 45 well-appointed bedrooms, each one individual and slightly different from the others.

B&Bs
Cobbles 26 Nethergate St, Clare CO10 8NP ✆ 01787 277539 🖱 www.cobblesclare.co.uk. A cosy B&B in a listed 14th-century cottage close to the centre of historic Clare. Breakfasts cooked using local produce are served in an oak-beamed dining room.

Lavenham Priory Water St, Lavenham CO10 9RW ✆ 01787 247404 🖱 www.lavenhampriory.co.uk. Stylish luxury B&B in a medieval Lavenham house with four-poster beds, beamed ceilings and period-piece fittings.

Milden Hall Milden, Lavenham CO10 9NY ✆ 01787 247235 🖱 www.thehall-milden.co.uk. In a grand 16th-century hall farmhouse near Lavenham, this has elegant, old-fashioned large rooms with tapestries, wall hangings and characterful furniture.

Mill House Cross St, Sudbury CO10 2DS ✆ 01787 881173 🖱 www.millhouse-sudbury.co.uk. Close to Sudbury town centre with views to the River Stour, this 500-year-old listed house offers two large comfortable rooms, one with a balcony, and a very small single suitable for a child.

Self-catering
Gilly Parva Gillyflower Cottage, Butt Rd, Stoke by Nayland CO6 4RD ✆ 01206 263237 (no website). Self-catering in a modern, timber-clad house in Constable country. There's a well-equipped kitchen and lake views from the outside terrace. The extensive gardens have exotic plants from all over the world.

6 WEST SUFFOLK & THE BRECKS
Hotels
Angel Hotel 3 Angel Hill, Bury St Edmunds IP33 1LT ✆ 01284 714007 🖱 www.theangel.

co.uk. Bury's best-known hotel – both Charles Dickens and Angelina Jolie have stayed here in the past. Located in the heart of the town's historic centre, this combines comfort and exotic grandeur and offers a wide range of accommodation that includes suites and family rooms as well as better-value classic rooms.

Ickworth Hotel Horringer, Bury St Edmunds IP29 5QE 📞 01284 735350 🖥 www. ickworthhotel.co.uk. Located within the Ickworth Estate at Horringer near Bury St Edmunds this elegant and well-appointed hotel has 27 rooms decorated in a variety of styles as well as 11 apartments for families. There's also a games and cinema room, crèche and swimming pool, and a wealth of country walks right on the doorstep.

B&B

Appleby Cottage The Green, Hartest IP29 4DH 🖥 www.clickbedandbreakfast.co.uk. Right on the village green in a beautiful west Suffolk village, this relaxed informal B&B is perfectly located for walking in the area.

Self-catering

The Old Manse Barn Chapel Rd, Cockfield, Bury St Edmunds IP30 0HE 📞 01284 828120 🖥 www.theoldmansebarn.co.uk. This large luxurious loft apartment overlooks lovely countryside seven miles from Bury St Edmunds. Despite being a converted timber-clad barn, the style is modern with an open plan kitchen, dining and sitting area.

UPDATES WEBSITE

You can post your comments and recommendations, and read the latest feedback and updates from other readers online at 🖥 www.bradtupdates.com/suffolk.

INDEX

Page numbers in **bold** refer to main entries.

INDEX OF ADVERTISERS